PAINTING ABSTRACT NATURE ON CANVAS

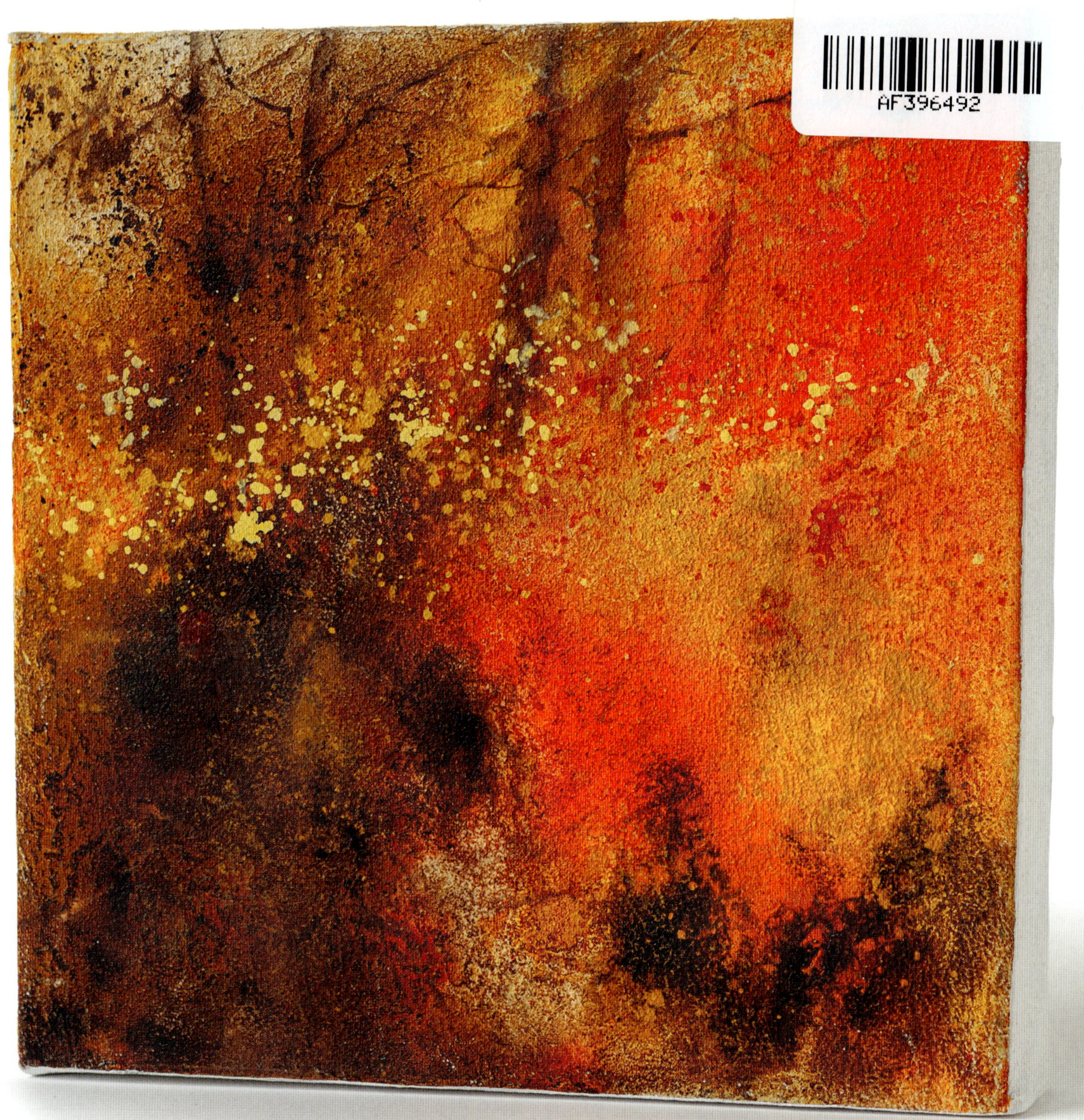

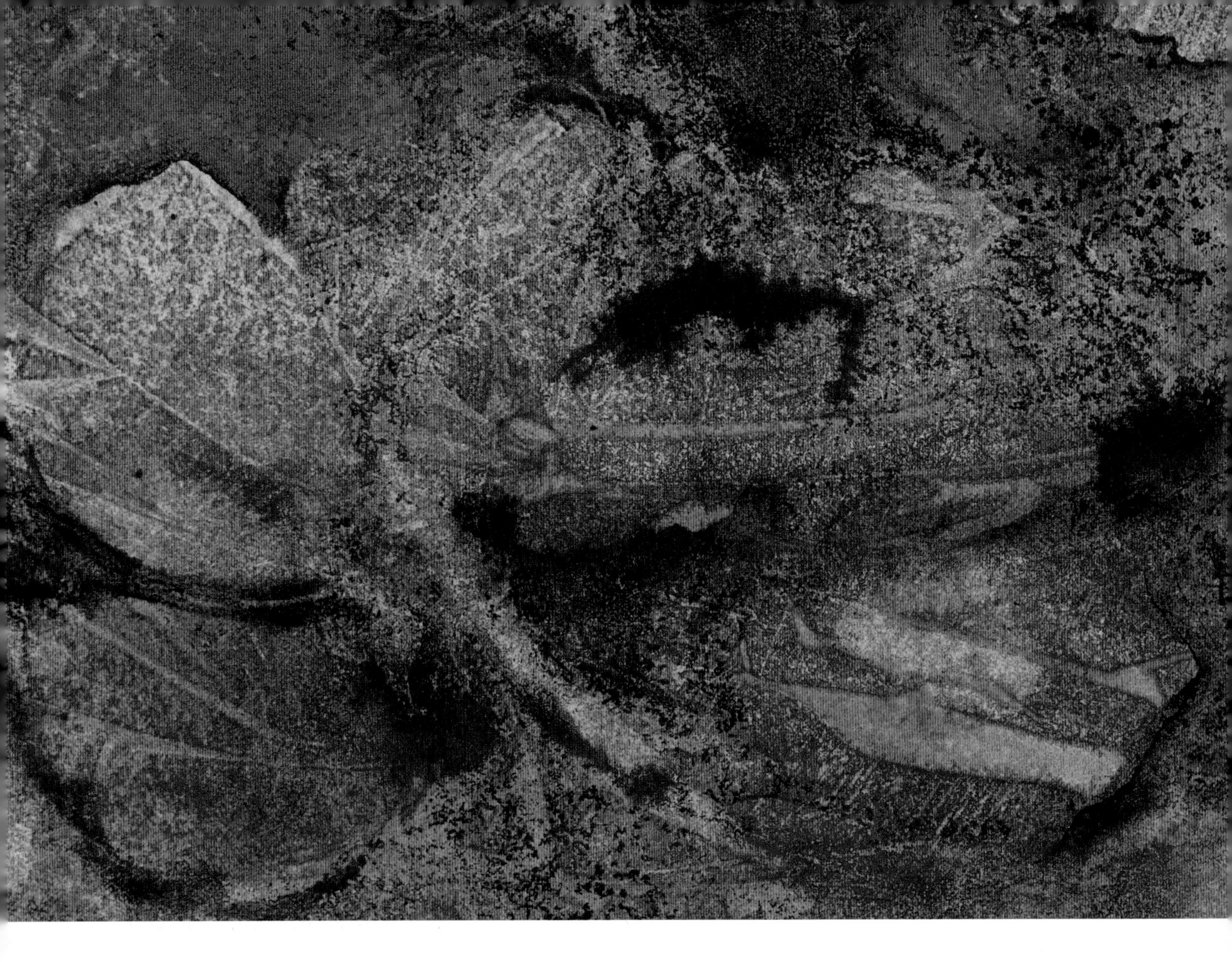

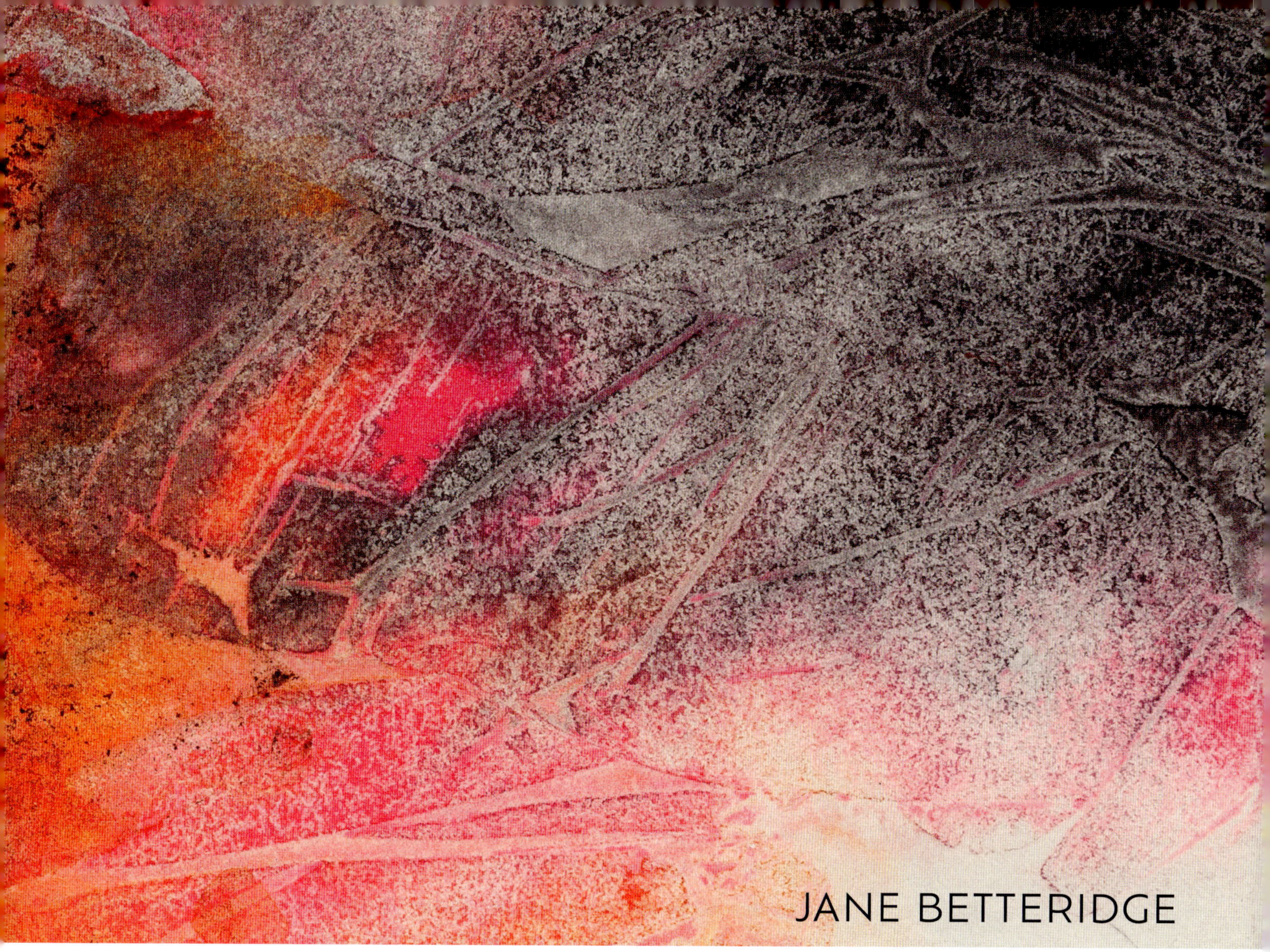

JANE BETTERIDGE

PAINTING ABSTRACT NATURE ON CANVAS

A guide to creating vibrant art with watercolour and mixed media

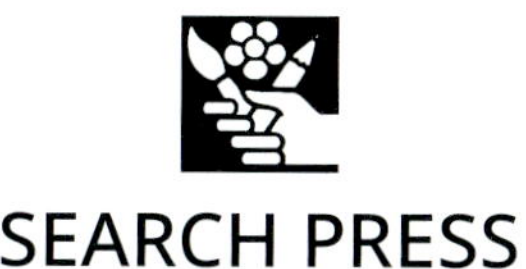

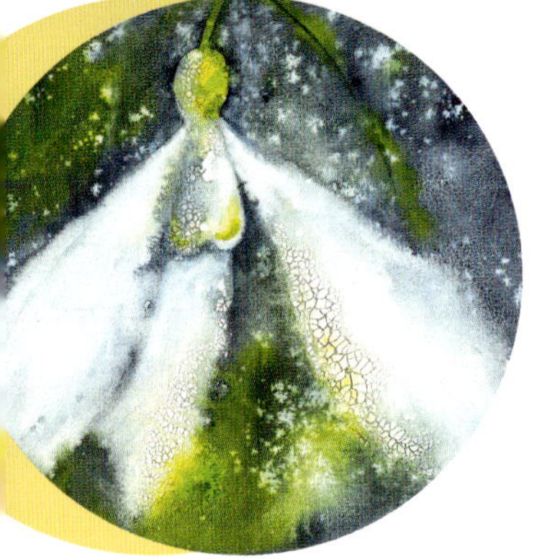

DEDICATION

This book is dedicated to Georgia Rose, my granddaughter, who has brought so much joy and love into our lives.

First published in 2023

Search Press Limited
Wellwood, North Farm Road,
Tunbridge Wells, Kent TN2 3DR

Photographs by Mark Davison at
Search Press Studios

Illustrations and text copyright ©
Jane Betteridge 2023

Photographs and design copyright ©
Search Press Ltd. 2023

ISBN: 978-1-78221-970-5
ebook ISBN: 978-1-78126-962-6

Suppliers
If you have difficulty in obtaining any of the materials and equipment mentioned in this book, then please visit the Search Press website for details of suppliers: www.searchpress.com

You are invited to visit the author's website: www.janebetteridge.com

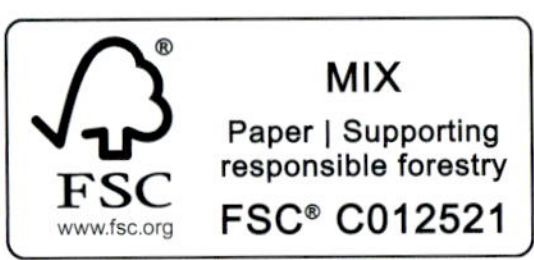

ACKNOWLEDGEMENTS

I'm lucky enough to have had the same editor for all three of my publications – Edward Ralph. Thank you Edd for your guidance, patience and support; and to all the team at Search Press, it's great to be in your stable of authors.

Thank you to my wonderful family, husband Alan and daughters Charlotte and Grace for accommodating me being shut away for hours, days, weeks and months at a time, beavering away in my studio and for putting up with me missing out on lots of their social occasions.

Thank you to all of my many students and also followers on social media whose kind words and positive comments always encourage me, thus giving me the confidence needed to produce this latest book.

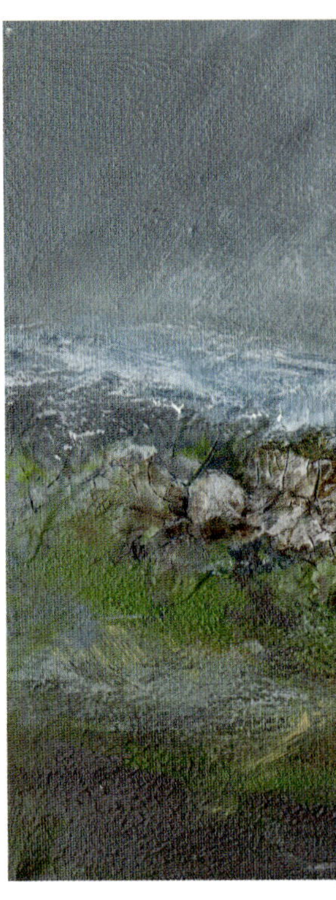

Page 1
Autumn Woodland
20 x 20cm (8 x 8in)

Nature's reds and golden hues were evoked here simply through washes and spatterings of watercolour.

Opposite, top
Bodmin Moor
80 x 50cm (31½ x 19¾in)

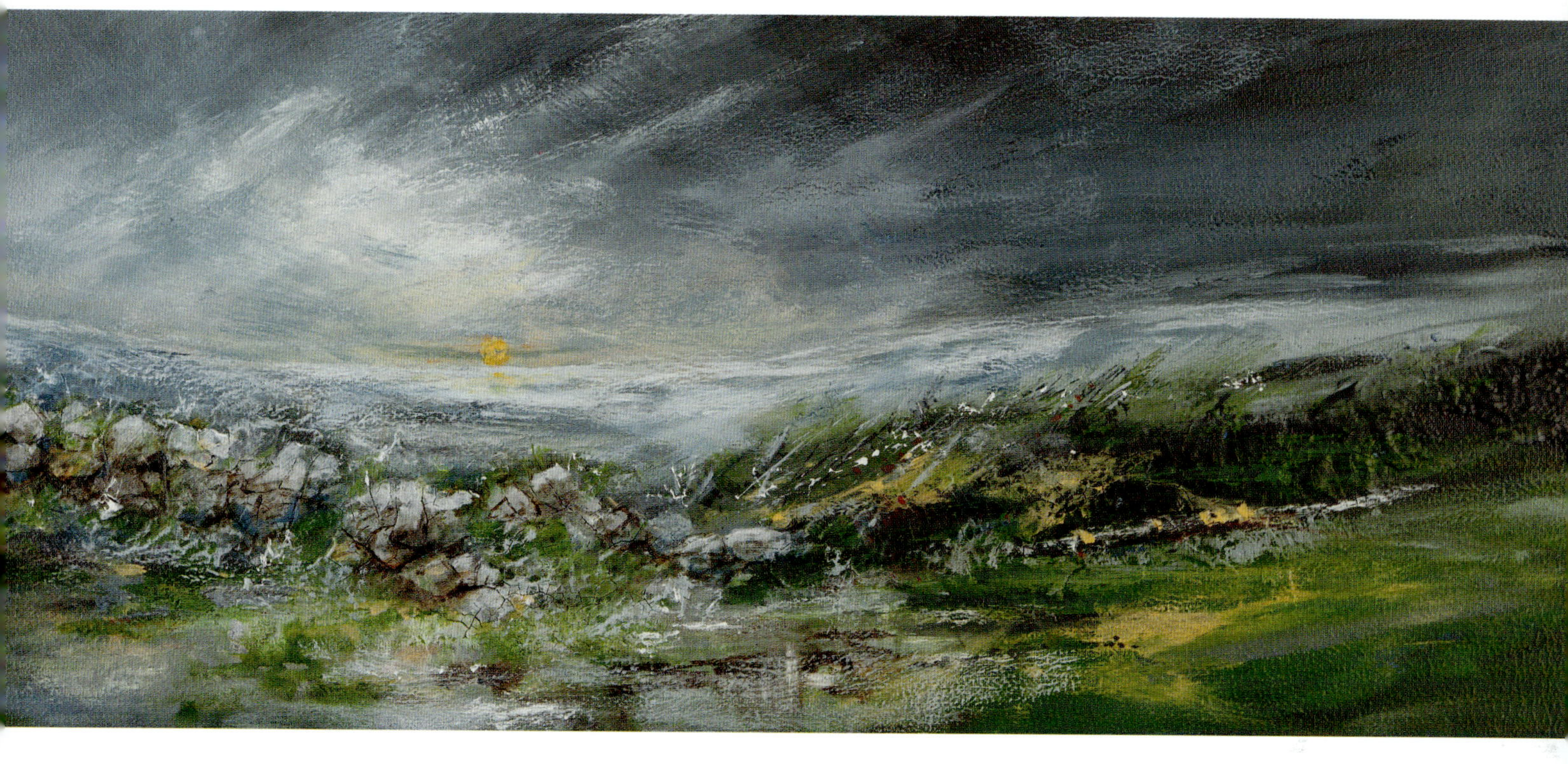

CONTENTS

Introduction   6

Getting started   8

First steps into abstraction   18

Texture   44

Colour   50

Swirling Tide at Porthmeor   58
Step-by-step painting

Deeper into abstraction   72

Magical Honesty   92
Step-by-step painting

Shape and line   104

Flowers and Fruit   116
Step-by-step painting

Afterword   126

Index   128

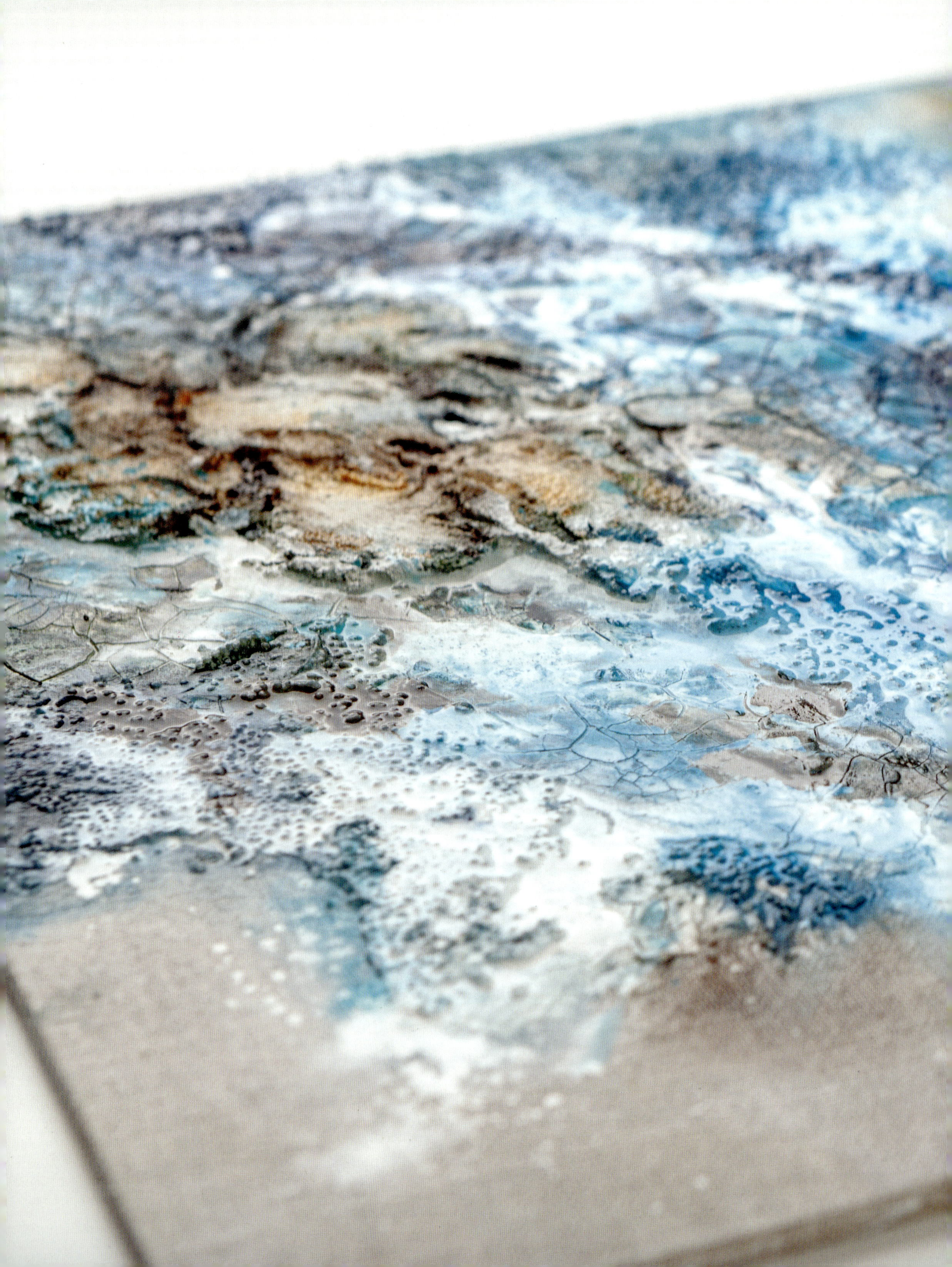

introduction

Abstract! A word that conjures up limitless ideas and possibilities – from minimal lines, carefully constructed dashes or randomly applied graphic marks, with no direct resemblance to any subject; to recognizable subject matter, painted in a looser, more exciting way than a purely representational approach allows.

In truth, abstraction was a form of art that I never took seriously. In fact, I hadn't intended to experiment with it at all – but my practice was clearly moving towards abstraction.

A friend happened to comment, while browsing my recent paintings, 'I see you're doing more abstract work now, Jane.' Looking at the painting she held was a groundbreaking moment for me. She was right. I had, quite unintentionally, begun to adopt a semi-abstract style. Looking over the past years' work, I could see that I had been loosening up a great deal – and I liked what I saw.

There was no going back. Later that day I ordered books by well-known abstract painters and turned to social media to find many more pieces from less famous artists. I found myself hooked. My experimentation accelerated and I loosened up still more. As my new style progressed, I realized that my studio time was becoming increasingly enjoyable and rewarding.

Thanks to watercolour ground, I found myself able to use watercolours on otherwise unpaintable surfaces, and in particular on the traditional artistic surface of canvas.

In this book I want to encourage you to take the same path – not gradually but headlong. Now! Let's prepare our canvas and get going.

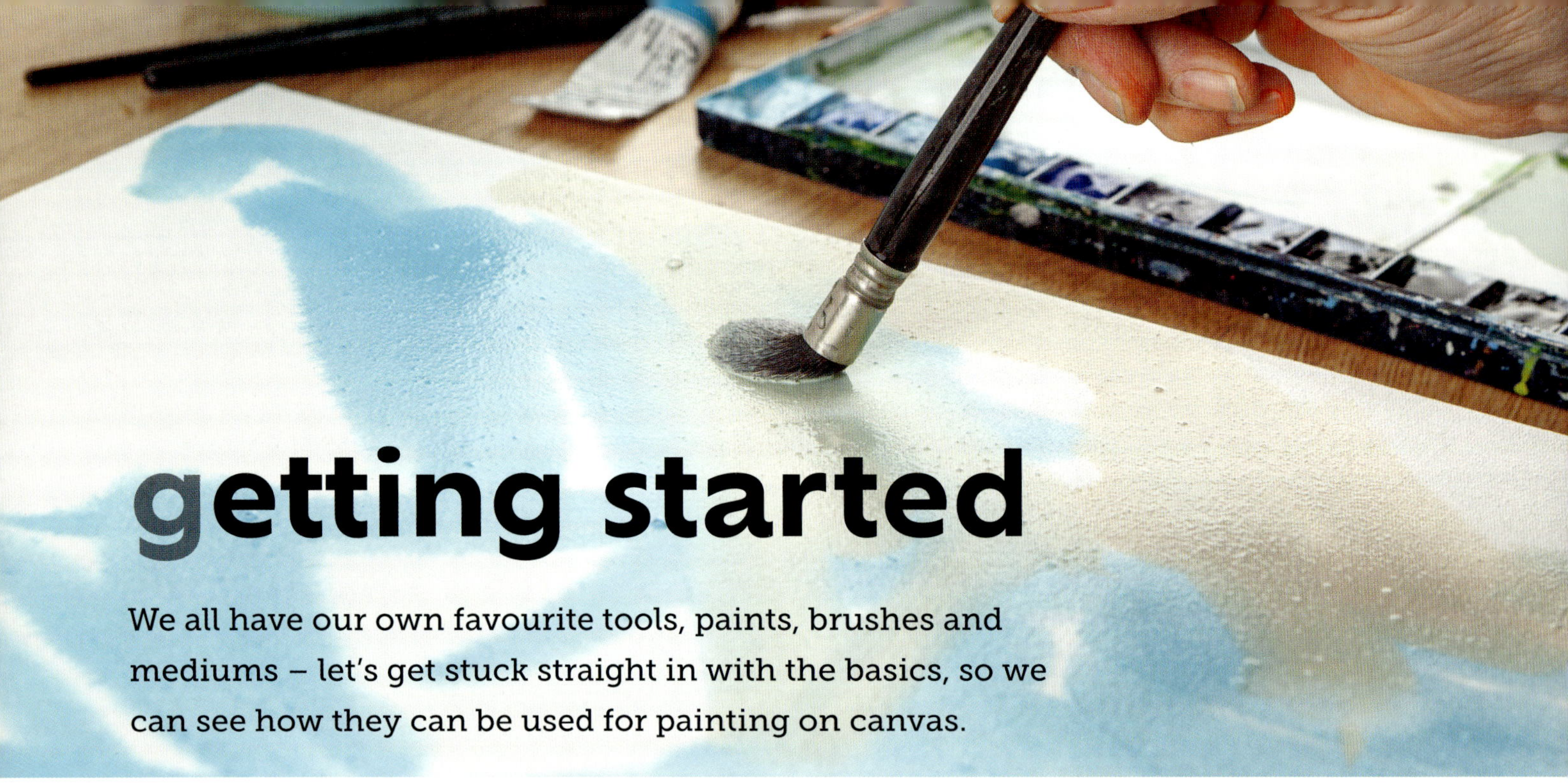

getting started

We all have our own favourite tools, paints, brushes and mediums – let's get stuck straight in with the basics, so we can see how they can be used for painting on canvas.

Canvas

If you have painted with watercolours before, you'll likely be more familiar with paper than canvas, which is more often associated with oil and acrylic paints. Artistic canvases are normally pre-primed with a few coats of gesso – ideal when using acrylics or oils, but not very good for use with watercolour paints. Fortunately a primer product called watercolour ground has been developed. This can be applied with a brush or a roller over the gesso surface, to make the canvas suitable for use with water-based media.

Canvas just means a heavy-weave fabric. The majority are made from cotton and linen. Cotton canvases are cheaper and perfectly suitable – it's what I generally use. Linen is better for fine, detailed work as it is woven more finely. Hessian canvases are also available. These are really textured, and are useful if you want to emphasize or explore more textural qualities in your work. Canvases are available in different forms:

Box canvases Sometime called canvas blocks, these are wooden frames covered with pre-stretched and primed canvas, ready to paint upon. Available in many shapes and sizes, the quality varies depending on how much you want to pay. Because there is nothing behind the majority of the canvas, there is a slight 'bounce' when working upon it.

Canvas boards Thin pieces of board with fabric glued to the front, canvas boards are primed and treated in the same way as a box canvas. If you want a firmer, more solid surface than a box canvas, these are a good choice. Canvas boards usually require framing. The easiest way is by using a tray frame, where the artwork literally sits inside the frame. No glass is required as the surface should be protected with a shielding spray or a finishing wax when the artwork is completed.

Loose canvas Canvas is also available to buy in rolls. It can be cut to any size, then stretched onto a wooden frame and nailed into place. Some artists prefer this method as they are not restricted to generic sizes.

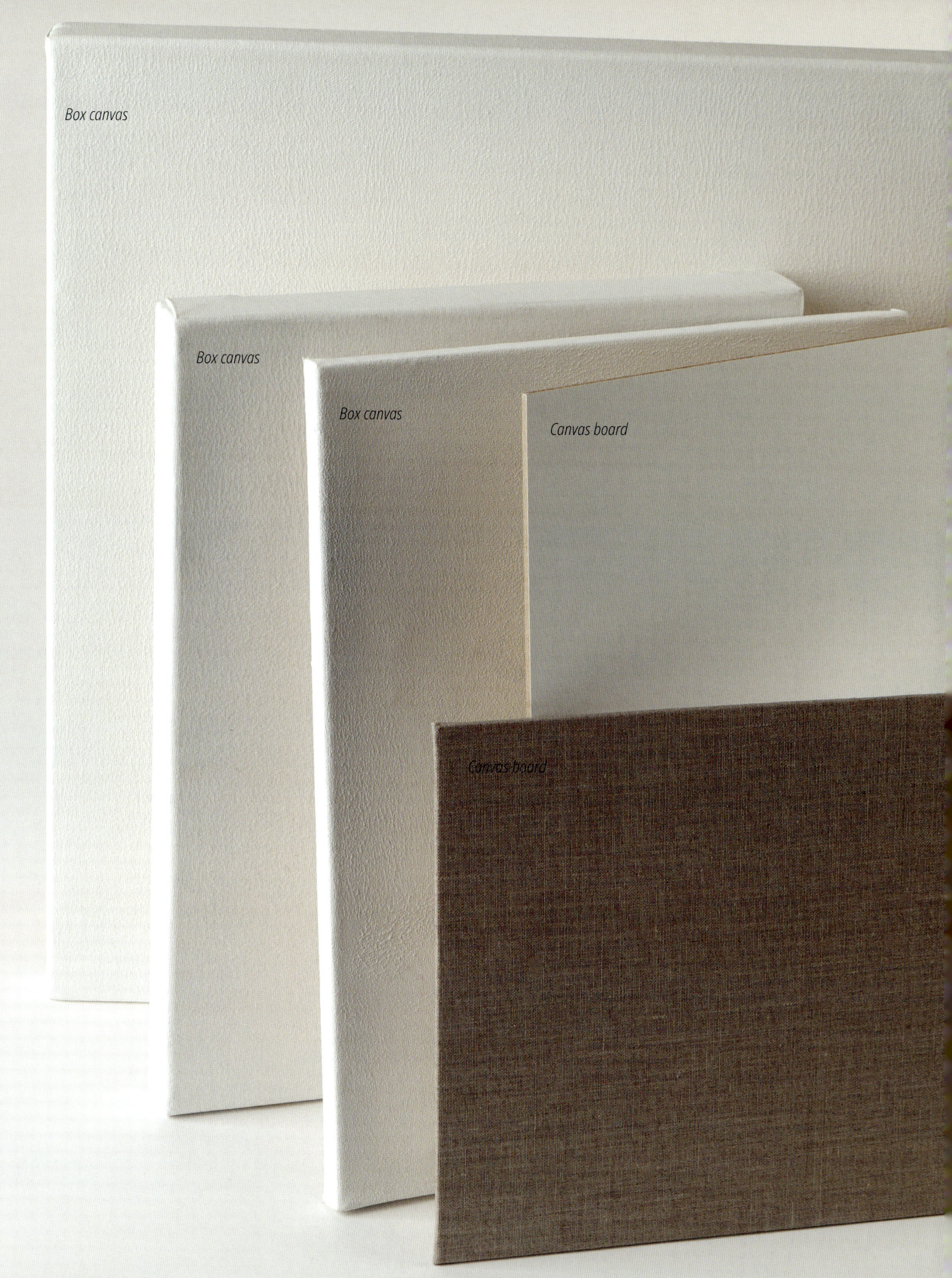
Box canvas
Box canvas
Box canvas
Canvas board
Canvas board

Preparing canvas for watercolour

Watercolour applied to canvas will either bleed and
sink in (if unprimed), or bead and run off (if primed).
To enable us to paint on it, we need a primer called
watercolour ground. This is painted onto the canvas
surface and allowed to dry. After that, watercolours
applied to the surface will behave much like
on paper.

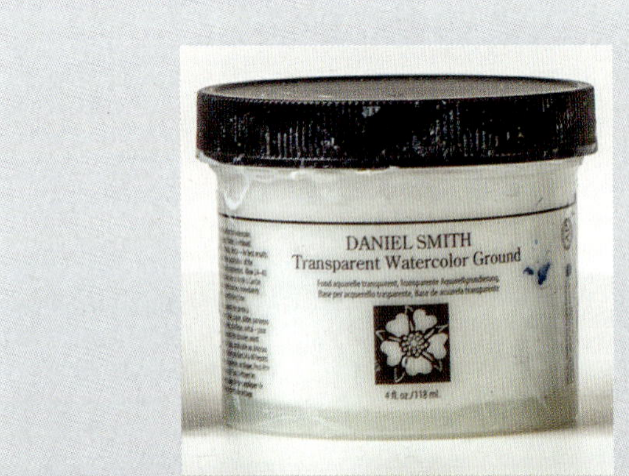

Watercolour ground

Watercolour ground is bought in large and small plastic
bottles and tubs. I favour white or transparent ground but
it is also available in black, buff and gold; as well as two
different surface textures – coarse and fine. It really is so
versatile, so experiment to find out what works best for you.
I find that the finer ground is best applied with a brush and
the coarser ground with a palette knife.

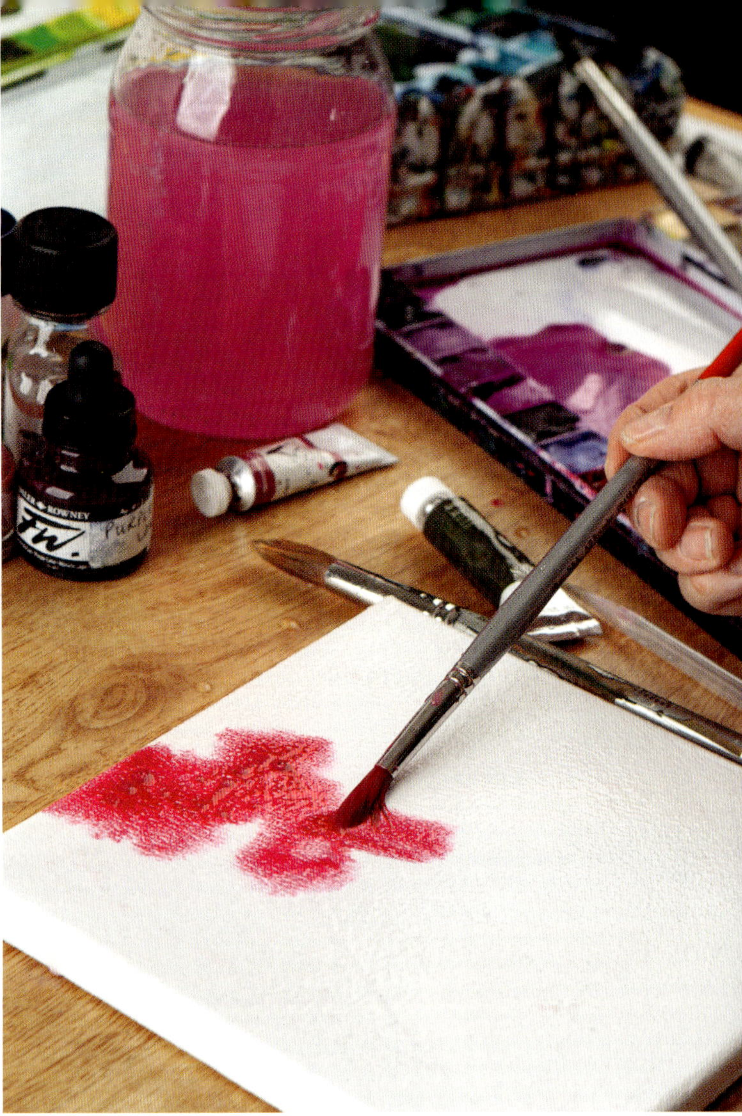

*Watercolours being applied to a box canvas prepared with white,
fine-textured watercolour ground, as described opposite.*

What else can I paint on?

Other surfaces such as plastic, wood, metal,
ceramics and leather can also be primed with
watercolour ground and painted on.

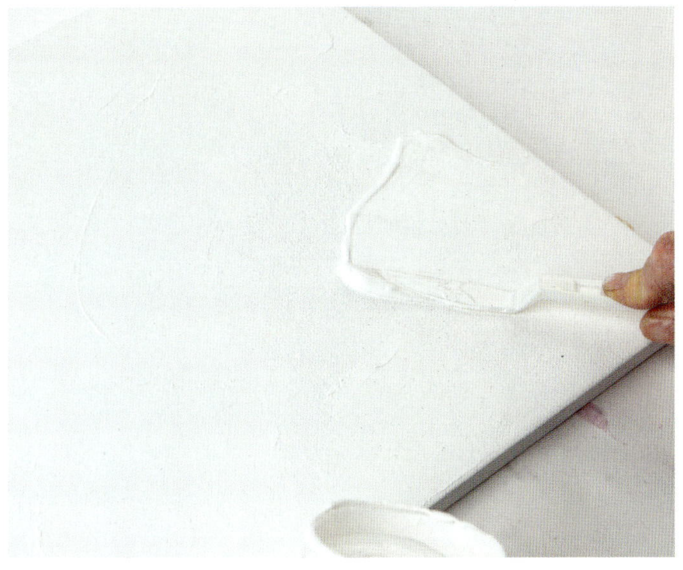

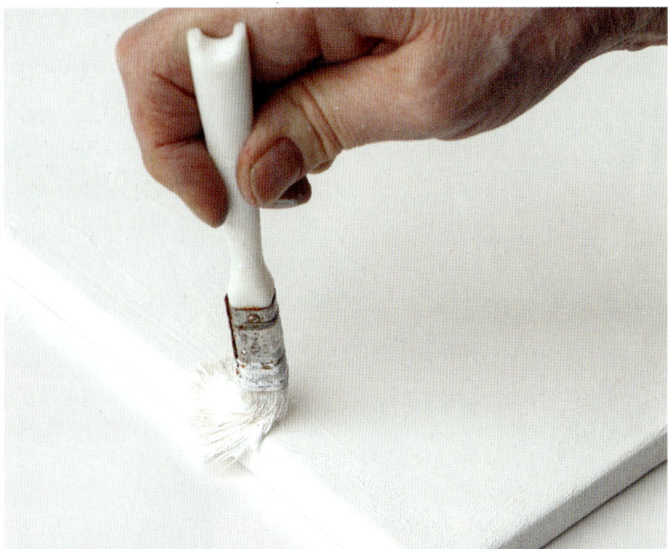

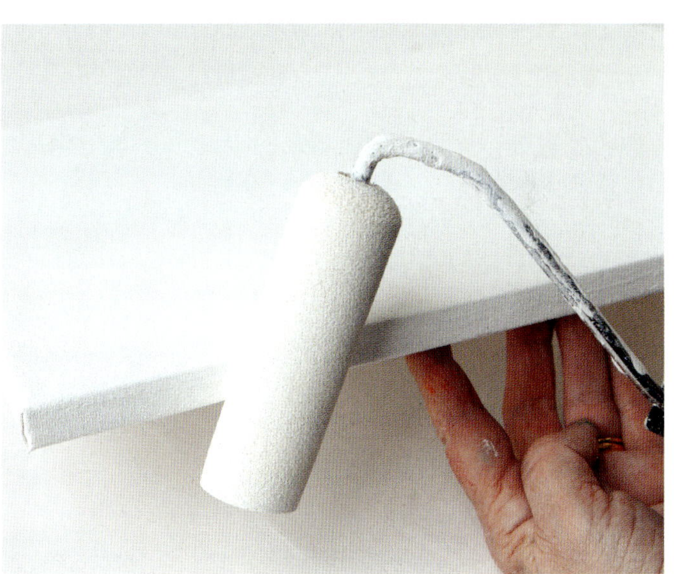

1 Use a palette knife to apply the watercolour ground, and spread it out evenly, as though buttering toast. Two thin coats are better than one, so spread it quite thinly.

2 Swap to an old household brush to work right round the edges of the canvas. Don't feel restricted to what's already on the canvas – apply more with the brush to ensure good coverage.

3 Once the front and sides of the canvas are all covered, use a foam decorating roller to smooth out the surface and obliterate any brushmarks.

4 Leave to dry overnight, then repeat the process to ensure the canvas is well covered with watercolour ground. It'll then be ready to work upon.

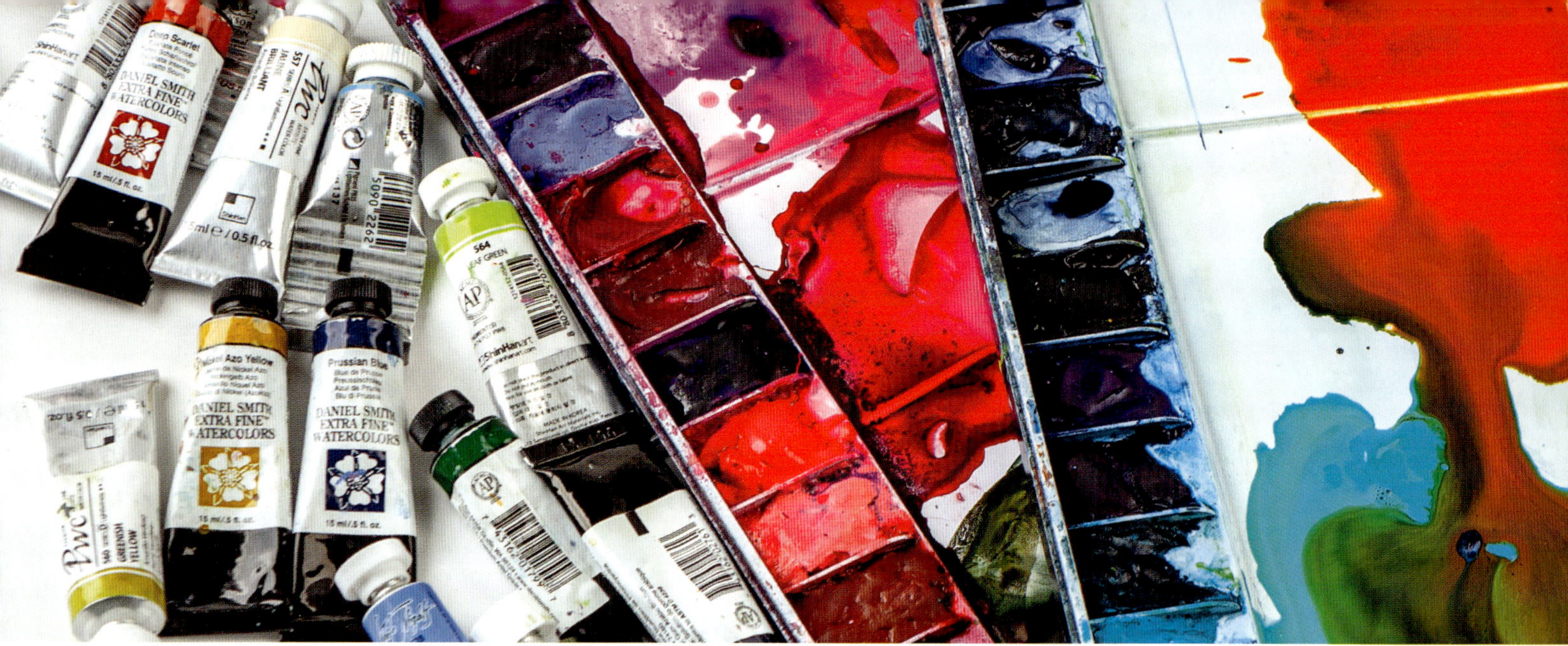

Watercolour paints

Watercolour paints consist of very finely ground pigments bound together in a carrier solution that – thanks to the presence of gum Arabic – allows the paint to be heavily diluted with water to make thin transparent washes of colour without losing adhesion to paper.

Canvas won't absorb the watercolour to the same extent as watercolour paper. As a result, dry paint on the surface is easy to accidentally lift off or remove. You can add a drop or two of Aqua-fix to your mixes to make it more resilient (see right).

Depending on the pigments used and combination of other ingredients, some paints behave differently from others. Some granulate, for example, which means that the particles of pigment form visible grains as they settle into the surface – this can be particularly effective on the heavy textures we will explore in this book.

Watercolours are classified as transparent, semi-transparent or opaque. This will be noted on the packaging. Transparent colours allow more light through, and opaque less. At one time I only used transparent or semi-transparent paints but, as I've moved forward with my work, I find I'm using a lot of opaque colours – especially when painting on canvas.

Watercolours can be bought in tubes, which can be squeezed out onto your palette, or in pans. Pans are solid blocks of paint designed to fit neatly into tailor-made metal or plastic paint boxes. Colour is released from the paints by stroking it with a wet brush. Pans are fine when working on a small scale and for taking out on location, but I favour tubes for painting bigger pictures so I can squeeze out larger amounts of paint.

There are several manufacturers that make good quality paint ranges. My favourite is Daniel Smith as their colours are highly pigmented and luminous. Another – much cheaper, but still very good quality – brand is ShinHan.

Aqua-Fix

Aqua-Fix forms a waterproof barrier that allows you to glaze or paint several washes without lifting the earlier layers – effectively fixing the main problem of working on canvas. This is a very useful product and one that I recommend adding to your painting kit.

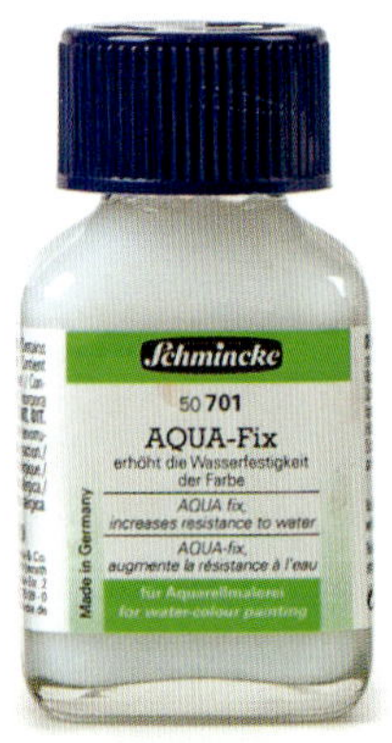

Preparing watercolour for canvas

Watercolour needs to be mixed a little stronger when working on canvas, so don't dilute your colours as much as you would when working on paper. The consistency you're looking for is double cream (US: heavy cream).

Optionally, add a couple of drops of Aqua-Fix to make the resulting mix more water-resistant, allowing you to use wet-on-dry techniques, such as glazing, later.

Get the consistency right

Shown above is watercolour paint prepared to the correct consistency on the left: rich, vibrant and full of impact. Above right, the paint has been thinned too much initially, giving thin, insipid results.

Keeping paint clean

Use a pipette to add water to your colours. It gives you control of exactly how much water you add, and, as you're not adding a loaded brush to the water every time, it also helps to keep your water clean.

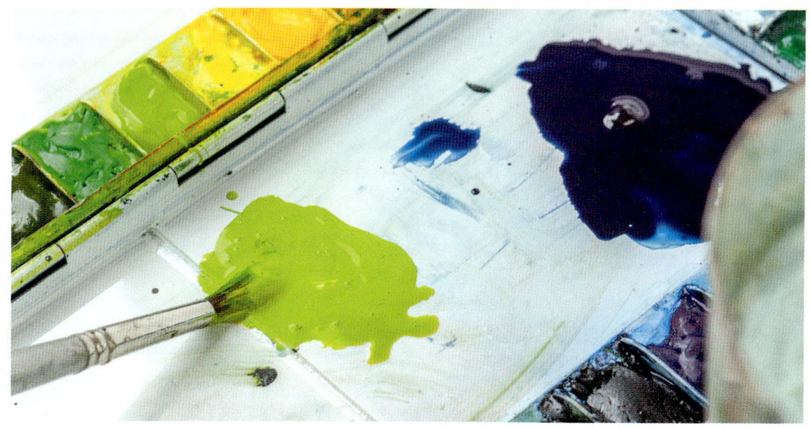

To ensure vibrancy, prepare wells of colours separately on the palette, leaving space between them.

Mixing colours

When mixing, prepare each paint in a separate part of the same palette well, then draw each into the middle. Don't combine the colours completely – leave some space between pools of colour, and allow them to merge naturally. This will help you to get vibrant effects.

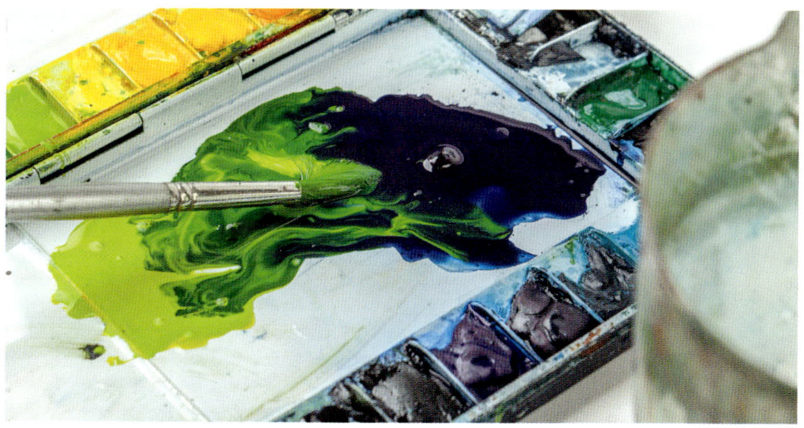

Draw the colours together into the space in the middle, and don't overmix them. Leave them like this, and they'll continue to mix on the canvas surface.

Brushes

I use both flat and round brushes. I find rounds more versatile. They hold plenty of water or paint and have a good point. Large flat brushes, on the other hand, are ideal when applying large amounts of paint – when doing washes, for example. Smaller flat brushes are useful for painting sharp edges or shapes like poppy petals, and also for dragging across silver birch tree trunks.

Paint with as large a brush as possible. This will naturally make your work more loose and free, as you will be unable to paint in too much detail. I use a range of sizes, from 4 to 16, along with a really big wash brush and a size 1 rigger. Riggers have long fine hairs and so are especially useful for painting fine lines and delicate subjects such as stamens in flowers and tree branches. I also have a small hog hair brush for scrubbing out any mistakes and a very useful slanted chisel brush for lifting stems or distant tree trunks from background washes.

However careful you are, brushes wear out with use – but that's not to say they are no longer useful. I save all of my old brushes to use with materials that may damage new brushes, such as masking fluid and various grounds.

Look for brushes with a mixture of sable and synthetic hair that keep their point and springiness, that last well and are reasonably priced too.

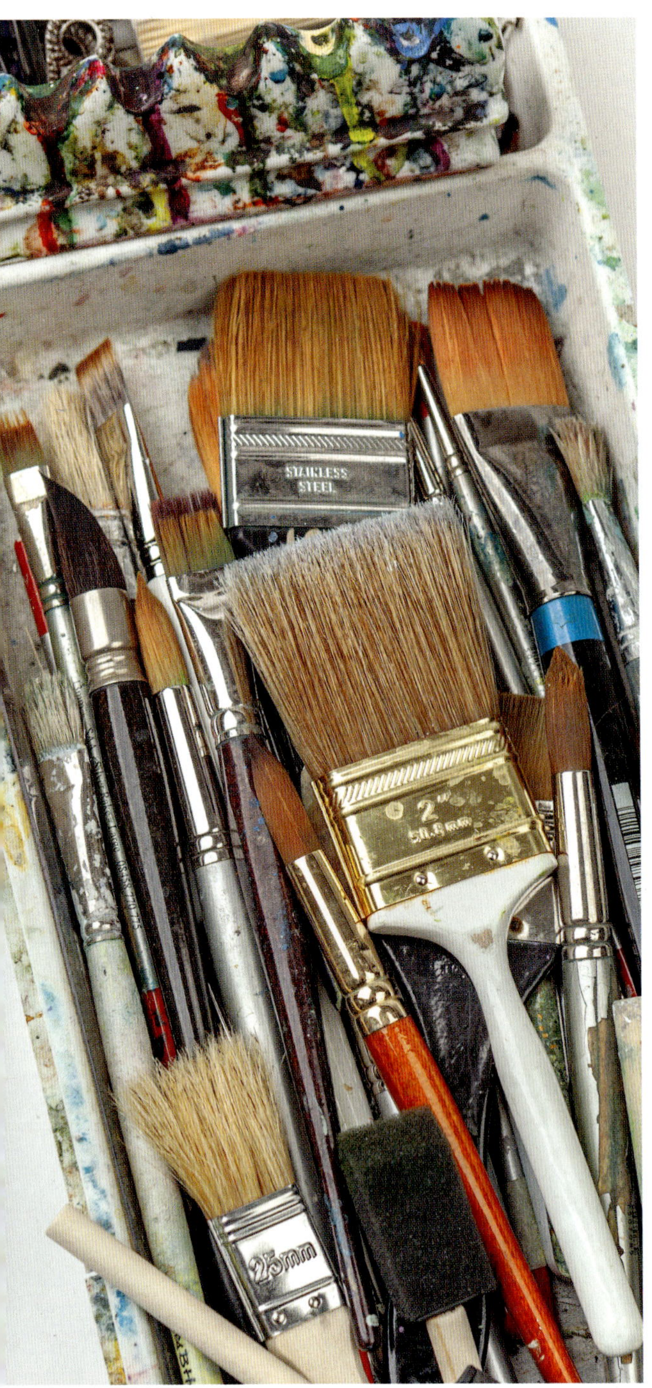

The SAA and Davinci brushes have the qualities I like and they are the ones I have used in this book. Experiment to see what type of brush suits you best.

False economy

I never buy very expensive brushes as I use them with many different types of painting media and, beyond rinsing and cleaning them, do not treat them as well as perhaps I should. Having said that, I never buy cheap brushes either. They are a waste of money, and usually lose hair which can then take up residence on the painting surface. This can be difficult to remove without spoiling your painting.

Applying paint to canvas with brushes

I prefer to work on a wet surface, so before applying the
paint, use a large brush to wet the canvas with clean water.
The water won't soak in as it would on watercolour paper, so
be careful not to apply too much water.

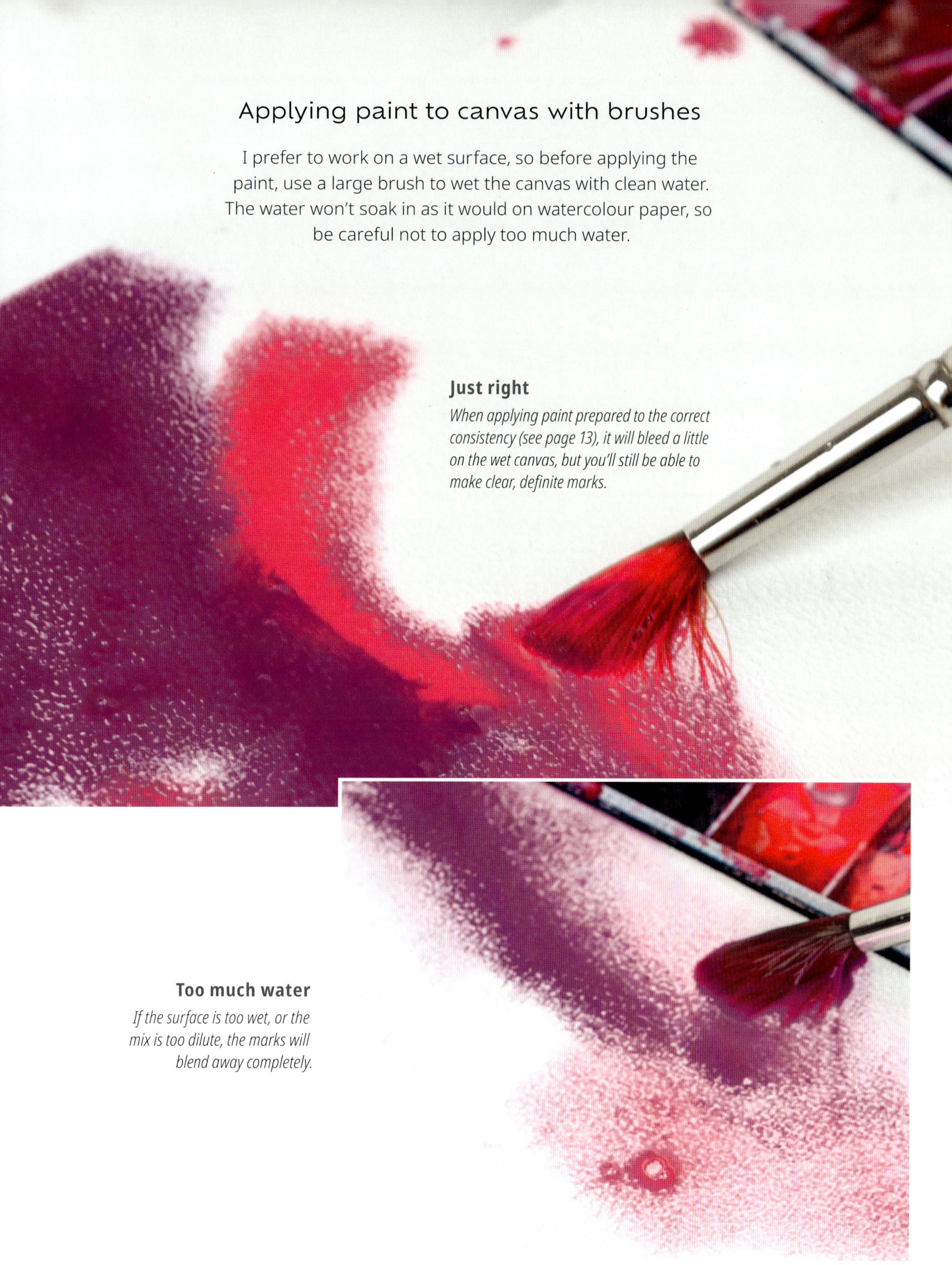

Just right

*When applying paint prepared to the correct
consistency (see page 13), it will bleed a little
on the wet canvas, but you'll still be able to
make clear, definite marks.*

Too much water

*If the surface is too wet, or the
mix is too dilute, the marks will
blend away completely.*

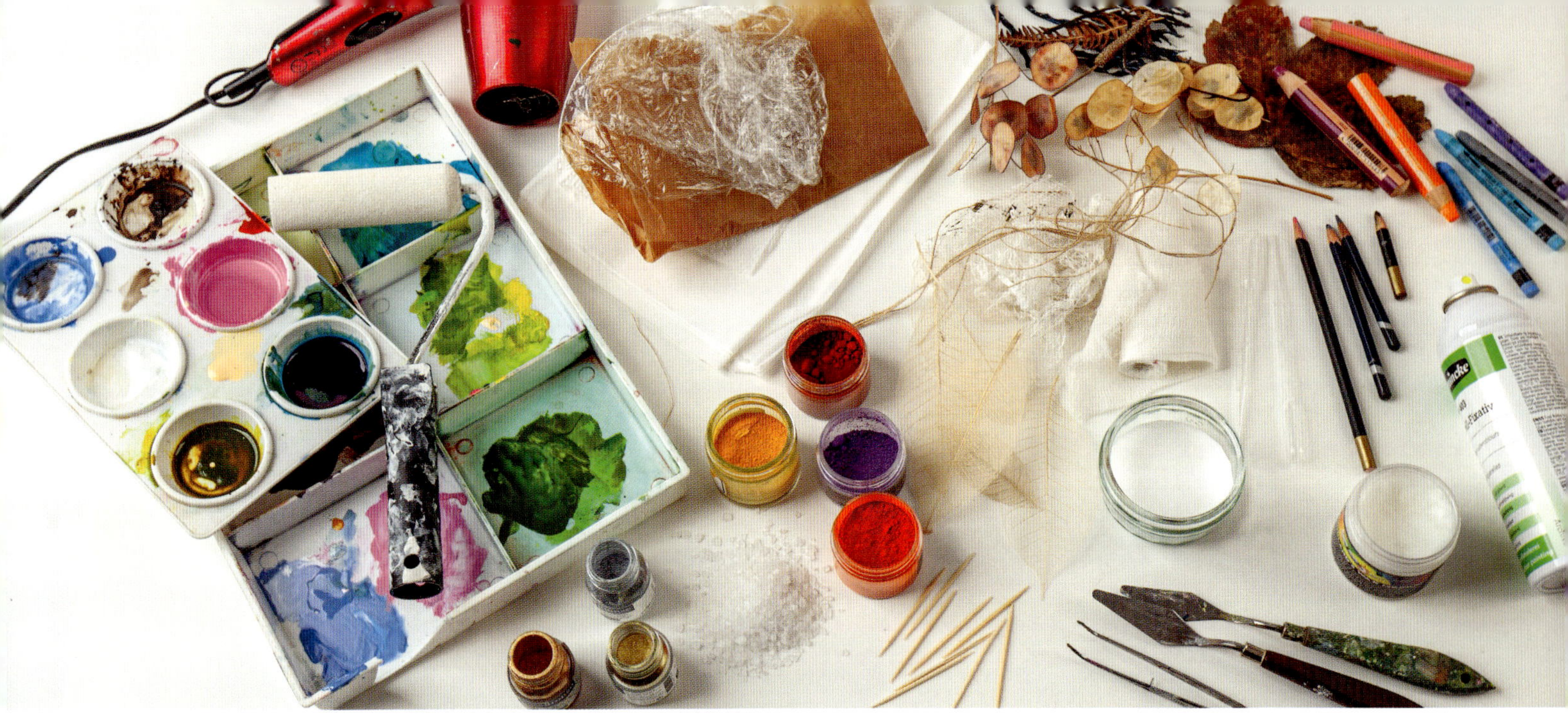

Other materials to explore

With a prepared canvas, paints and brushes, you're ready to go –
but before we start, it's worth considering what else you can bring
to your artwork.

Palettes For outdoors use, I have a small palette
with loose, interchangeable pans that I fill with
colour depending on where I'm going and what I'm
painting. The palettes I use in the studio are larger,
my favourite being two metal ShinHan palettes
which hold thirty-six colours each and have large
mixing areas. If I'm doing large washes, I'll use a
cheap old-fashioned muffin palette. These hold a lot
more paint and keep the colours separate too.

Bronzing powders These sparkly, luxurious,
metallic powders are wonderful – a real must-have
in your painting kit. They come in various shades of
silver and gold and also a bronze colour.

Rollers and foam wedge applicators Using
foam rollers to apply watercolour ground to
canvases (see page 11) gives a really smooth, even
finish; but they can also be used to apply paint or
various mediums. I also use them to roll over collage
materials to get them to stick down.

Skeleton leaves, gauze and thread To add
extra texture to my work I often introduce cotton
thread and gauze (old-fashioned cotton bandage) to
replicate branches in tangled hedges, ditches and
interesting foliage.

Salt If you are a traditional watercolourist and
reluctant to try new approaches to your work, the
application of a sprinkling of salt might tempt you. It
requires little effort to achieve big results.

Mark-making materials I use watercolour
crayons, Derwent Inktense blocks and watersoluble
sticks to draw into my work, to add lines or
squiggly marks. Ideal to take out sketching, they
are made even more interesting when water is
added. They are also good for running over the
surface of texture materials to highlight the raised
areas. I also use a variety of both watersoluble and
waterproof black pens for sketching and mark-
making in a painting.

My process

Pure experimentation is at the heart of my process. I always work with the colours first and then composition, deciding what to focus on, what to include and what to leave out. These tips will help to give you some ideas for experimenting.

Don't over-plan I doodle more than draw accurately – my main aim is to get down on paper the shape and form. Once you've got that, you can expand to develop the composition as much or as little as you need.

Colour I use whatever colour I feel like – it may be representational or it may be nothing like the colours I saw when out seeking subject matter. If it's a particular colour that has inspired you to paint a particular subject in the first place, ensure you emphasize that colour. Try painting swatches of different colours, and trying different options together to create harmony or drama, depending on what you want to happen.

Texture It may be that textures I experienced when out and about made me want to get painting – if so, what better to use than what's right there? Play around with different materials and found objects in your sketchbook and try several possibilities. You might try stamping a few leaves or grasses into some watercolour ground to make organic-shaped indentations. Once this is dry and paint is added, it will create some really unusual effects. You might also try shredded gauze or dried seedheads – even tiny shells and pieces of seaweed.

Bronzing powder tips

These are prepared by being mixed with water. They can be mixed very thinly to give a hint of a sparkle or to the consistency of single cream for excellent coverage – the latter is usually the approach I take. I love to see them spattered in the background or used to emphasize the light catching leaves on trees or birds' wings. The gold is really good to use when painting autumn leaves or atmospheric skies. They can be used on top of inks as well as paint and sprayed with a touch of water for a more subtle effect, if required.

Salt tips

Ideal for use in skies, seascapes, landscapes and flower painting, salt can give textural results as well as adding sparkle and interest. After applying pigment to a wet or dry surface, the salt should be added just as the paint is starting to dry and lose it shine. When the salt hits the paint it pushes the pigment away, leaving unusual white markings. The salt residue is brushed away after the painting is completely dry.

Table salt gives smaller markings whilst the larger, coarser granules of rock salt give a more exaggerated effect. If you are after a subtle effect try sprinkling fine salt sparingly. A more random, dramatic effect can be achieved by adding generous amounts of the rock salt.

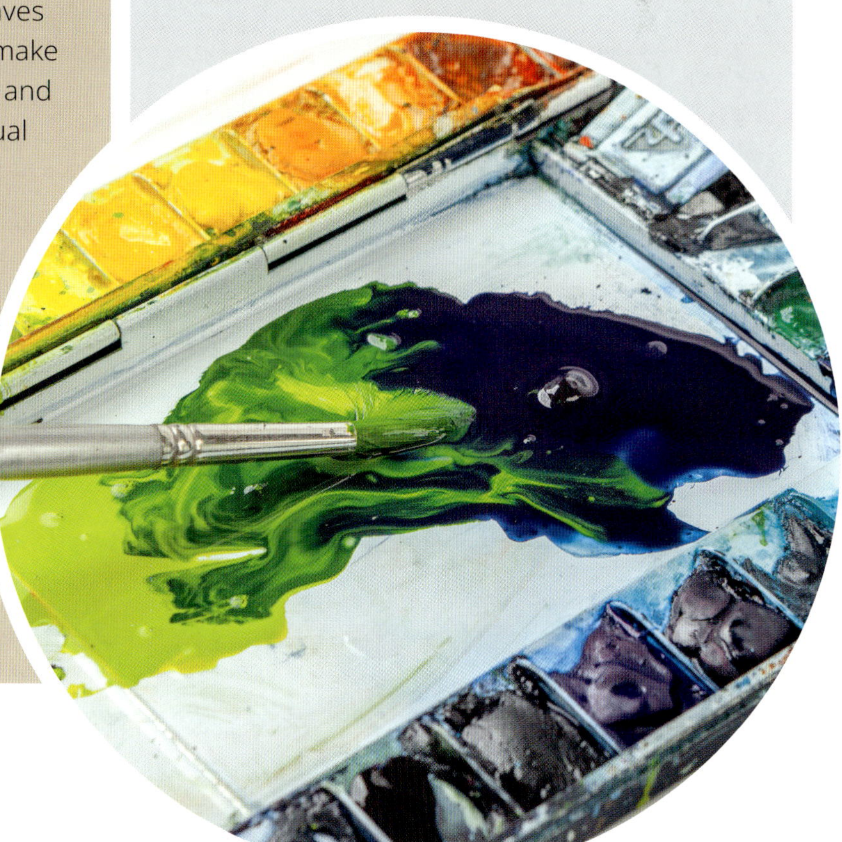

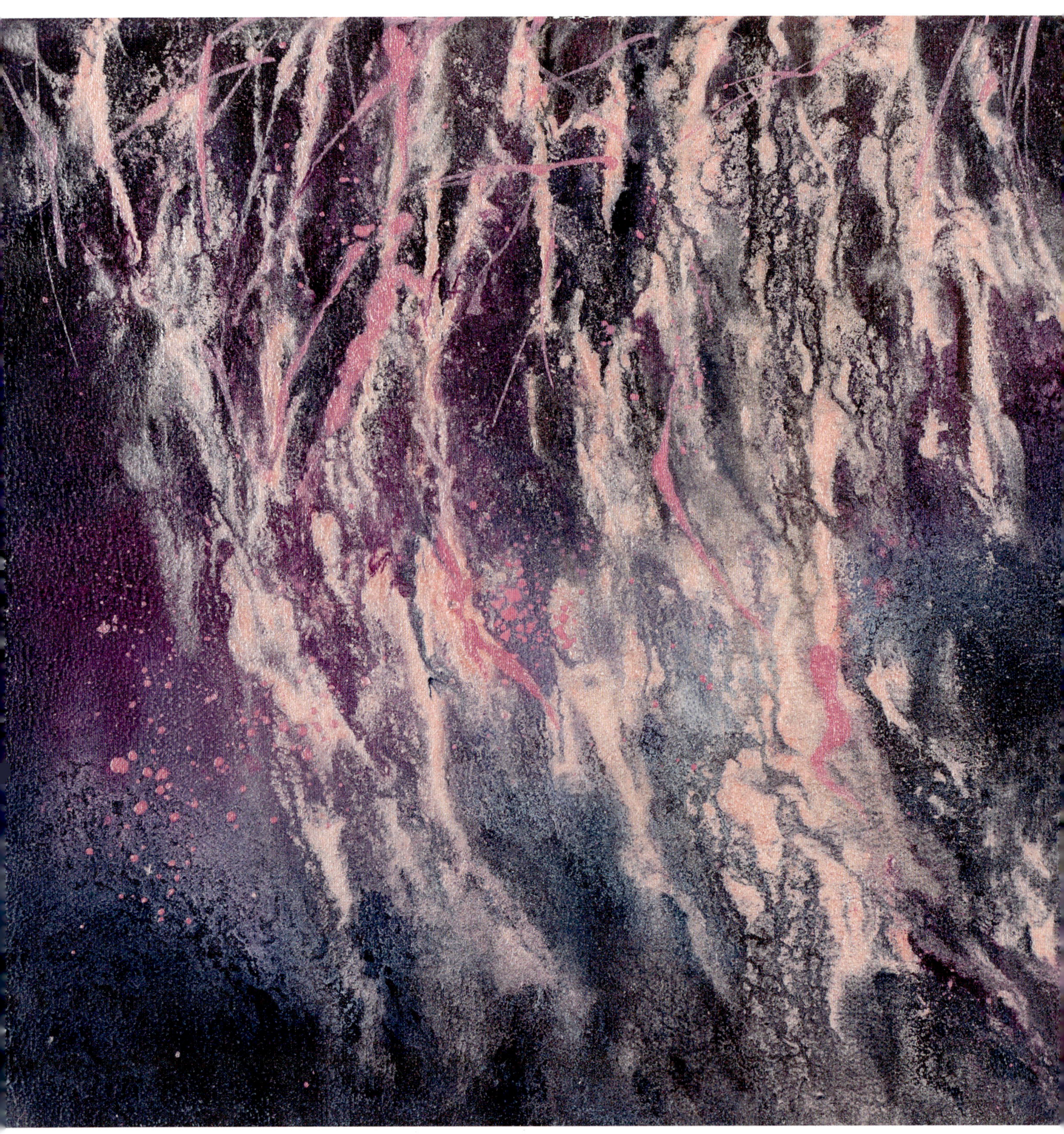

Mystical Woodland

25 x 25cm (10 x 10in)

first steps into abstraction

With your canvas prepared and your paint and brushes at the ready, you're all set to begin your journey into abstraction. The exercises and ideas here are intended to get your energy up, and allow you to get familiar with how the paints and canvas interact. Don't worry too much about 'how abstract' to go just yet – we'll explore that later on.

What is abstract art?

Abstract art is much more than laying down haphazard splotches and smears of paint, random lines and shapes – it provides you with the freedom to withdraw from the restictions of representational qualities. The elements and characteristics of the subject remain, but they are conveyed in a different, freer, way.

An abstract approach gives the artist more freedom and expression in interpreting their subject matter; from the way they perceive it to the practicalities of painting it.

With regard to colour, lines, shapes and textures, abstraction allows artists to show their personality. The work relies on personal reactions and responses; feelings of emotion, intuition, creativity and spontaneity as well as personal response to shape, colour, mark-making, composition and so on.

These characteristics lie at the heart of all forms of any art – abstraction simply gives you the perfect opportunity to free yourself from traditional and common ways of working, to take a fresh approach and develop your own personal style.

Taking an abstract approach in your artwork stimulates you to experiment, break down barriers, discover and create. It enables us to look at the world around us in a different way, allowing ourselves freedom without boundaries or preconceived ideas. This is both challenging and exciting – and well worth experimenting with. Abstraction paves the way to originality and individuality.

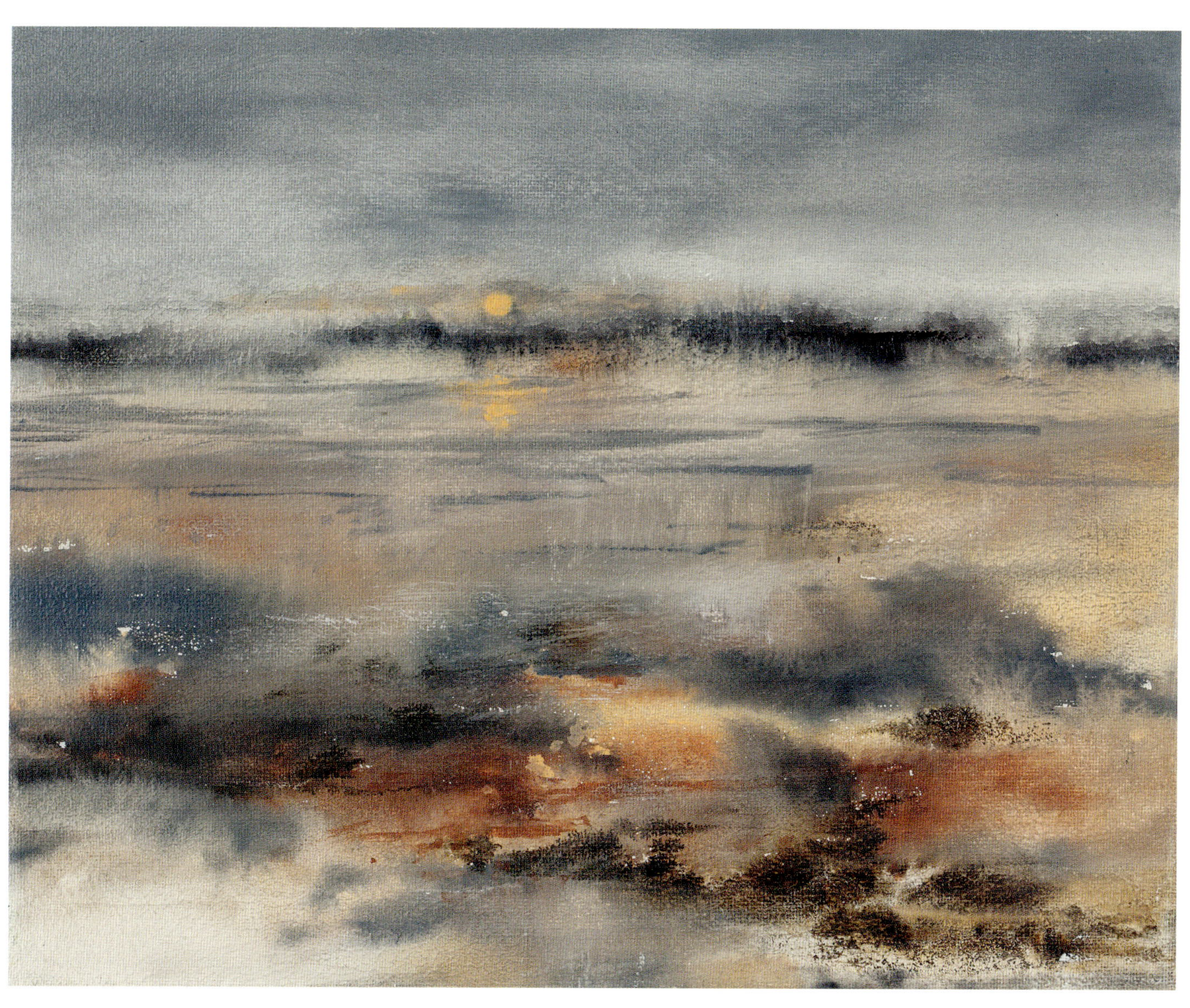

Last of the Sun
30 x 25cm (11¾ x 10in)

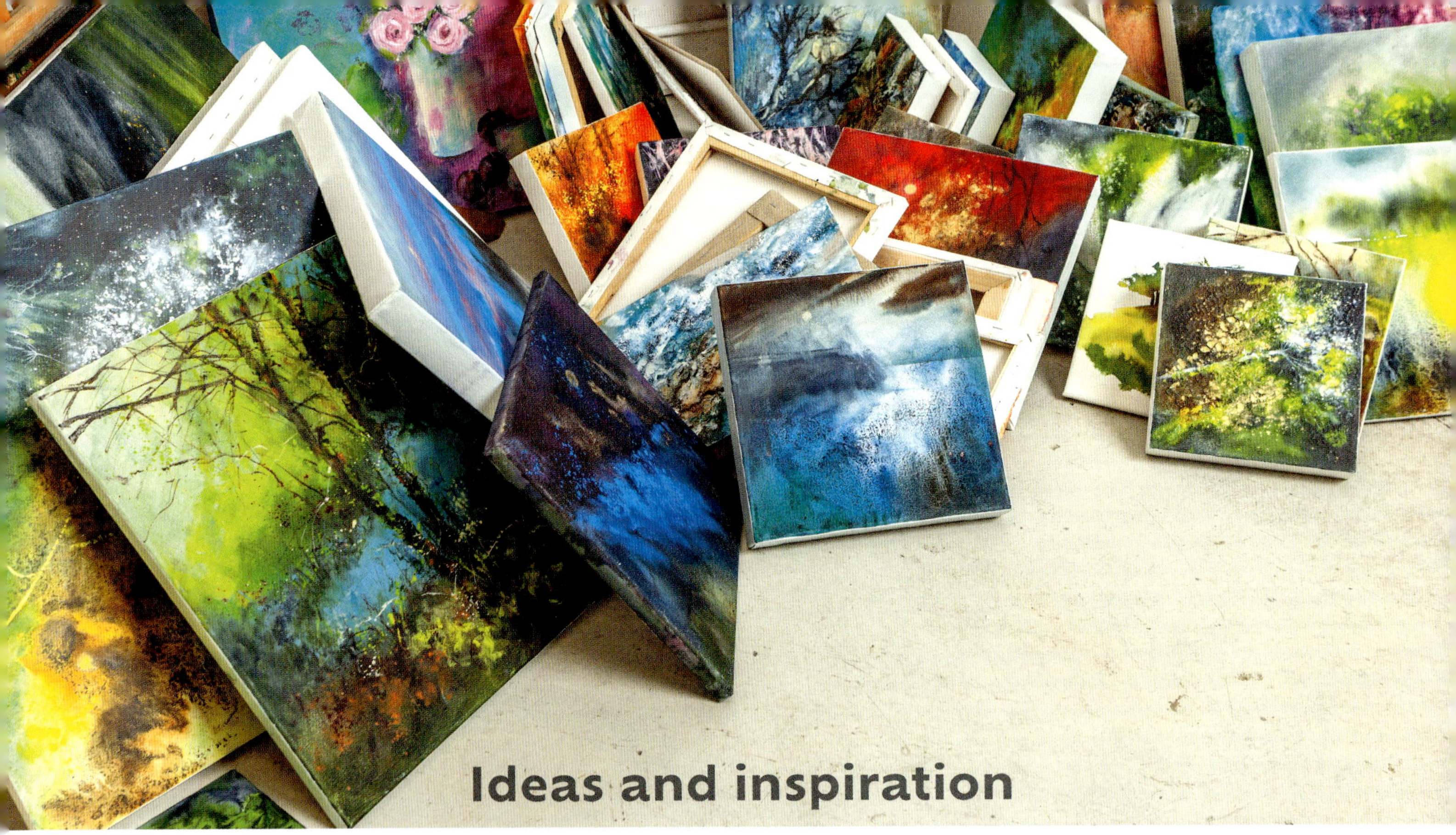

Ideas and inspiration

Deciding what to paint is a very personal thing. What inspires one artist to paint may not inspire another, and it can be challenging to know where to start with abstract art. What should you use as inspiration? How you will develop your work?

Here I share three different routes into abstraction – try them all, and see which works for you. As always, experimentation is key. Don't regard these as the only routes in. The exercises on pages 38–43 will help you to explore and practise responding to these entrance points.

My inspiration

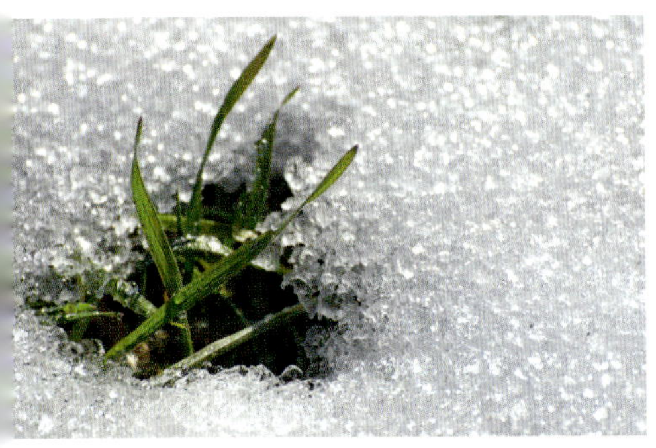

Nature provides the majority of my inspiration, and it has a huge scope. Seascapes, landscapes, flowers, plants – indeed, flora in any form. Whether it is new shoots popping their heads through the ground in spring; flowers in full bloom in summer; the gradual changing of the colours in autumn; or stark, bare, raggedy remnants of plants trying hard to survive in winter – all inspire me.

Object as starting point

Perhaps the most obvious way to approach an abstract painting is exactly as you would a representational painting: by picking an object or image that appeals; such as a leaf, then identifying and focussing upon the exciting quality that attracted you to the object – perhaps the texture, pattern, colour or surface.

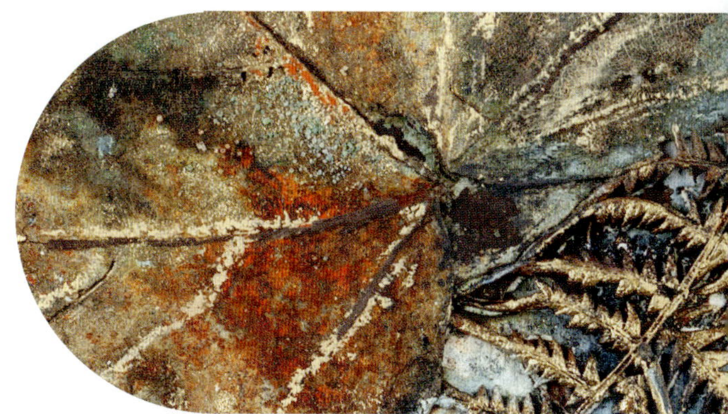

Detail from Winter Leaves *on page 25, which was inspired by fallen leaves.*

Location as a starting point

We've all found ourselves amazed by a scene in front of us, and if you take a moment to take in as much of your surroundings as you can, you'll find it really helps to put your finger on how exactly it makes you feel – and this in turn can be a powerful starting point for an artwork.

That feeling can be joyful, exciting or inspirational – or quite the opposite. Your choices of colour and how you approach the detail can reflect this.

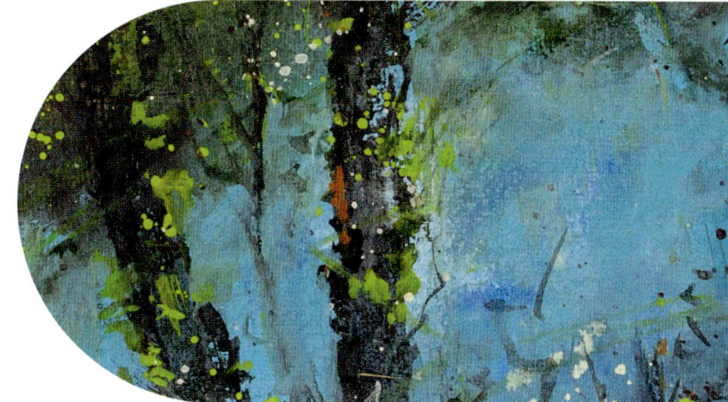

Detail from Dimminsdale Wood, *shown on page 27, inspired by an unfamiliar sight in a local wood.*

Technique as starting point

Some artists choose a concept, such as 'happiness', or 'struggle' to explore, rather than an object. If this seems too nebulous, you might find that looking at particular techniques – such as loose, free washes, or dense texture – offers another route in.

Experimenting with new materials, taking one step at a time, can lead to some new experiences in how you apply paint and use colour.

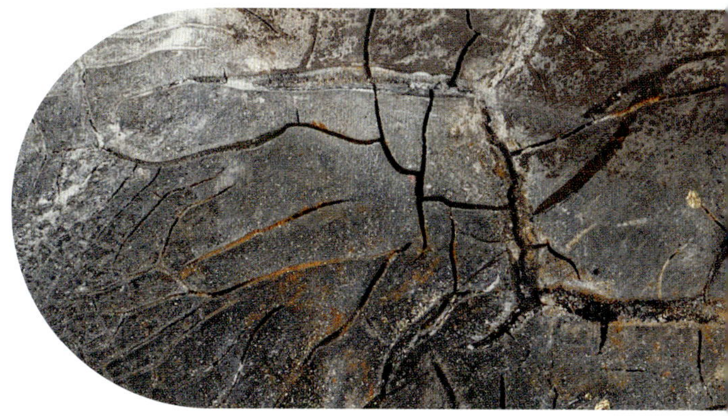

Detail of Above and Below, *shown on page 29, a semi-abstract work that was the result of explorations with crackle paste.*

Starting point: object

Once you find an object that you think might be a good starting point, examine it really closely, then take several close-up photographs. If appropriate and you are able to, you might gather up some of the object for later reference. Jot down your observations in a sketchbook, too.

I try and get down some notes about colours on the spot, then work more on the sketchbook once back in my studio. This will help you to focus and identify exactly what appeals to you. I have occasionally filled a whole sketchbook with my notes and scribbles from just one walk.

Next, try printing off several of the photographs you have taken and experiment with textures, shapes and mark-making and then work on colours and composition.

Painting *Winter Leaves*

The leaves that inspired – and feature in – the painting opposite were nearly frozen to the ground when I came across them, and I can remember being cold and yet stimulated by the frosty weather. This experience added to stirring up the senses and was a great point of inspiration for my work.

Since they were plentiful, I picked up a few to feel their texture – running my fingers down the veins to see how prominent they were allowed me to experience their crinkled, scrunched-up dryness. It felt almost as though they might shred in my hands. It struck me that this quality might make it possible to use them as collage material later.

I gathered some up and pressed them between the pages of my sketchbook so that I could look at them closely once back home.

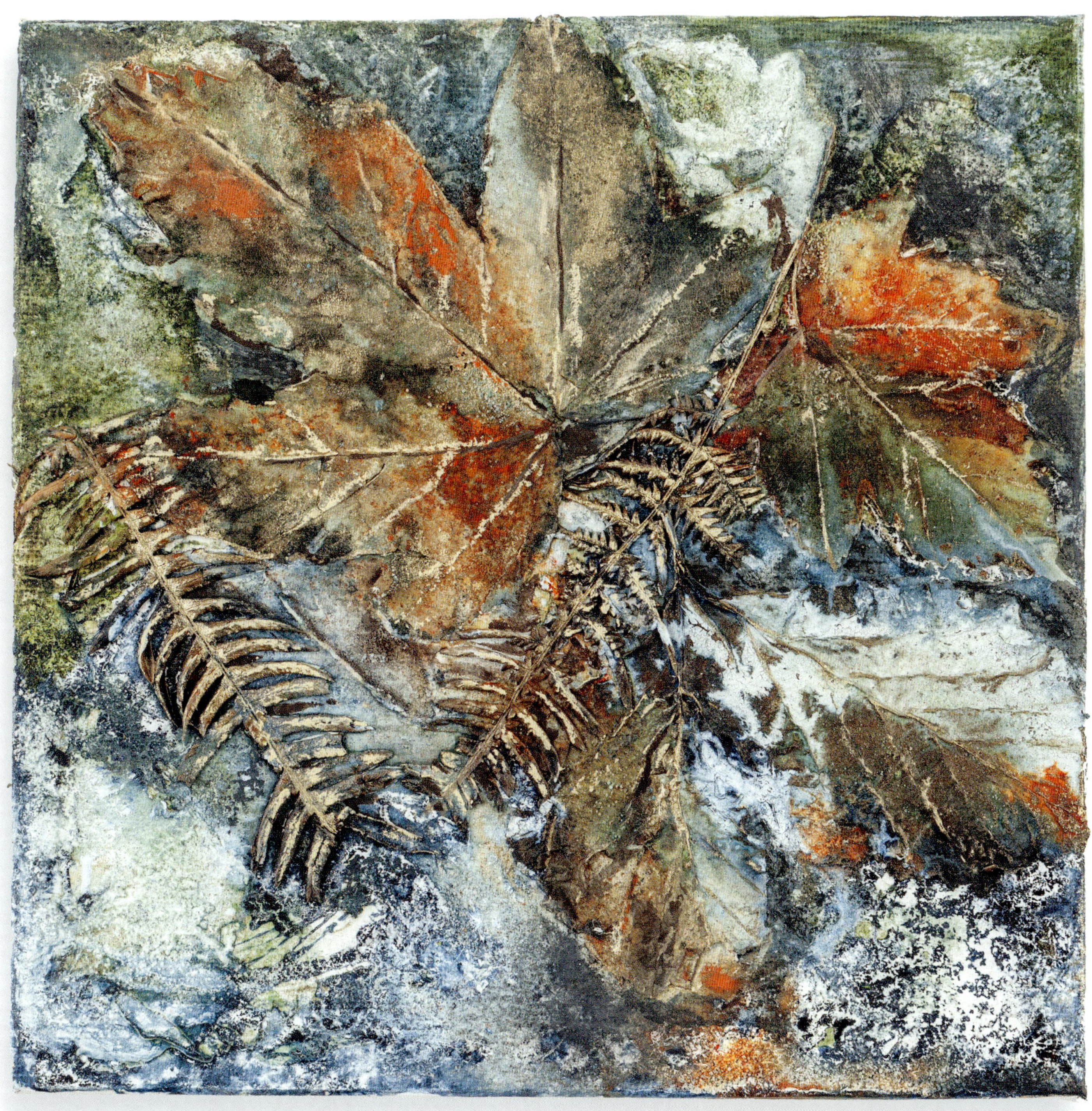

Winter Leaves
20 x 20cm (8 x 8in)

Starting point: location

If I'm out with the intention of deliberately looking for scenery to paint, I'll carry several light sketchbooks, loose sheets of watercolour paper and a small limited palette of paints, the odd ink and some crayons.

Often it is the overall scene that appeals to me, but it might equally be a particular element or aspect within the scene that speaks to you. When you are simply walking, take your time to soak up the atmosphere of the place, so you're alert to the potential it offers. Smell the air, listen to the birdsong or other sounds – or it may be that it's the silence and solitude of a place which inspire you. Think of these sensations when you are back in the studio, ready to start planning your painting. It will stimulate your creative juices and help to reignite the stimulus that excited you when you were there.

Of course, if you've visited a place before and felt inspired, the chances are it will work again. Even here, try to look through fresh eyes and remember that different weather conditions can change the mood, the light, the colours and the overall feel of a place. This is true with the changing seasons too.

Painting *Dimminsdale Wood*

When a potential painting presents itself, it is often by surprise, so I try to have my camera, or at least my phone, handy at all times.

The woodland painting opposite was the result of a wonderful walk close to my home, where I am a frequent visitor. This particular day was cold, but the sun was shining and the stagnant pond, normally a green/grey on a dull day, was transformed as it reflected the bright blue of the sky.

The sight uplifted my spirits as we'd all been through a very difficult year. The wonderful blue sky and the new bright green shoots of the bushes and trees made me feel that we were moving forward in the world. I knew that nature was beginning to flourish and, hopefully, so would we. I stood and soaked up the atmosphere, the bird song, the wind rustling some of the grasses and a few leaves. I took lots of photographs, and couldn't wait to start painting when I got back to the studio. Everything else is subsidiary to the eye-catching central area of vivid colour, and is rendered as though out-of-focus. Only a few linear marks suggest trees and undergrowth so that the eye-catching blue stands out as the focal point. Soft edges and the light overall key help to create a calm and safe atmosphere to the finished painting.

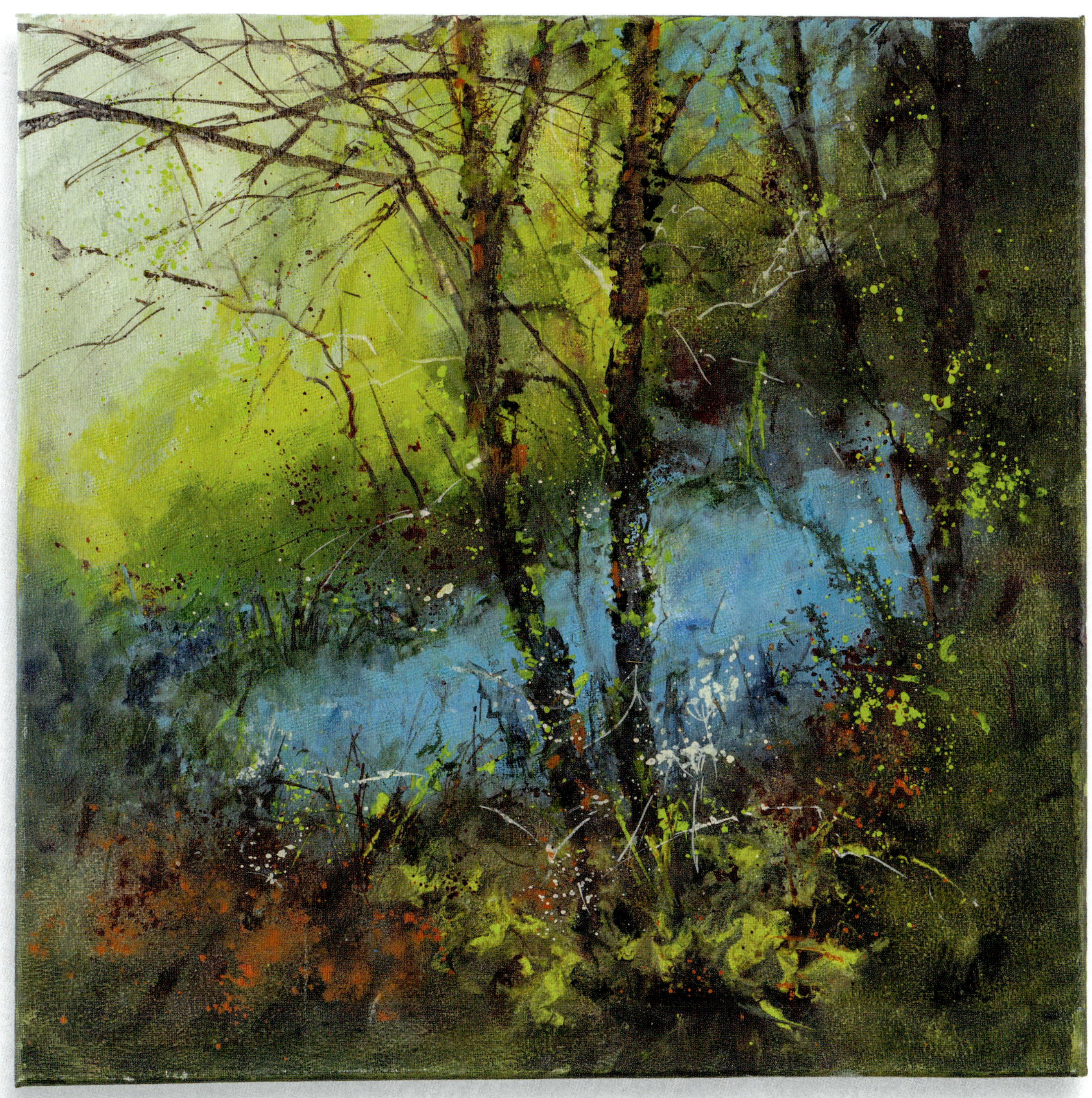

Dimminsdale Wood

40 x 40cm (15¾ x 15¾in)

Starting point: technique

If you've got a subject in mind, choosing a suitable technique for a representational painting depends at least somewhat on the subject matter. You need to try and choose something that reflects or enhances the characteristics of the subject. For example, to depict a dried, barren landscape, you might look to crackle paste.

However, abstract work can free you from this restriction by flipping things around – by taking a particular tool, technique or even colour as your starting point, you are free to explore as you wish.

When you discover a new paint that you really like, especially one that has an interesting property such as heavy granulation, or a particularly vibrant colour, start playing around with it. Start by letting it run and mix with other colours, or adding a dribble of granulation medium. While it's starting to dry, try adding salt, sprinkling in some gold bronzing powder, or drawing into it with a pipette, twig or pencil, to drag out fine lines of colour. See what comes of these experiments and discover whether a subject starts to suggest itself from what you explore.

I sometimes use a sponge applicator, scraper or roller to pull the paint around and across the surface of my support or try glazing over it with a transparent wash. I will try using a palette knife with a thicker mix, using impasto techniques or flattening it into some inks. I really enjoy playing and experimenting with different ideas – it's so rewarding.

As an example, I experimented with manufactured raw pigments to make my own paint a couple of years ago. Using a sheet of glass and a palette knife, mix a little pigment with gum Arabic and then add a few drops of honey to stop it cracking when it has dried. You can then pour it into empty pans and let it set. I built up quite a selection and enjoy using them. I also rub dry pigment into textured marks on paper and canvas and then spray with AquaFix; this creates a lovely effect.

Painting *Above and Below*

Crackle paste is a great favourite of mine. Over the years, I've used it as a base to enhance and give unusual, exciting results to many landscapes and seascapes and even flowers. The structural, organic marks it makes are reminiscent of dried, cracked mud, but in experimenting, it also reminded me of the bark – and structure – of trees, so I pursued this idea.

Some techniques will captivate you by creating added interest. Others may not suit you or your style of work – but you won't be sure until you give them a try – and just when you thought there couldn't possibly be anything else to try, you can be sure that your next experiments will bring something to mind.

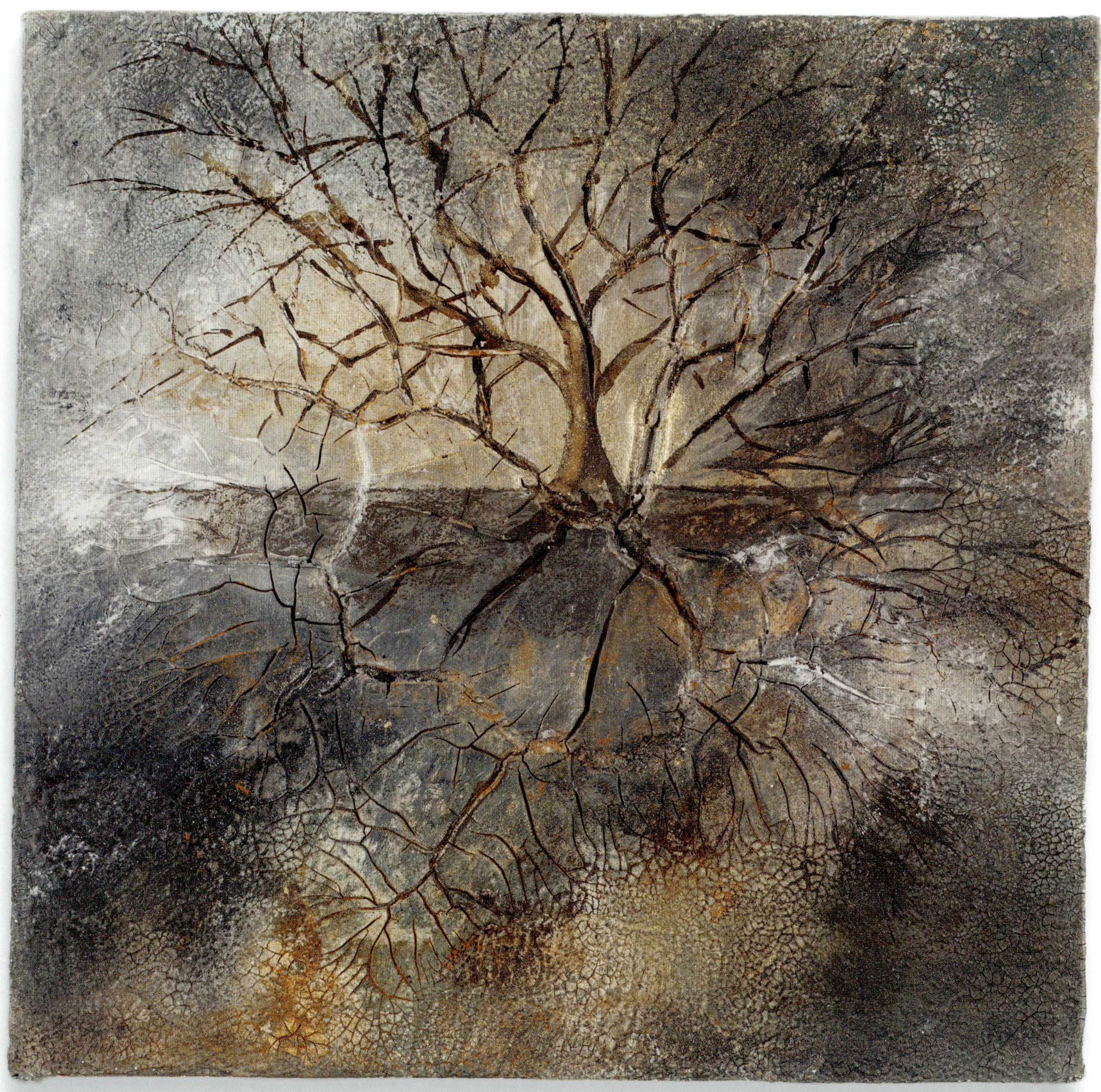

Above and Below

20 x 20cm (8 x 8in)

Here the crackle paste depicts deprivation: dried earth and tree roots struggling to get through a harsh winter.

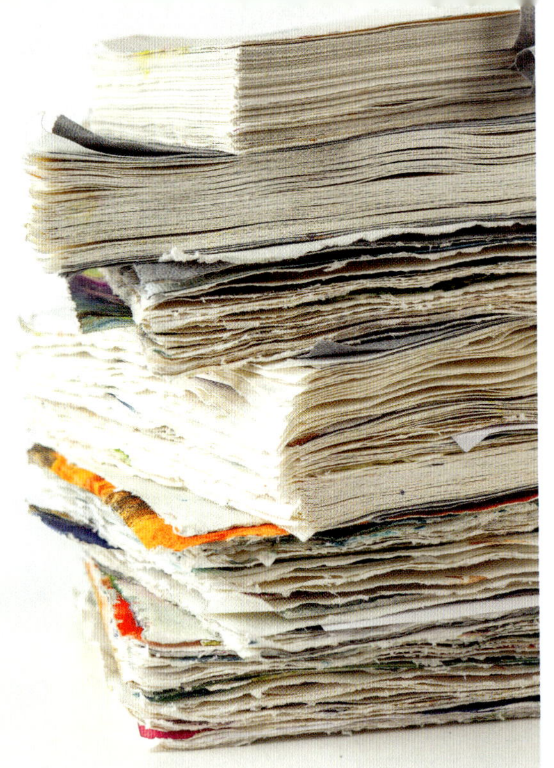

The importance of sketchbooks and reference

Whatever starting point you come from, keeping notes and sketchbooks will not only provide invaluable reference later on, but will also encourage you to practise – and enjoy the process of painting.

   Sketchbooks are wonderful souvenirs of your time spent out on location or in the studio. Here, all of your ideas and inspiration are down on paper to be considered carefully before embarking on a finished piece of work on canvas.

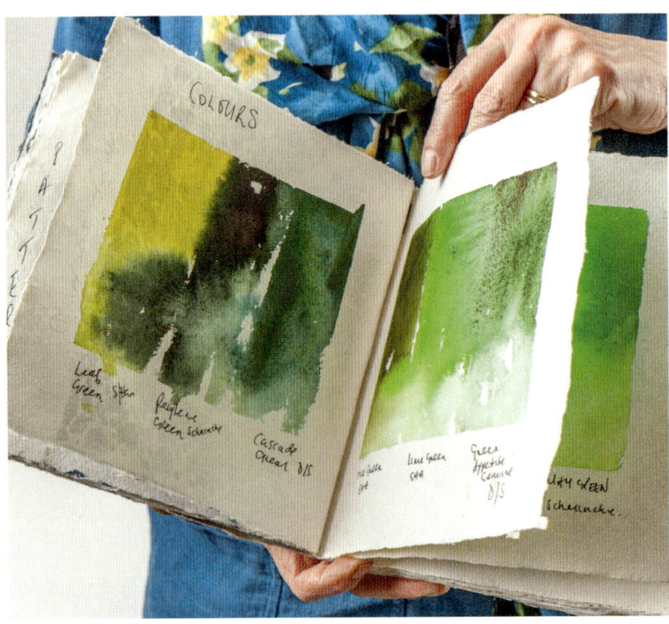

Purpose

I have subject-based sketchbooks, experimental texture sketchbooks, flower sketchbooks and colour theory sketchbooks. Whatever you want to keep a record of, a sketchbook can help.

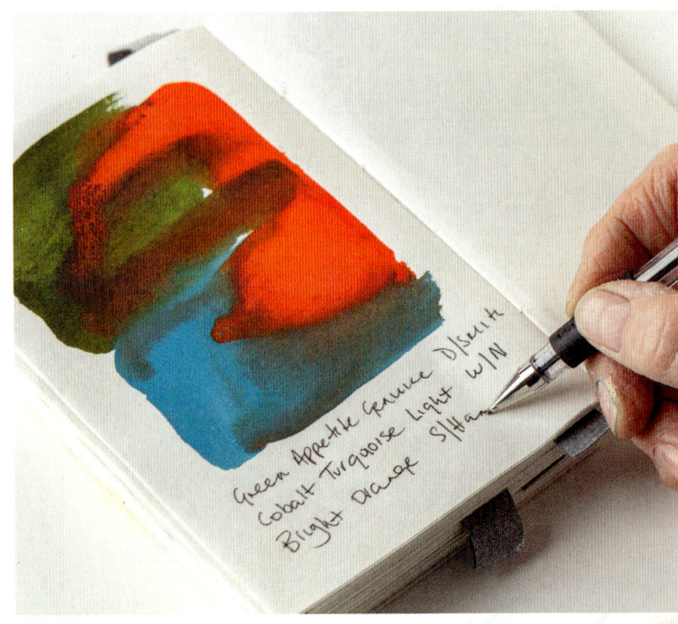

Colour details

If you do not want to display your sketchbook, then feel free to make more extended notes directly onto the page.

EXERCISE: Taking photographs

Getting good photographs for reference is so important. We have the
capacity to store thousands on our phones so you can click away to
your heart's content, making sure you have covered everything from
wide-angled vistas to various close-up surface textures and different
angles of flowers and leaves. Having said that, don't get too carried
away with the camera and forget to actually experience where you are
what you are seeing, hearing and feeling.

  Here are some tips to get you started:

- Try and get as much detail as you can, zoom in on details and textures.
- Look out for cast shadows and bright sunlight. Try not to get any glare.
- You may have to climb up slightly or lie down to get the type of shot
  you need.
- Water can be fascinating to photograph; the reflections from its
  surroundings make it so important – but make sure you don't forget to
  photograph the actual surroundings too.

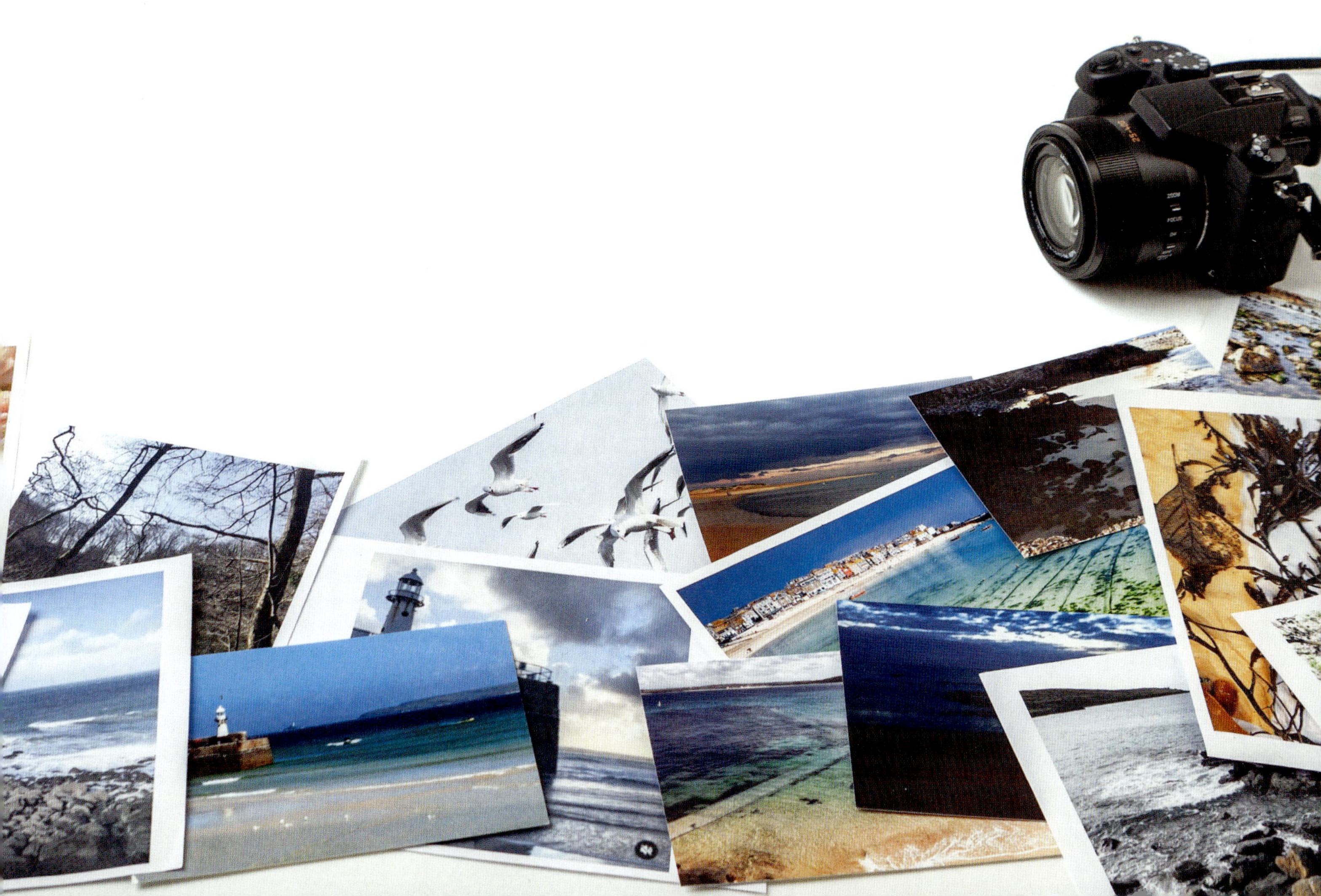

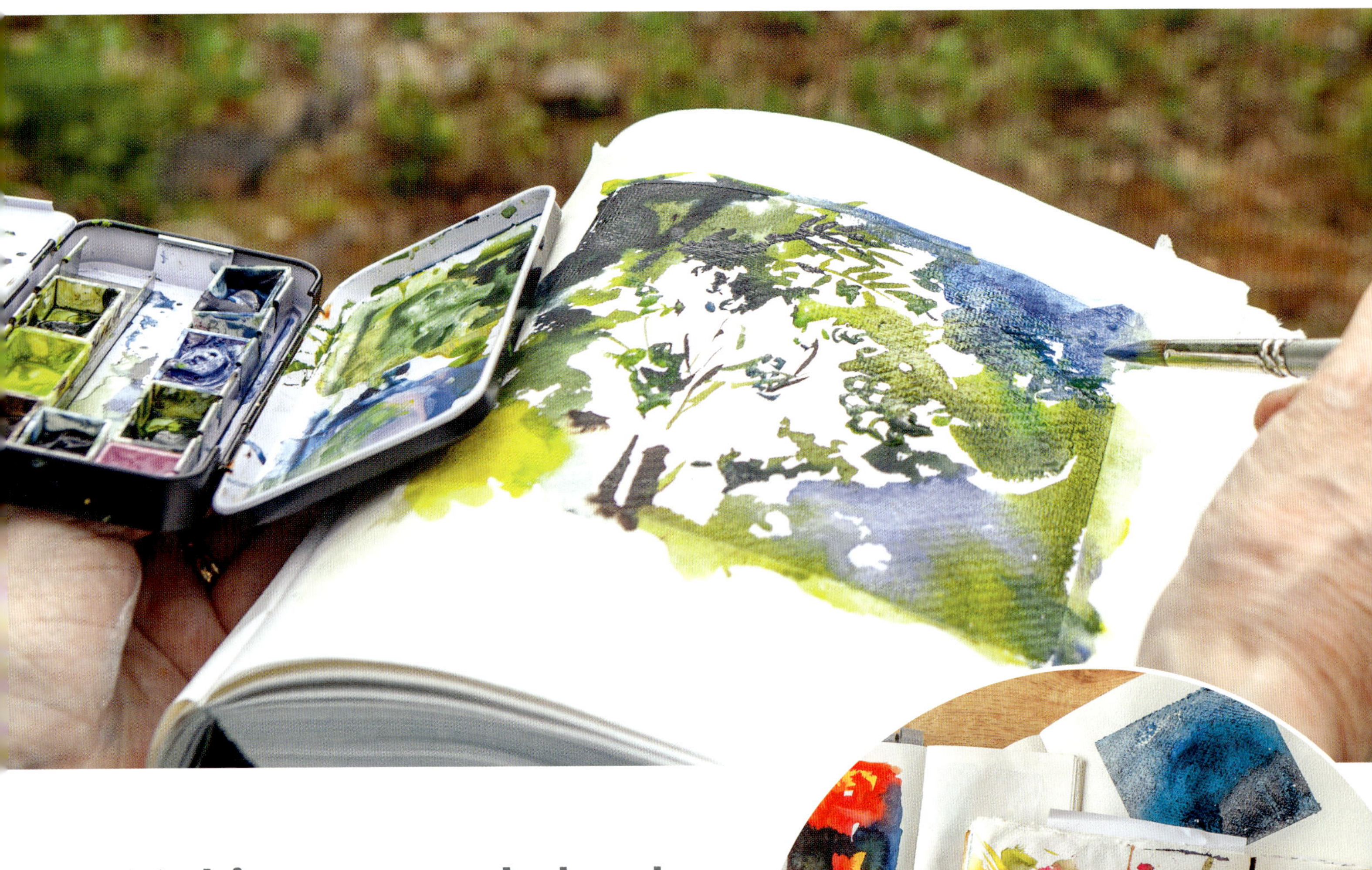

Making a sample book

I spend lots of time making my sketchbooks as interesting as I can. They are a work of art in themselves. I like nothing better than flicking through some of mine from time to time to give myself more inspiration when I'm embarking on making another one. I always present them in the best way I can and find that, at exhibitions, people are as interested in looking at them as they are my paintings.

This project will give you a helping hand to develop a really interesting sketchbook that is a joy to look at. Once you've got used to working in this way, you will find yourself encouraged to use it more and move on to working on canvas – and you'll have a wealth of reference material, too.

These sketchbook pages are examples of the sorts of quick sketches and references I create while working outside.

Portable kit

When taking a walk to seek out subjects, I carry a select few art materials with me. It's important to remember that you need to be able to carry (and handle!) everything, so lighter is better.

All you need is a small number of paints – pans are ideal for this purpose as they're light and compact – along with a sketchbook or some loose sheets of paper. One or two inks and a few crayons will increase your options.

All of this will easily fit into a small rucksack along with a bottle of water and a couple of paper cups. If there is a natural source of water where I am, I will use that – this all adds to me getting into the sense of place. This is true with seascapes too. I love using seawater, it really does some interesting things to your paint, especially if you incorporate some sand as well.

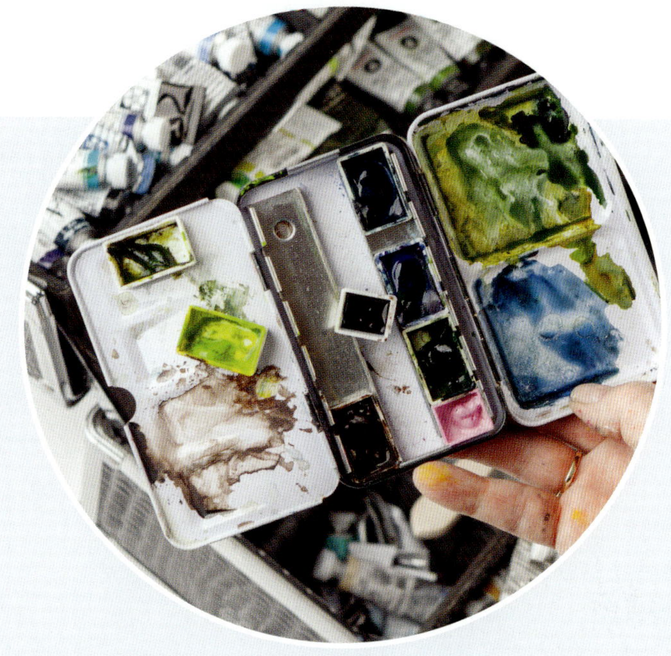

The essentials

I take just the following with me: small palette; two brushes (one large, one small); a bottle of water and a paper cup. This is deliberately minimal; if going out to make sketches is a big hassle, it'll put you off. Keep things simple.

1 – Preparing to go

Before you set out, use masking tape to mark out squares on each page. This sort of sketchbook is as much an art piece as a reference guide.

Next, fill your portable kit. There's no need to take everything (in fact, this will be distracting and spoil the enjoyment), so select colours appropriate to the environment you'll be sketching in – or that you want to play with. For the moment, let's stick with pure watercolour; we can experiment with other media when you come back.

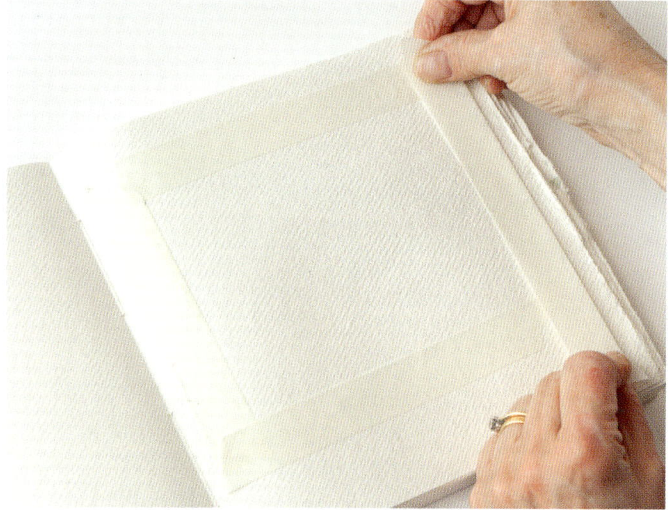

Marking out squares

Clean squares help to present your experiments in the best way, and make it much easier to compare them back in the studio.

tip

Take some additional loose sheets of paper with you. This allows you to work while the watercolour in your sketchbook dries.

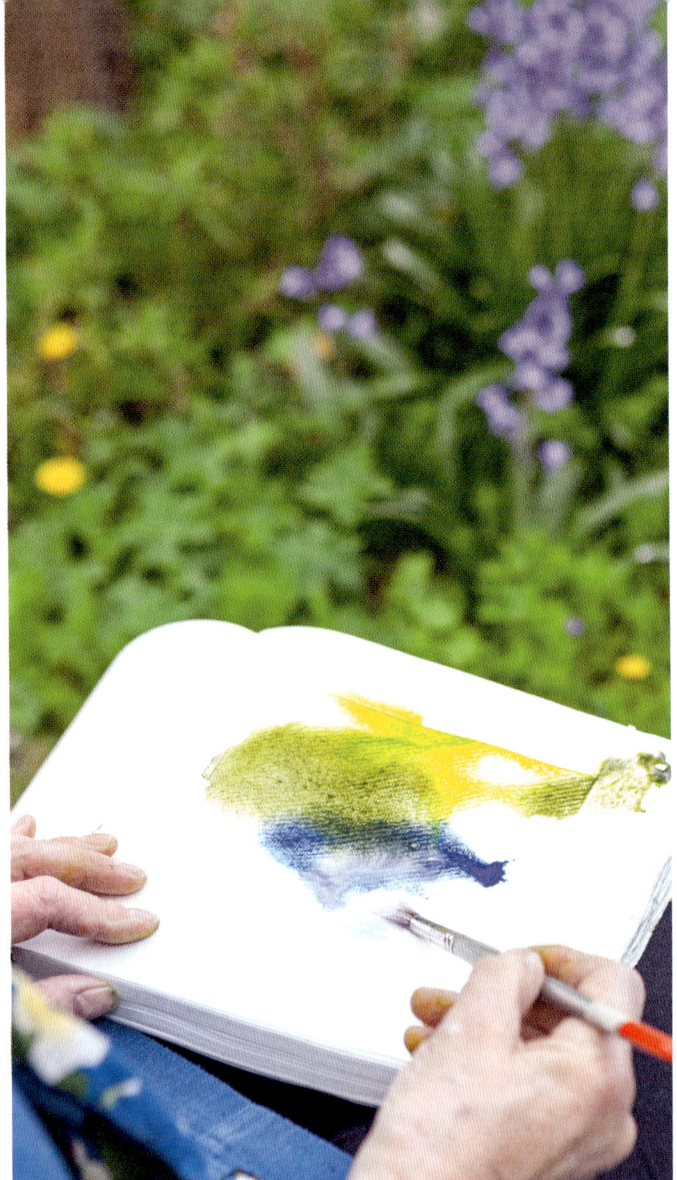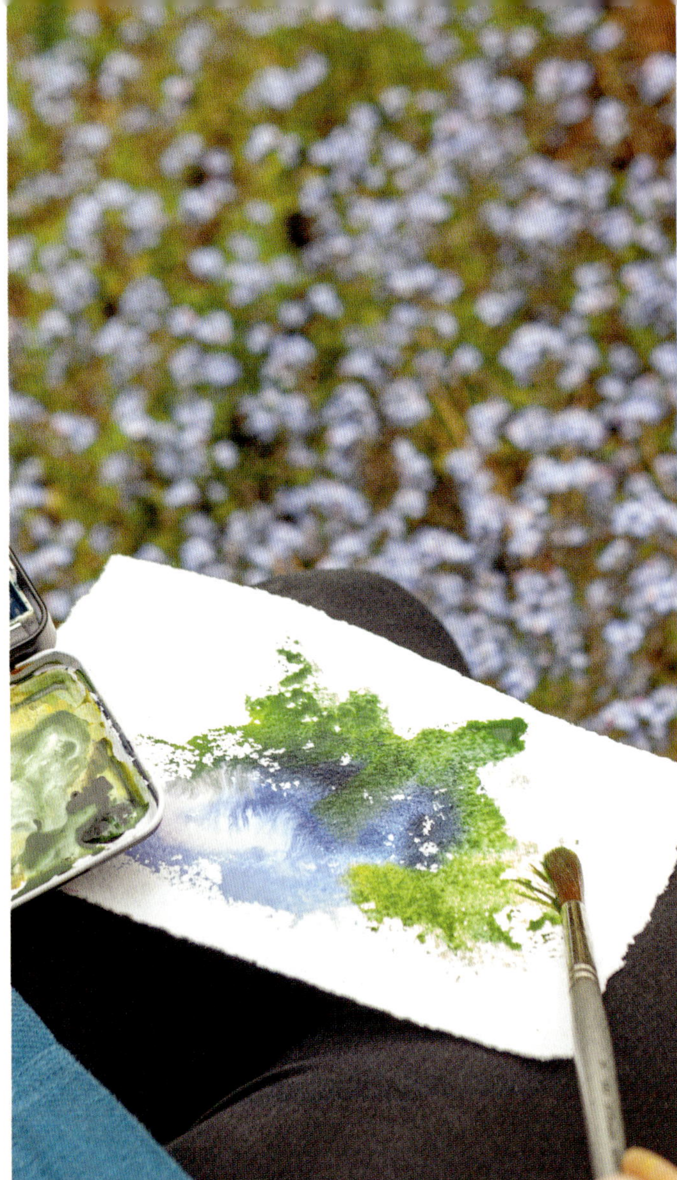

2 – Field experiments

Once in the field, concentrate on a particular aspect of the scene in front of you, such as colour. It's easy to feel tentative when you first start working, so try not to feel under pressure. You're just filling in a small box with colour, after all. Don't spend ages looking for the perfect spot to start; just get stuck in, with whatever's in front of you. Keep things simple. Aim to get nothing more than an impression of your surroundings in colour.

Once you've filled the first box, allow it to dry, or carry on with a loose sheet. Working on a clean area, try changing positions, to look at the same subject from a different angle; or perhaps somewhere completely new.

3 – Further experiments outdoors

If you find something that you want to sketch, but are lacking the right colour, aim to capture the shape and area, and make notes or take supporting photographs or samples back to the studio with you.

Even if you do have the right colour, it's worth changing tack anyway, perhaps concentrating on shapes, texture or the general atmosphere instead of colour.

First pages

Remember, you're not trying to paint every part of the scene in front of you. Aim simply to capture the colours – or whatever aspect of the view you want to concentrate on.

Opposite:
Further impressions

Concentrating on colour will have allowed you to focus. Take a breath and wait for a few moments. Enjoy the experience of being outdoors in the moment, and aim to capture that impression on your paper.

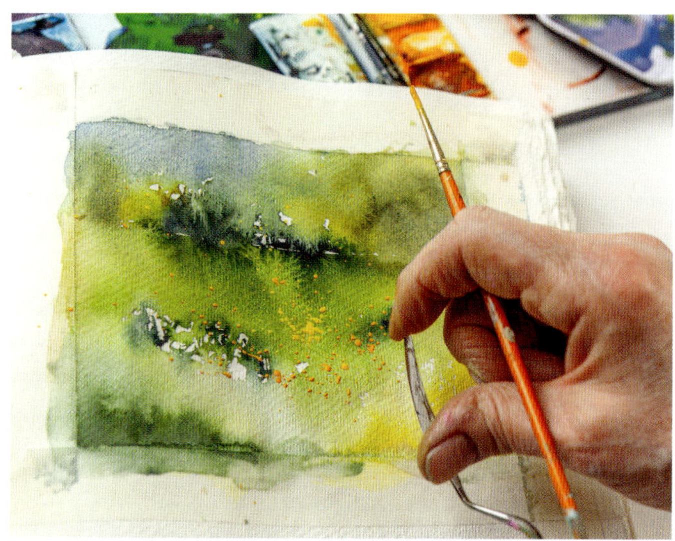

Explore in the studio

Experiment with different techniques, as well as colours. Here I'm using spattering (by loading a palette knife with paint and flicking it onto the surface) to capture the loosely scattered dandelions of the location.

4 – Back in the studio

Once back from the location, continue to make sketches while the impression of the place is still fresh in your mind. This is a great opportunity to bring in some new colours from your larger palette, using your notes and reference to help. Keep working quickly, and don't over-think things – these sketches are here to give you a feel for the area and capture your initial impressions.

Once you've finished, allow your sketchbook to dry, then carefully remove the masking tape to reveal clean, crisp edges to your work. This is a way of working that gives a lovely suprise at the end – a bit like unwrapping a present. Some of these sketches will result in satisfying mini-paintings; and that can spur you on.

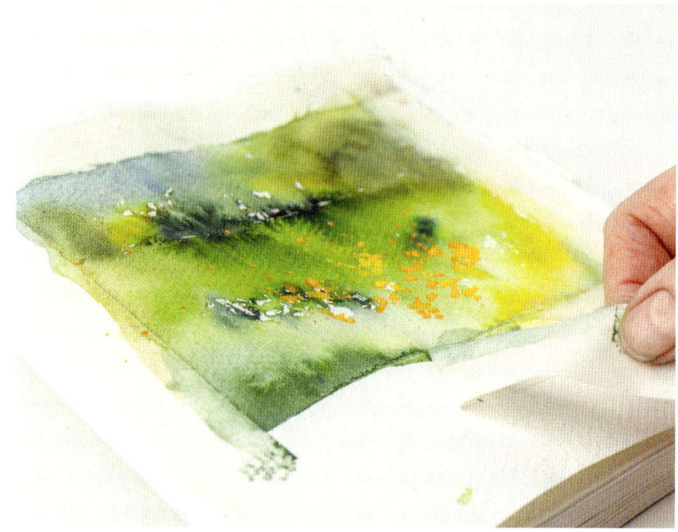

Removing the tape

If the paint has crept a little under the masking tape, don't worry. If you want, you can try lifting it out or scratching off, but these are really just reference pieces – think of it as adding a little character to a particular sketch.

5 – Making notes on your experiments

While the sketchbook will be an attractive art object in its own right, it's also a practical tool to help inform your later, larger work on canvas. With that in mind, it's worth taking some time to ensure your sketches are useful to you.

You can add notes and reference details to the sketch – these details might be quite formal, including location, time of day, the paints used and so forth; or you might prefer a more casual or poetic approach. Work out what exactly is the inspiration in front of you and pick out the main colours and shapes.

You may feel like adding some drawing into the paint, picking out the odd branch, twig or suggestion of a horizon line. Equally, you may ignore what you choose to and, in so doing, discover some unexpected detail that jumps out at you once you've put some space and time between you and the outdoors experience.

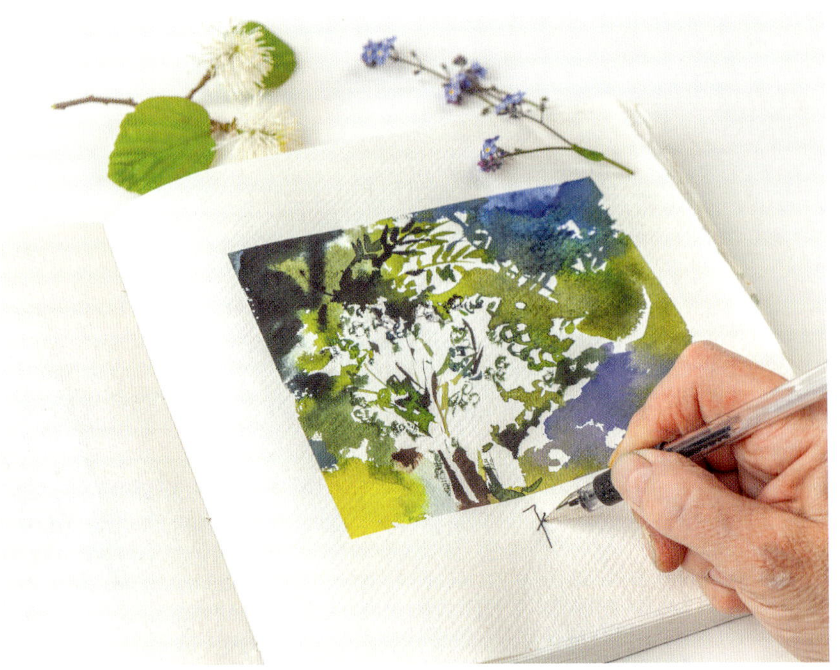

My reference
I favour keeping the pages clean, to allow the sketch to stand on its own merit. I add just a simple number, as that keeps things uncluttered. I then reference the number at the start or end of the sketchbook, giving all the details there.

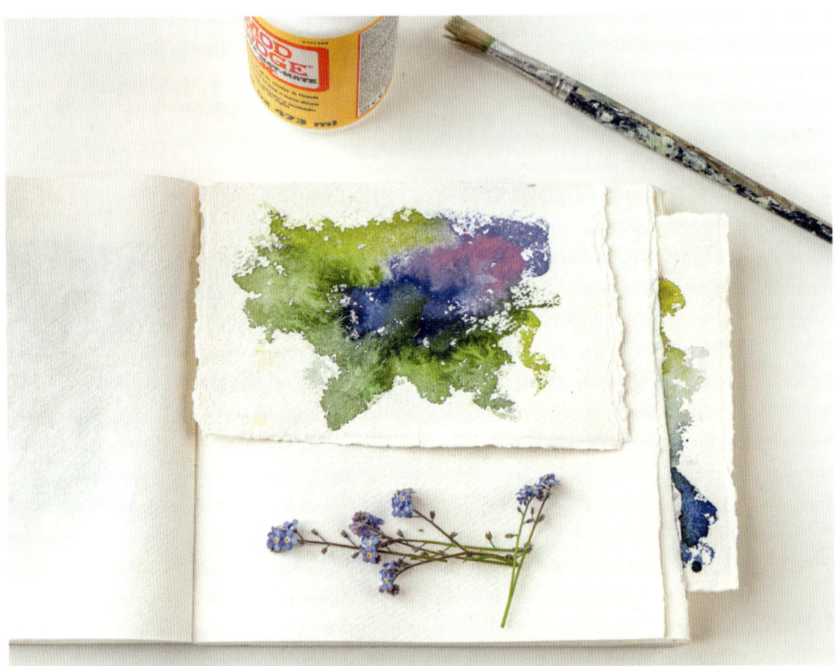

Loose sheets and found materials
Use white glue to secure any loose leaf sketches or additional reference into the sketchbook. You can trim them down to fit, but I quite like an occasional sketch overhanging the edge. You can also incorporate any reference material – like these flowers – with white glue.

6 – Filling your sample book

From here, it's now down to you to fill your sample book with reference. Try to get into the habit of taking it with you and filling each page with loose, free marks. It's precisely because your sample book is so informal that it's useful later on: without the pressure of a clean blank canvas, you're free of the burden of expectation, and can just enjoy the process of painting. It's all valuable experience at working quickly and loosening up.

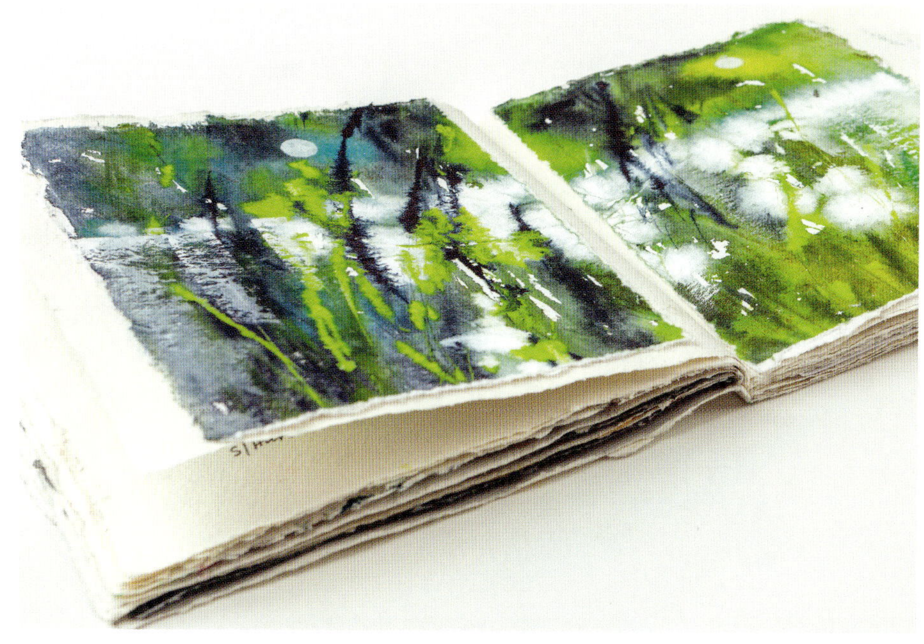

Light catching on a lake near to where I live. Through half-closed eyes I saw how the light hit the water and honed in on it.

These two sketchbook pages show lovely old trees with their surroundings picked out using colours and textures of different times of the year.

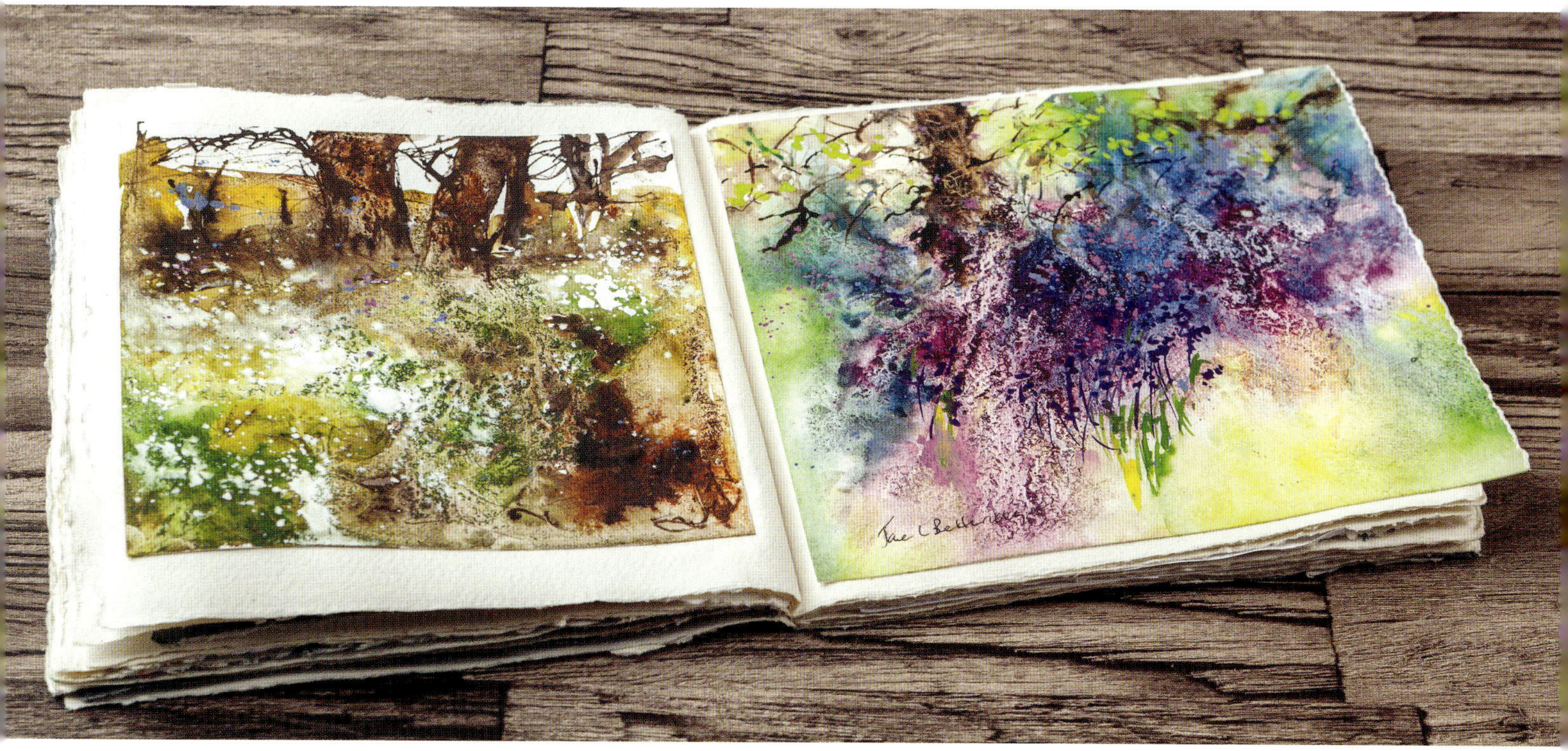

EXERCISE: Getting your impressions down while fresh in your mind

As well as photographing your surroundings, you must remember to get some notes down about various colours, shapes and relationships of subject matter to neighbouring objects, such as rocks or plant life, ponds and trees, where the light is coming from, what the sky looked like, and so on. This is very easily done by some quick rough sketches; start by drawing the most exciting thing that made you want to paint that particular subject or vista and then add other material.

I usually carry a little plastic bag when I'm on the beach so I can take back seaweed, shells, or bits of lichen-covered stones. I sometimes press leaves or seaweed into mud and press them onto the paper or use a stick dipped in mud or dirty water to doodle shapes and make marks to remind me of what I saw.

While on location, work out what colours you think would suit a particular idea for a painting. Try preparing one or more colours from your small palette, then mash a broken-up leaf into the well and let the juices run into your mix to bring a little of the area into your work. Consider picking up any found objects you stumble over, too – it is so important to get these impressions down whilst still fresh in your mind.

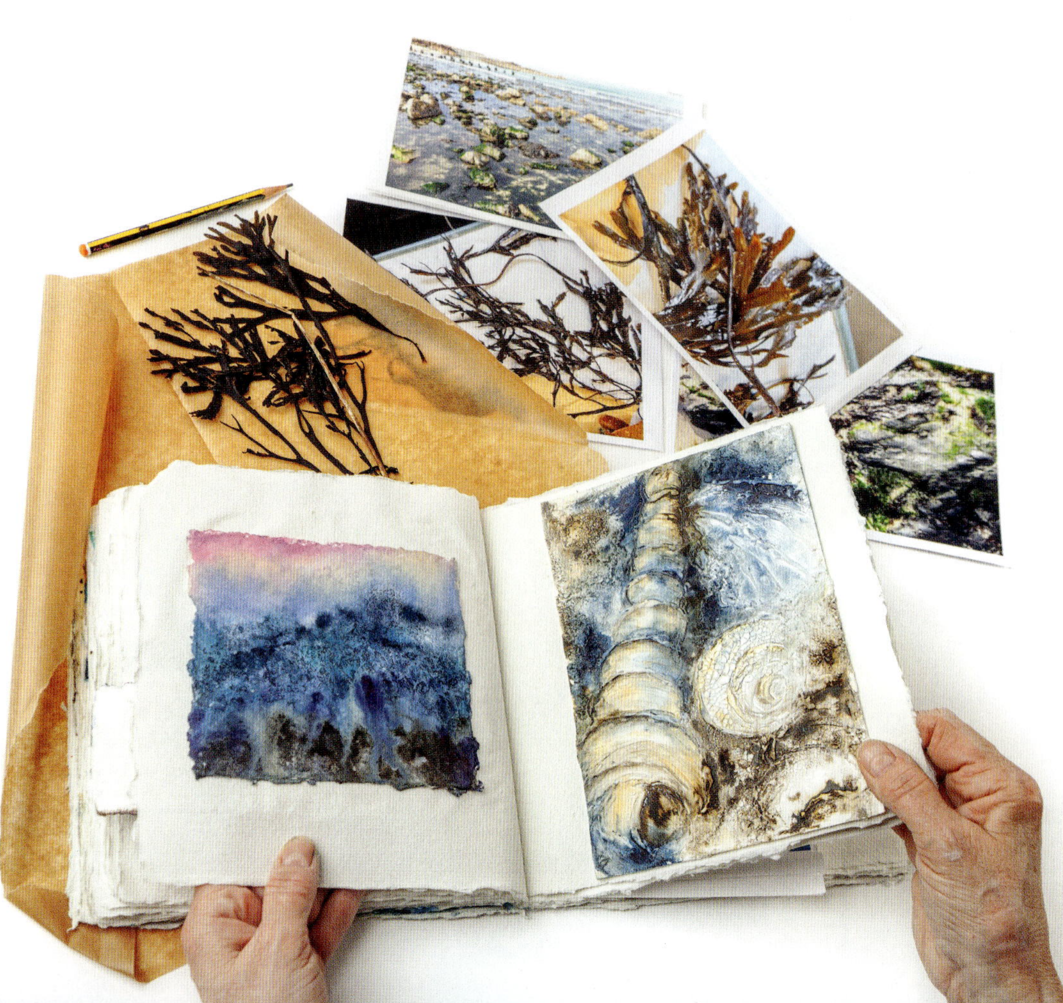

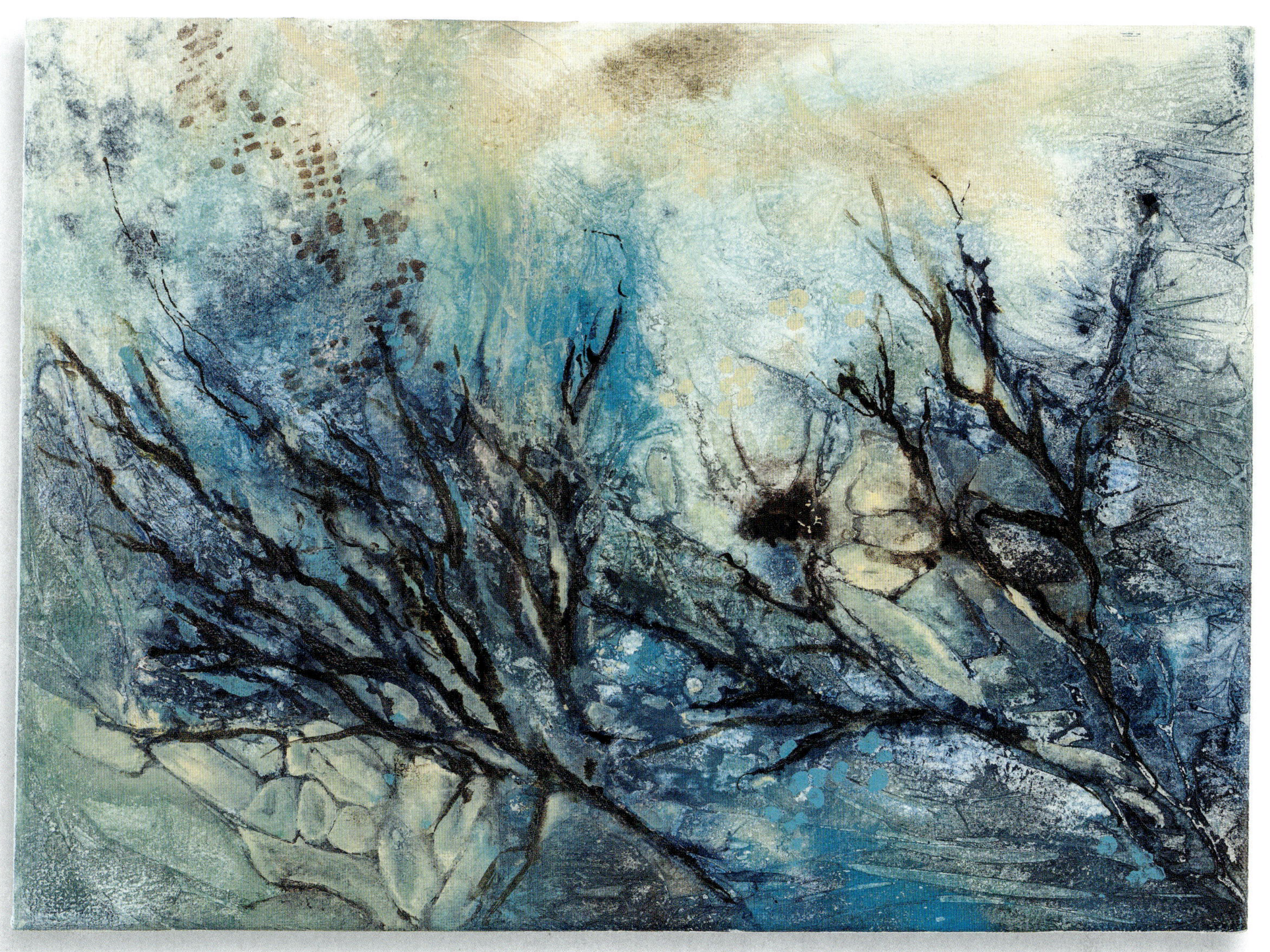

Seaweed on Canvas

40 x 30cm (15¾ x 11¾in)

*After collecting seaweed from the beach and making sketchbook references, I stuck some
seaweed into watercolour ground as I was preparing the canvas. I placed plastic wrap
over the top and weighted it down with some books. After leaving it a good 48 hours,
making sure it was completely dry, I started adding paint and ink and picked out some
other organic shapes created by the plastic wrap.*

EXERCISE: Movement and energy

Maybe, like me, you like the coast. Rocks and sea on a blustery day provide a gushing fountain of ideas and inspiration – and this never fails to charge my creative batteries. Angry clouds rolling in, flurries of rain and hail, sand whipped up like a mini tornado into your face, holding tight to the hood of your coat or pulling your hat further down around your ears... It all makes you wish you were warm and safe inside with a hot drink – but the experience will have touched your senses and this will come out when expressing these feelings in your work. The invigorating experience is just the same on a bright sunny day, when the sea appears angry and the tide is rushing in, spilling over and frothing in little pools around the rocks, turning them a shiny silver in the strong sunlight.

Using object, location or technique as your starting point, and using your sample book for reference, try creating a painting that's full of movement and energy. To convey this sense of movement and energy through your work, use bigger, bolder brushstrokes than usual; and quick, short, confident mark-making. The energy you experienced is much easier to convey when standing up and using big arm movements, as though conducting an orchestra of colour and texture, so let your inhibitions go and you will see movement and energy come to the forefront of what you are trying to deliver.

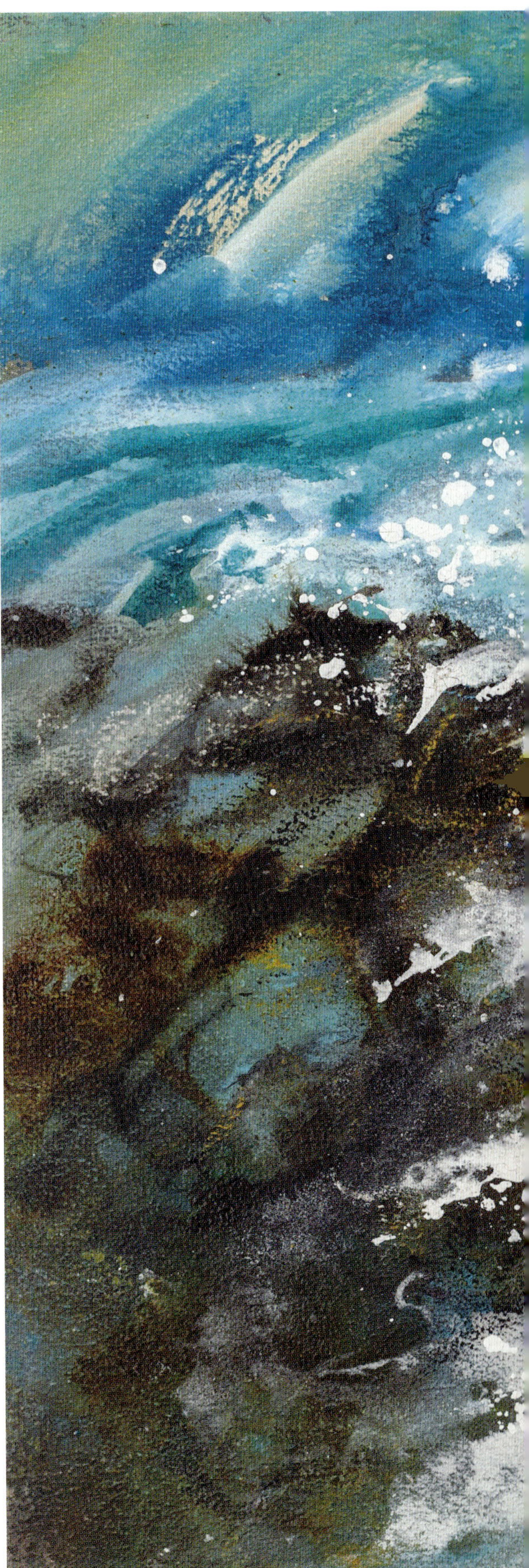

Crashing Waves at Porthminster
30 x 25cm (11¾ x 10in)

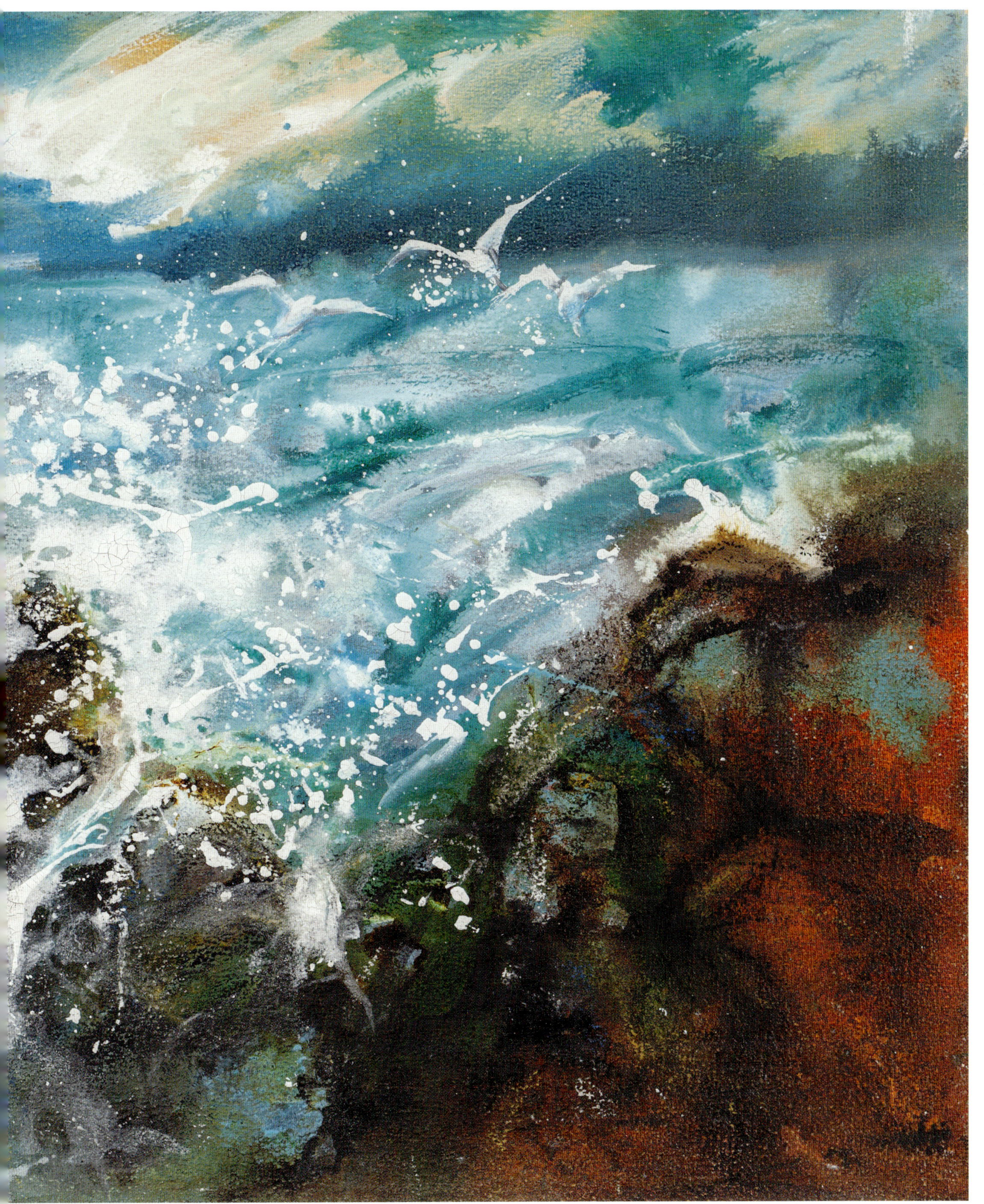

EXERCISE: Evoking peacefulness and calm

Picture it: a secluded walk on a calm, quiet day, with nothing but
the birds to keep you company. A time for reflection, a time to
appreciate all that nature has to offer, and to seek out its little
nooks and crannies, to find those hidden gems just waiting to be
found – and to be observed. Such times are like gold for the artist.

The small, ordinary, subjects in front of us every day – those
we think of as insignificant – can be really quite something if you
stand, stare, listen, smell and absorb all nature has to offer.

As with the earlier exercises, using one of the starting points
(detailed on pages 24–29) and your sample book for reference, try
to create a painting that evokes peacefulness and calm. Softness
is key to getting across a sense of peacefulness in a painting.
Using muted colours and just hinting at detail is the main aid in
achieving this.

You painting could be a distant view of some fine golden grasses,
all bending and blowing in the same direction as the gentle breeze
sways them from side to side, or it could be the trunk of a very
old gnarled tree trunk with its pathways of marks, colours and
crevices running up and down its body like a wizened old man.
Perhaps you might focus on how astonishing it is that something
half-dead can grow new shoots, sprouting new life for generations
to come.

The Edge of Dimminsdale

30 x 30cm (11¾ x 11¾in)

*At eventide, a gentle stroll, when the natural world is quiet and still,
offers a sense of peace and a chance to reflect; to think deeply about the
thoughts in your head. Problems can seem less serious, if you are at one
with the natural world.*

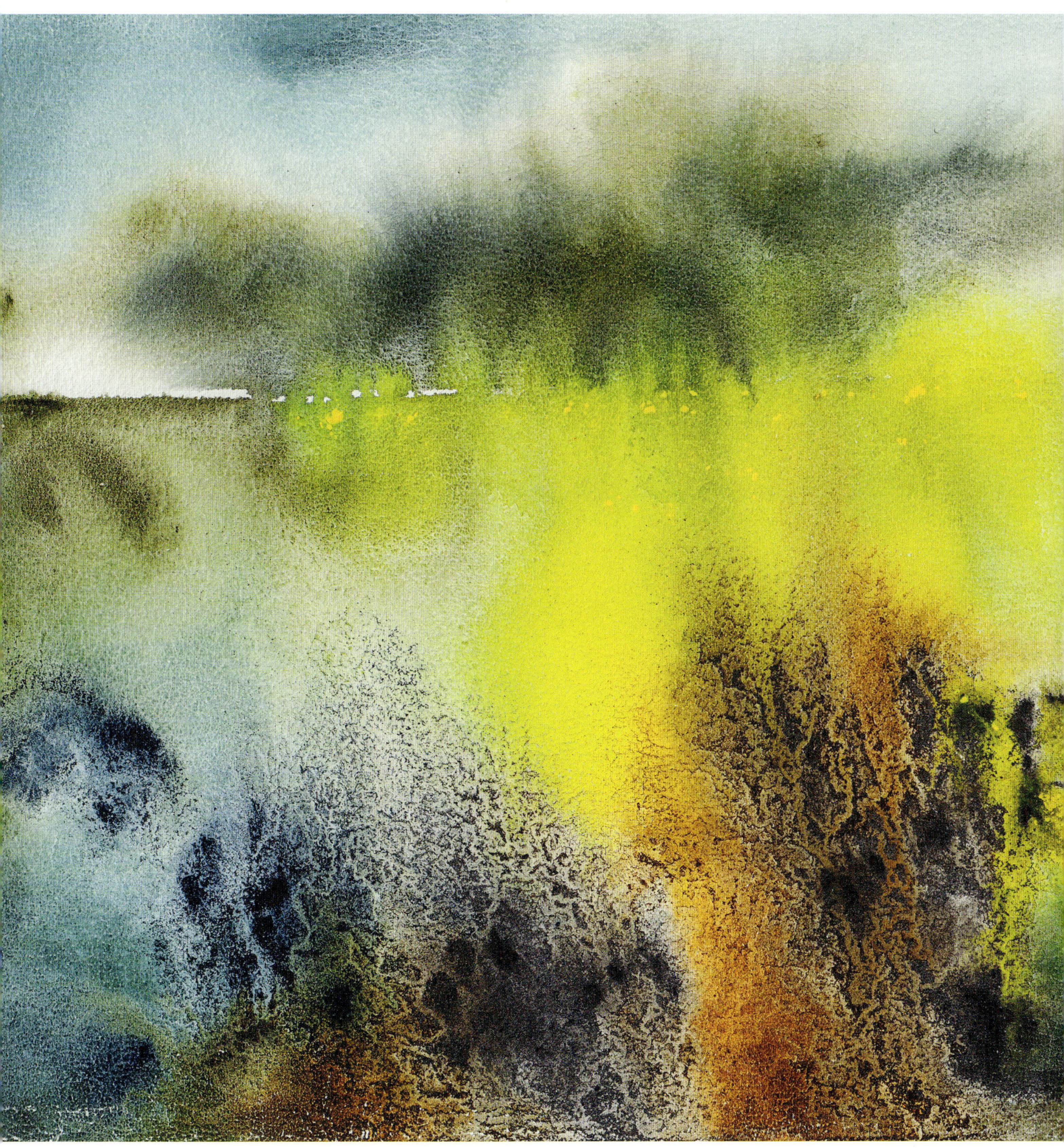

texture

Texture is uncommon to see in traditional watercolour, but it offers so much to the artist – particularly when working on the already textural surface of canvas. Before we launch into the projects, then, let's spend some time looking at how we can develop and enhance the surfaces we'll be working upon.

‘Properly prepared paint on properly prepared canvas gives you perfect pictures’

Symphony of Texture

20 x 20cm (8 x 8in)

The physical textures you apply to the surface can be enhanced and developed through the textures suggested by your paints. Here, crackle paste has been applied in different thicknesses, leading to larger and finer areas of physical texture. These have been enhanced through the use of inks and fluid paints, which flowed into the resulting fissures. Gold bronzing powder has also been used to draw attention to the deep physical cracks.

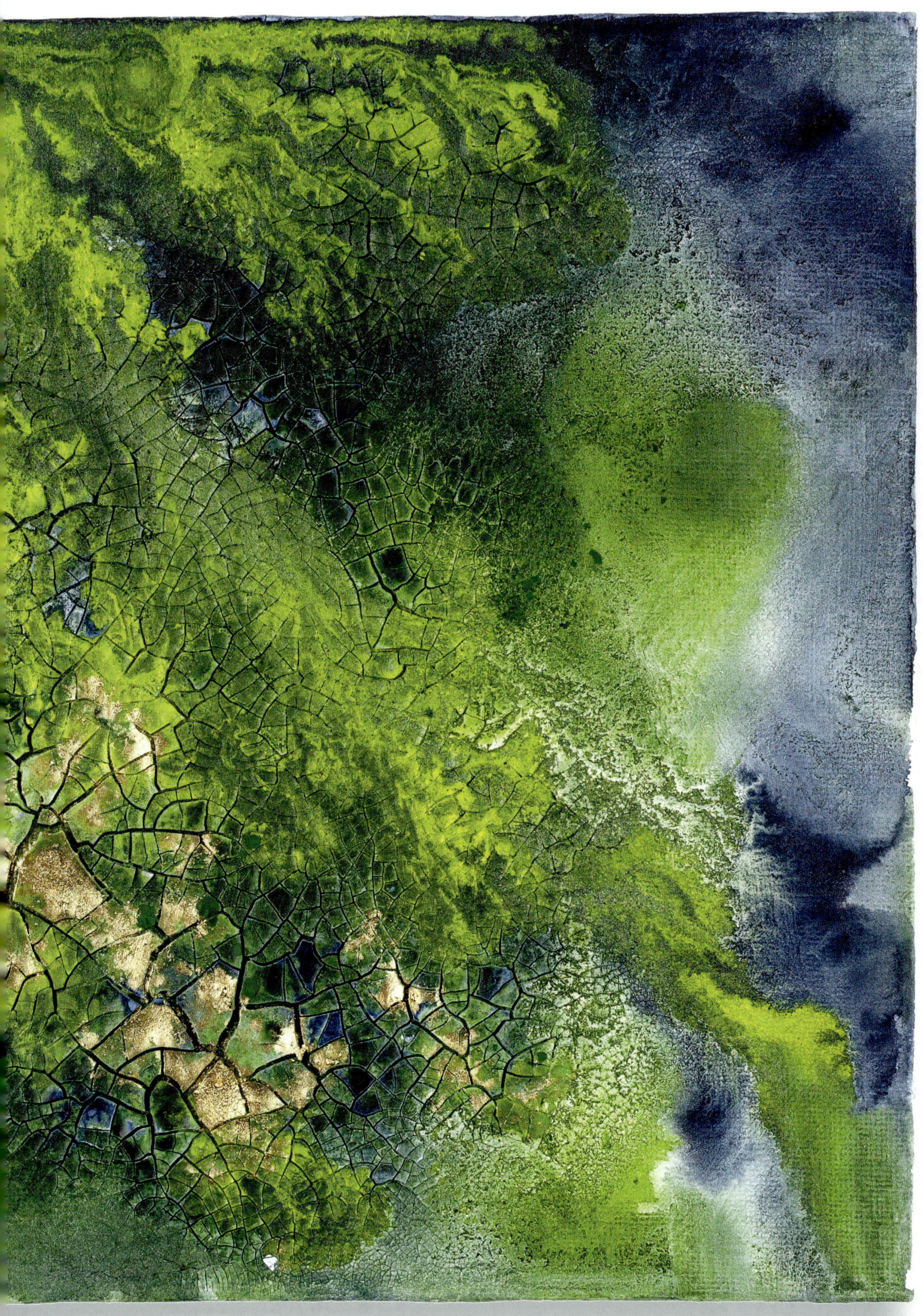

Primers and mediums

'Medium' is a catch-all term for materials you add to the surface or mix with paint for different special effects, as in the example opposite. Here are some of my favourites to use when working with watercolour on canvas.

Glass bead gel This medium is a paste incorporating hundreds of tiny glass beads. It is best applied to the canvas with a palette knife and left to dry. When painted over, a really interesting textured surface is created. I love to use it to depict swirling, frothing sea water.

Masking fluid A latex gum that can be applied to the canvas with an old brush. Once dry, it will protect the surface from paint, which allows you to preserve your highlights. Once you have finished the painting, you simply rub the dry masking fluid away to reveal the clean canvas underneath.

Granulation medium One of my favourite products to use, granulation medium is a colourless liquid bought in small bottles. When added to paint or acrylic ink, it splits the pigment and creates remarkable effects. It can be added to your paints when preparing a mix, or dribbled directly into wet paint on the surface using a pipette. There is a more intense, powerful result when it is used with acrylic inks.

Crackle paste There are several different types of crackle paste available from different manufacturers. Some require a two-stage process, but I prefer the simpler types which just require time to air-dry. I tend to use Golden's Gel Acrylic Medium crackle paste when I want larger, more noticeable, cracks on the painting surface, and thinner layers of DecoArt Media White Crackle Paste when I want a more subtle eggshell type of effect.

Modelling pastes Modelling pastes are similar to watercolour grounds but thicker, which allows them to be shaped and built up for textural effects. They are available in two finishes, fine which is smooth and coarse, which has a wonderful graininess.

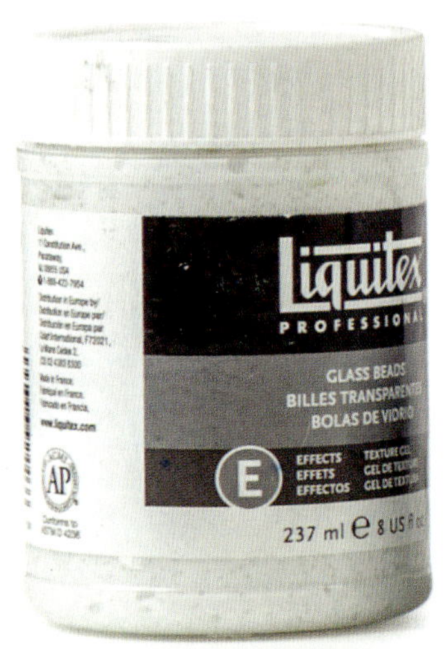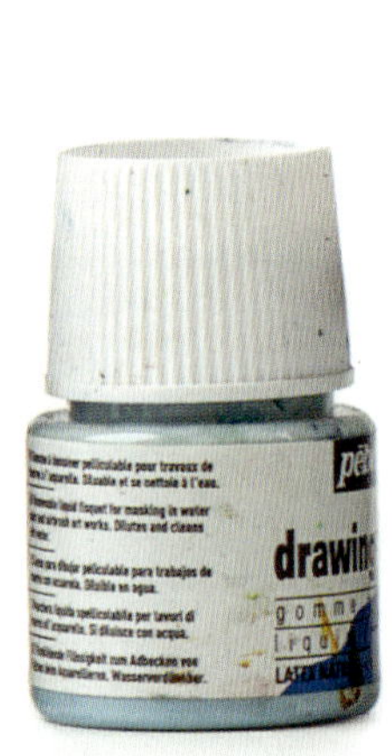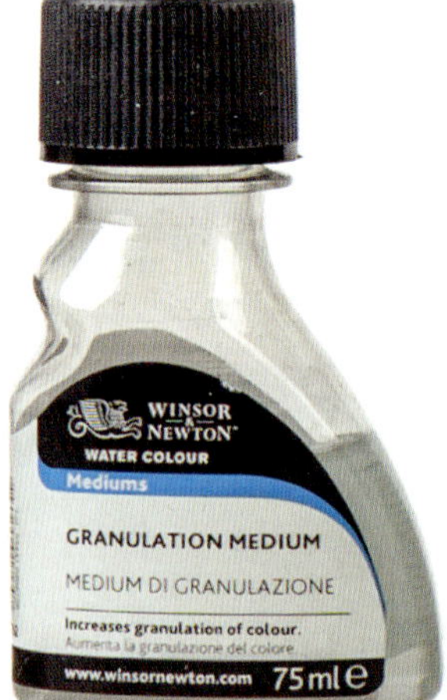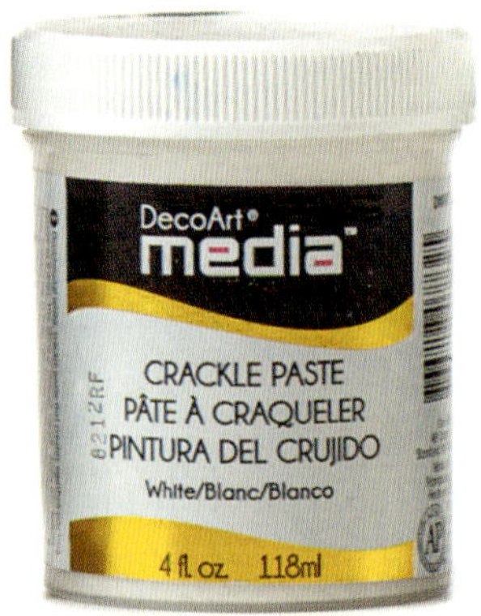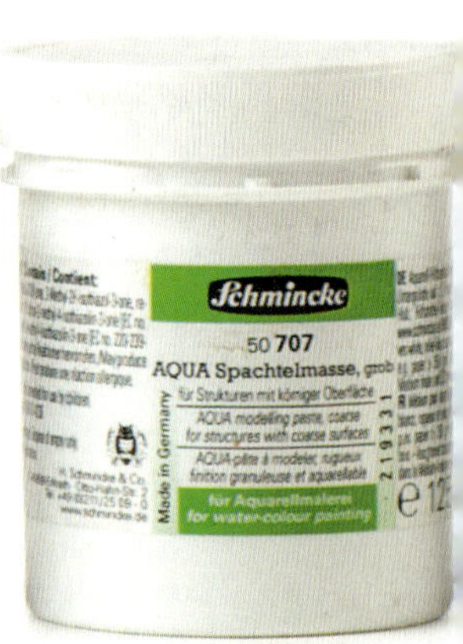

From left to right: Glass bead gel, masking fluid, granulation medium, crackle paste and modelling paste.

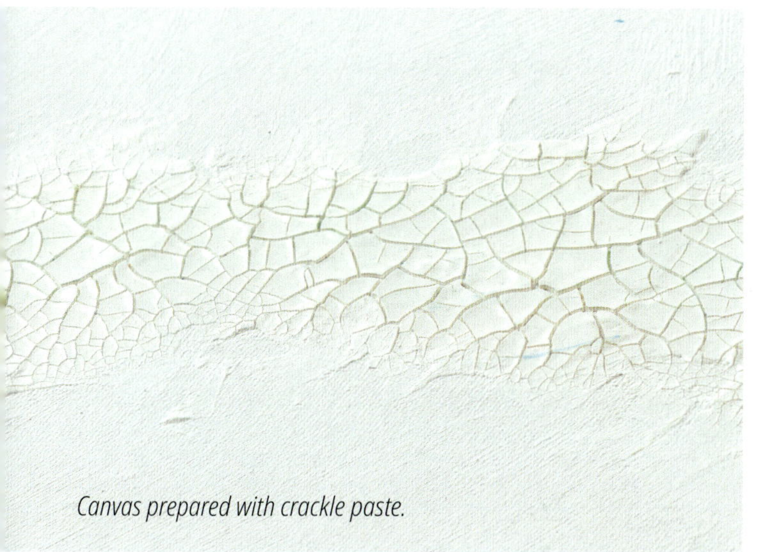

Canvas prepared with crackle paste.

Crackle paste tips

Crackle paste is best applied to canvas that has been pre-primed with gesso (a primer used to prepare surfaces for acrylic and oil paints, which makes the surface non-absorbent) as the medium won't work on an absorbent surface.

Crackle paste doesn't like being messed around with, so the less you handle it, the better. For this reason, I apply the paste with a palette knife. The medium must be allowed to dry completely before you can paint over it. I normally add a very thin wash of watercolour ground over the top to make it more accepting of watercolours.

Modelling paste tips

Apply the pastes with a palette knife and build up and mould the shape you require. Once dry, these mediums are water resistant, and they must dry thoroughly before being painted over. My preferred paste is Schmincke's Aqua Modelling Paste, which is designed especially for the watercolour artist.

Canvas prepared with modelling paste.

Protecting your textures

Because our watercolours will not be protected from the elements when painted on canvas, they need to be sealed to protect them. One of the easiest ways is to give them a few coats of spray-on fixative. This will keep them as safe as if they were framed behind glass. An alternative is to apply wax, such as Dorland's Wax Medium, with a brush or your fingers. When dry, use a lint-free cloth to buff it to a matt finish.

It's important to protect the texture in one of the ways described above as moisture in the air will penetrate the canvas over time and ruin the painting. This applies to any surface prepare beforehand with texture-making mediums – once paint is added on top it will need protection.

Embedding material

I love combining exciting techniques in my work. This can be anything from preparing the canvas with grounds and modelling pastes or tissue paper, or imprinting leaves and grasses, flower heads or found objects. I like to use gauze that's ripped and falling apart and adhere it to my canvas or board with watercolour ground – when dry and then painted over, the paint meanders in all of the little crevices giving exciting, uncontrollable results. A touch of gouache or gold powder gently rubbed over the raised part of the gauze really brings it to life and makes it even more prominent.

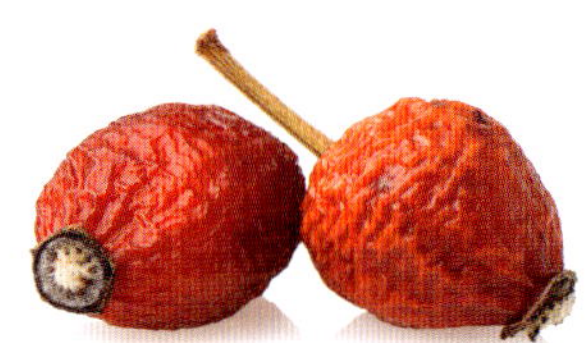

Further ideas

Found materials You might want to incorporate found materials or other additions to add interest to the surface before you paint. It's very similar to preparing any other canvas. Before you begin, apply a layer of transparent watercolour ground as explained opposite, then leave to dry.

Distressing I usually distress the gauze by pulling sections of it apart. Place these sections directly on to the canvas, and add a little water with a brush to help keep them in position before you add any paint. You can instead put the paint on first and then place the gauze or thread on top.

Thread and skeleton leaves Single strands of cotton thread and commercially bought skeleton leaves can be applied in a similar way to gauze. Skeleton leaves (pictured below) are really useful: you can use them as a stencil, drop them into wet paint or, after putting some quite thick paint on one, you can stamp their markings in areas that need some added interest.

Plastic wrap Gauze, thread and skeleton leaves can also create lovely shapes and patterns, particularly if used alongside plastic food wrap (see page 82). They should be positioned into the wash before the wrap is added. When using these materials on canvas, I always cover them in a white watercolour ground to give them strength, before placing them into the wet ground that I'm preparing the canvas with.

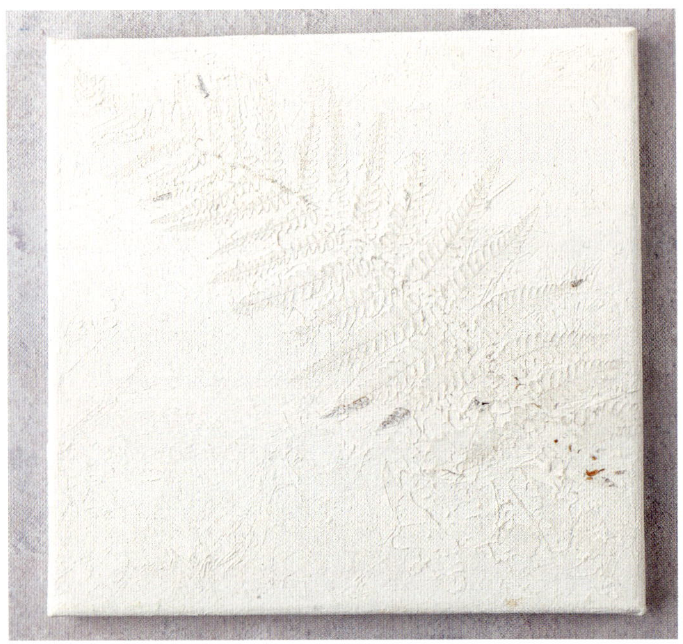

The canvas was prepared with watercolour ground. While wet, a fern leaf was embedded into it and then removed, leaving an imprint.

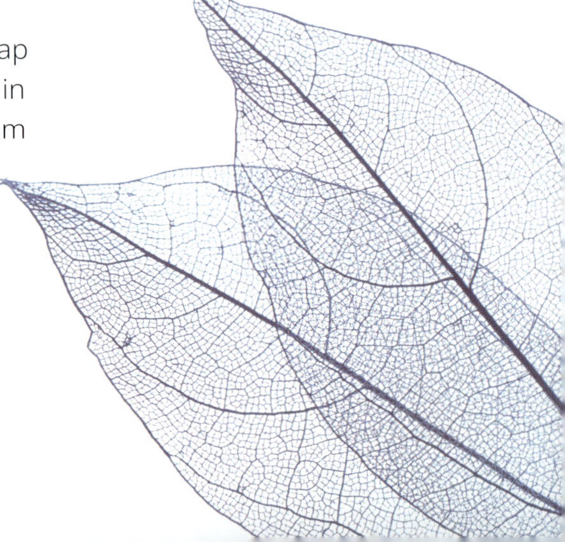

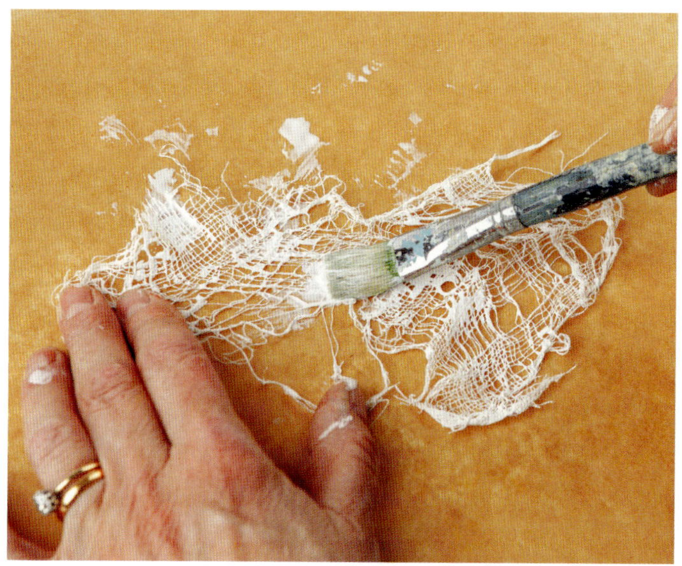

1 Place the material to be embedded (in this case, gauze) on a piece of greaseproof paper, then use a brush to apply PVA glue. Greaseproof paper is great to use for this, as the glue won't stick to it.

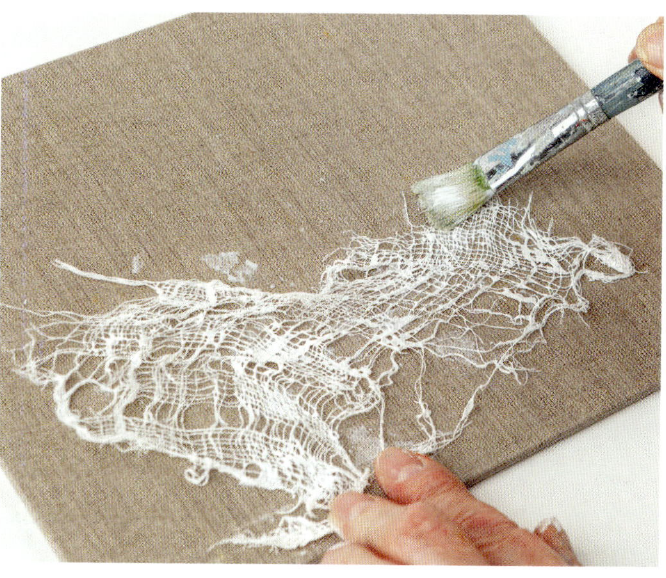

2 While the glue is still wet, place the material onto the canvas surface and press it loosely into place with your brush or some kitchen paper. Allow to dry completely.

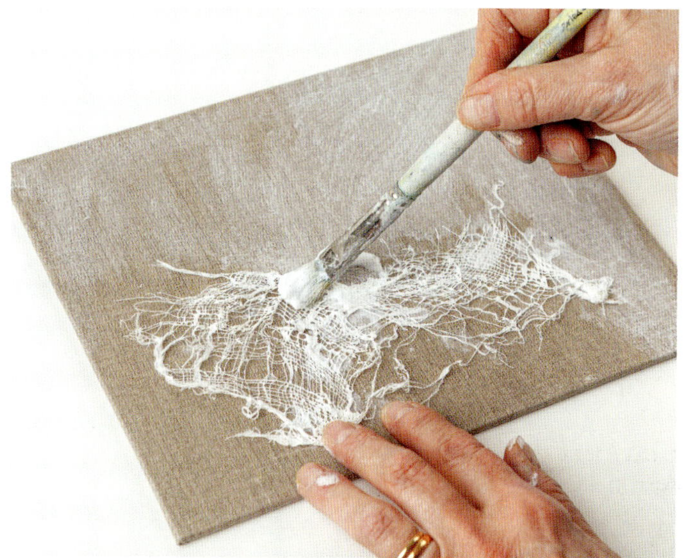

3 Use an old brush to apply another layer of watercolour ground over the surface. I've used transparent ground here, to help make things clear.

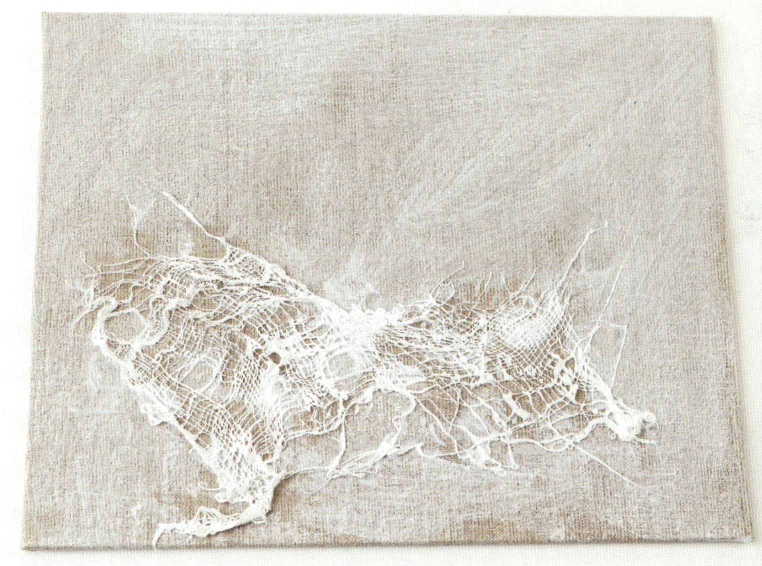

4 Once dry, the canvas is ready to work upon.

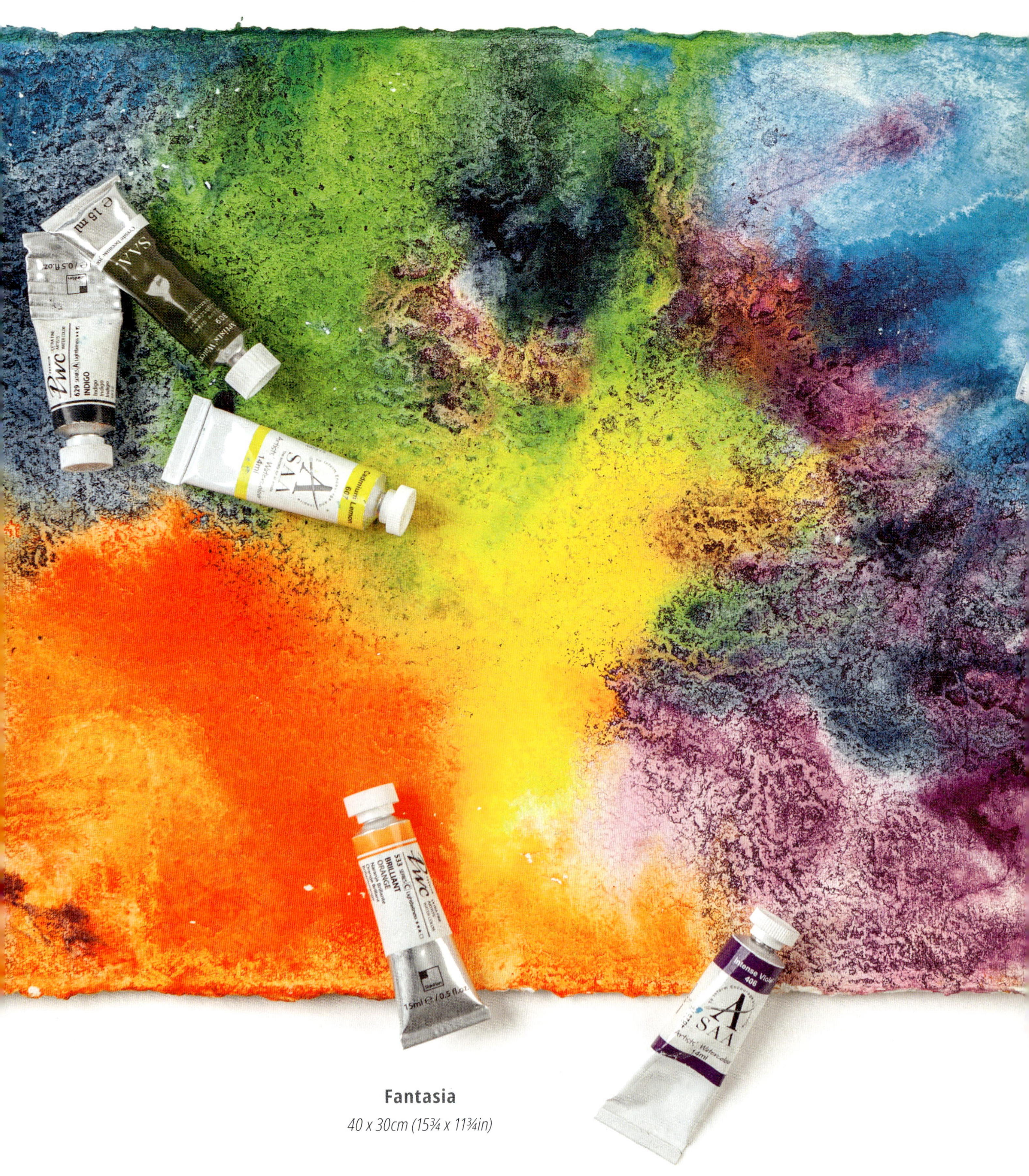

Fantasia
40 x 30cm (15¾ x 11¾in)

colour

When painting in a representational style, we usually stick to the colours we see in front of us to try and replicate the subject matter as accurately as possible. When painting in a contemporary abstract style, however, we can be a lot more expressive and experimental – and use whatever colours we wish.

Well-chosen colours can make all the difference between a painting's success or failure. It is up to you to experiment to see what colour combinations suit your taste and style and subject matter, but the advice on the following pages aims to give you some guidelines and starting points.

The artist's palette and use of colour

Colour choice is very personal. We are all different and, just as we choose colours for our clothes and decoration in our homes, the colours in our paintings will reflect a little of our own personality. It is the difference between our colour palettes that gives the world of art such huge variety.

Some artists have a natural and instinctive response to the subtleties of colour while others rely on a more analytical approach to help them appreciate its complexities. Some artists' work can be instantly recognized by their use of colour. We all have our favourite paints and, I suppose, we use those more than any others. The same can be said of brushstrokes and mark-making, as we'll see later in the book.

I have been complimented many times about my use of colour. Phrases like, 'Gosh, aren't they vibrant for watercolour!' are often said of my work. The old adage that watercolour is wishy-washy is no longer the case. There are so many new paints coming onto the market all the time that do amazing things such as splitting into two colours, as well as pearlescent sparkly paints and paints with silver and gold tones. Watercolour has never been so exciting! If you find you're a little disappointed with the vibrancy of a hue, you might try adding a little acrylic ink to give it some oomph.

Colour and dynamism

To achieve the optimum benefit when painting, always bear in mind, and be guided by, the colour wheel (see right). The colour wheel is an arrangement of colours that helps the artist to see, at a glance, the relationship between the colours and the effect they have on one another. Some colour terms you might come across are:

Primary colours Yellow, red and blue form the basis from which all the other colours are mixed, and cannot themselves be mixed from other colours. The primary colours are arranged in a triangle in the colour wheel.

Secondary colours Violet, orange and green are the three secondary colours, which can be created by combining two primaries. They sit on the colour wheel between the two primaries that make them up.

Tertiary colours Mixing a primary colour with a secondary colour that is adjacent to it – blue with green or red with violet for example – will produce a tertiary colour. Red can be combined with its neighbour to the right (orange), to get a red-orange. If you combine red with its neighbour to the left, which is violet, you will get a red-violet. By adjusting the proportions of the primary and secondary colours you use, you can create a wide range of subtle tertiary hues.

Complementary colours Any two colours that lie opposite one another on the colour wheel are said to be complementary. When used adjacent to each other in a painting, the intensity of each of the colours is heightened. Purple and yellow will look more intense next to each other, for example. The same is true for green and red, and blue and orange, amongst others.

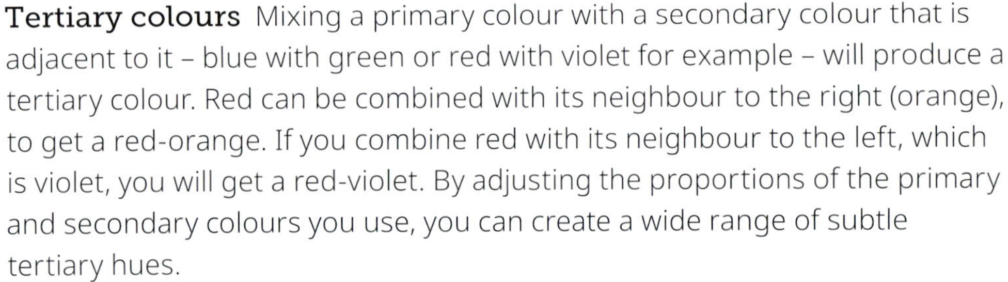

Colour temperature

Colours help with perspective. Cool colours, such as blues, blue-green and greys, recede into the background and make things look more distant – an effect called recession. Warmer colours, including reds, oranges, warm browns and yellows, appear to come forward or 'advance', and so are best used in the foreground.

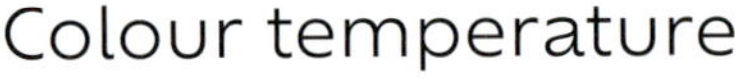

Autumn Leaves and Berries

40 x 40cm (15¾ x 15¾in)

Colour can be used as a tool to lead the viewer into a painting – pointing them in the direction you want them to take. In the painting opposite, the red berries lead the eye up and through the painting. You can read more about abstracting through colour choice on page 78, and more about leading the eye in the 'Shape and line' chapter that begins on page 104.

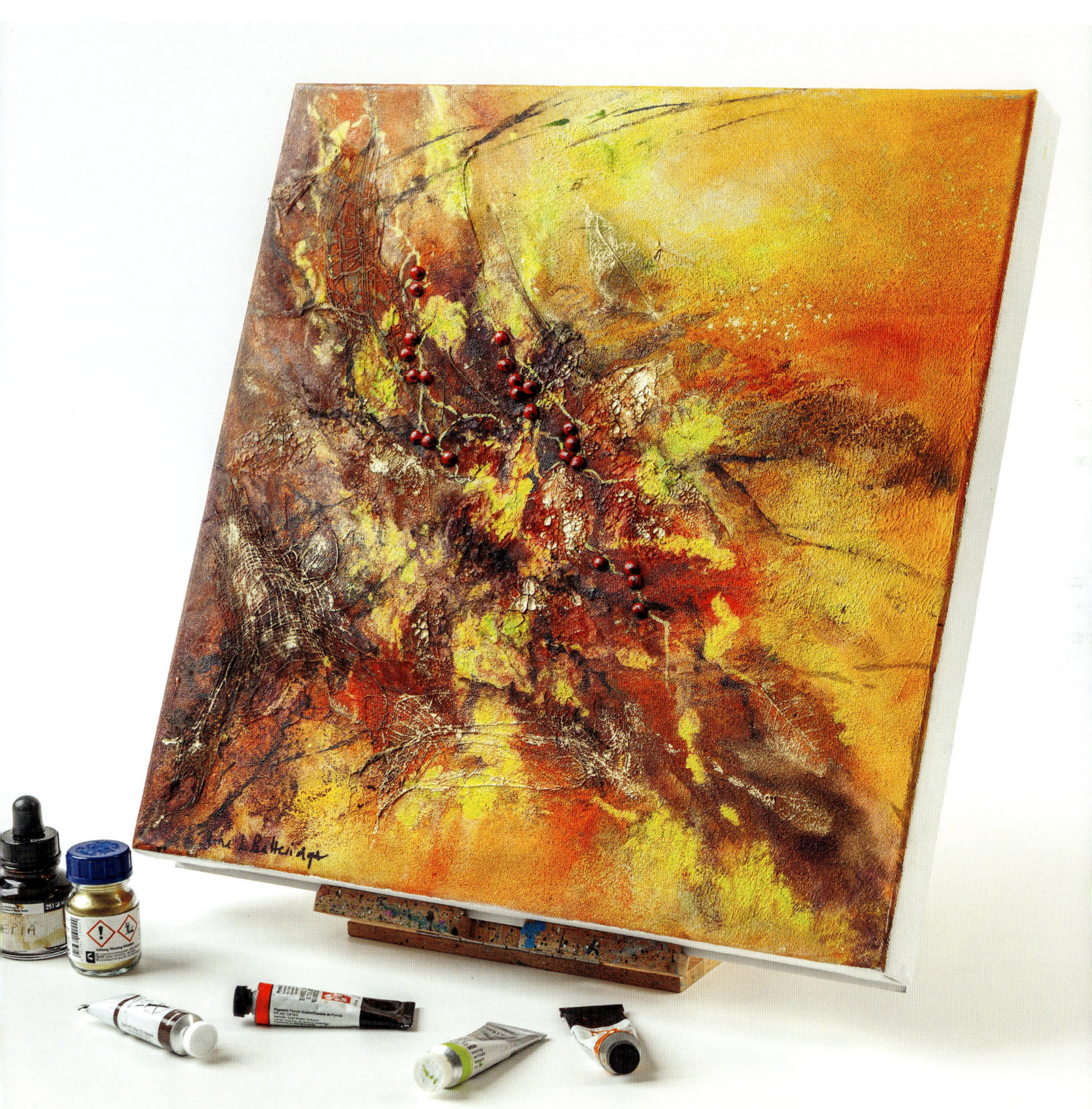

Colour and mood

Surroundings can affect our mood and feeling of well-being. They can make us feel happy or sad, uplifted or downbeat. Being somewhere that you don't want to be – a desolate wasteland, surrounded by shabby, run-down buildings – will affect you differently from being in a location that really appeals to you. Likewise, how we respond to our surroundings is influenced by the time of day and seasons of the year. A brightly lit field at the height of spring will evoke very different feelings in you than the same field at night in late autumn.

Whether walking through a bluebell wood and feeling energized by the fantastic colours of nature, seeing a field of poppies or sunflowers, or a turquoise shimmering sea against a golden sun, it is often the effect of the colour we are experiencing that affects our mood.

To convey this in a painting, you can use the paints you pick as a tool – and we don't have to just stick with warm, 'happy' colours. A barren landscape, for example, where the last remnants of last year's flora are now finally giving in and allowing new signs of life in the form of new shoots, might best be expressed through a cool, subdued, moody palette.

The colours you choose should reflect your response to your subject. Consider how your inspiration made you feel, and instead of aiming for realism, choose a palette of colours that evokes a similar feeling in your viewer. The greys, blues and neutrals used for *Blue Honesty*, opposite, for example, don't represent what I saw in front of me, but they reflect the stark, cold, wintry scene well.

Blue Honesty
20 x 20cm (8 x 8in)

This painting shows a cold, desolate area of my garden, where honesty seedheads remained so beautiful, shining silvery against the dark undergrowth and dead foliage. The cool blue I've used conveys a feeling of an icy, cold, frosty winter's day.

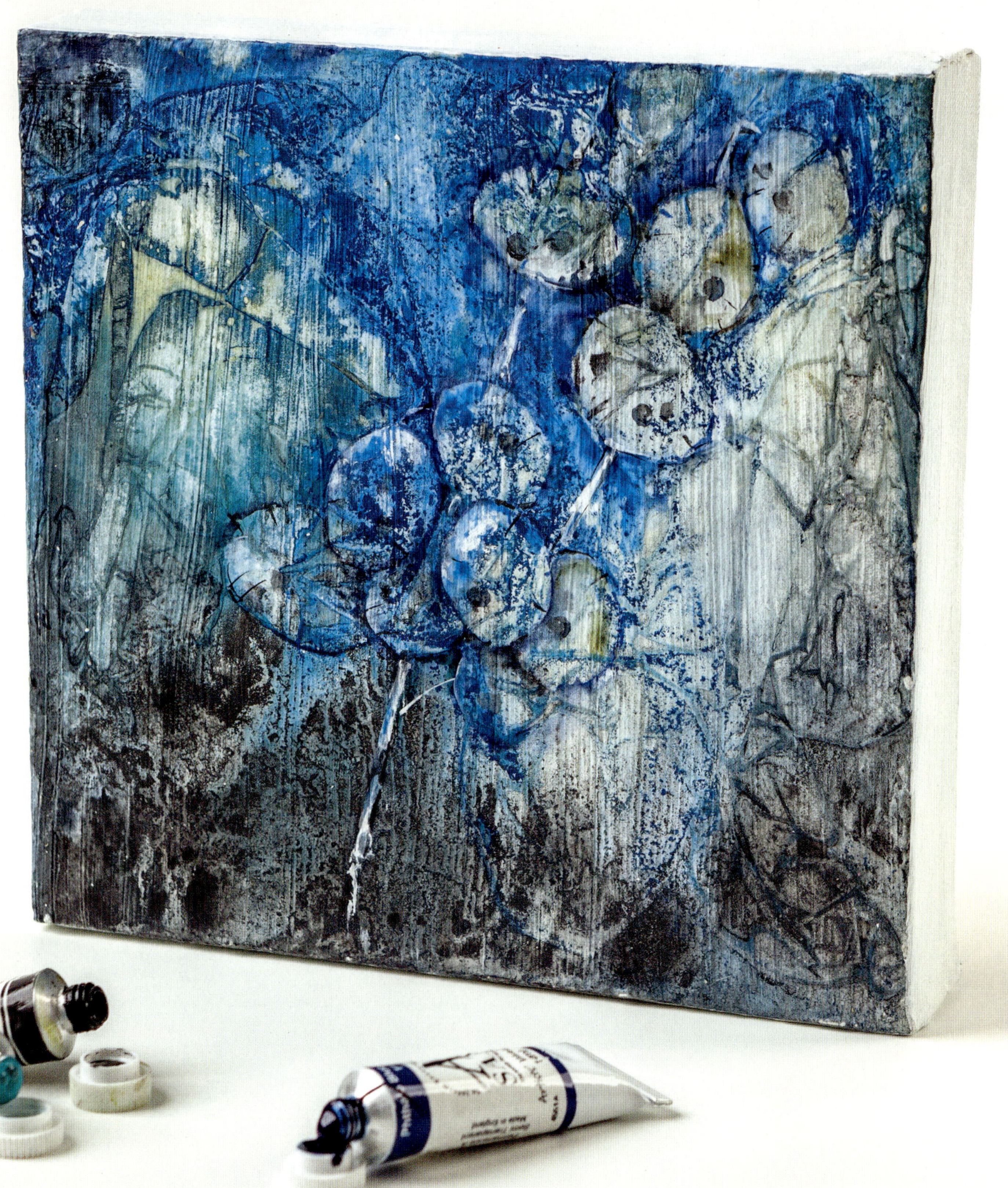

What to avoid

Mixing several colours together can start to dull down the vibrancy of watercolours, resulting in muddy, muted mixes. This is made even worse when semi-opaque and opaque colours are used. I always try to use transparent colours whenever possible, and avoid mixing more than two colours together. These simple steps help to make sure that my work stays fresh and vibrant.

Where you do need more subtlety – when using two or three really vibrant colours, for example – try adding a toned-down hue alongside them, or mixed into each (see page 52). This will help to anchor everything together. Simply remembering the logic of the colour wheel can turn your work around.

It should be noted that when complementary colours meet and merge together they mute each other and produce undesirable tones. For this reason, it is always best to apply a 'friendly' colour in between them to stop this happening. For example, yellow and purple are opposites on the colour wheel. Adding a blue where they meet stops each colour turning to mud.

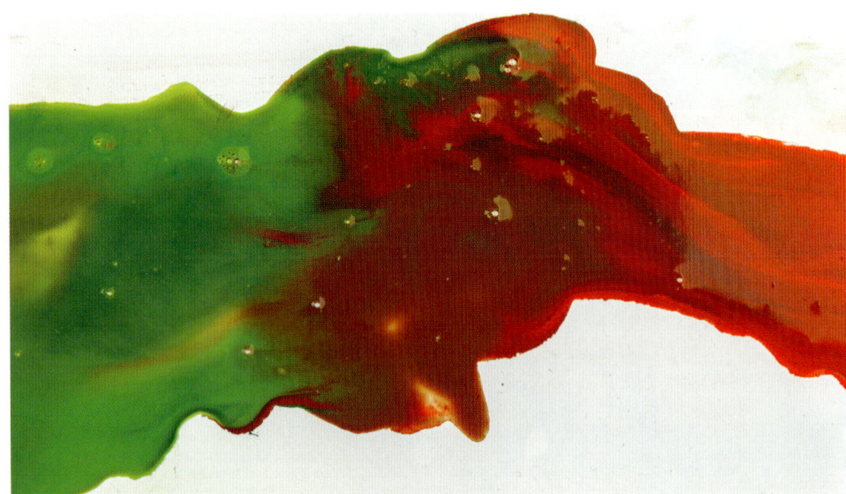

Muted mixes

Being complementary colours, Daniel Smith's serpentine green and pyrrol scarlet combine to make a muted, earthy tone.

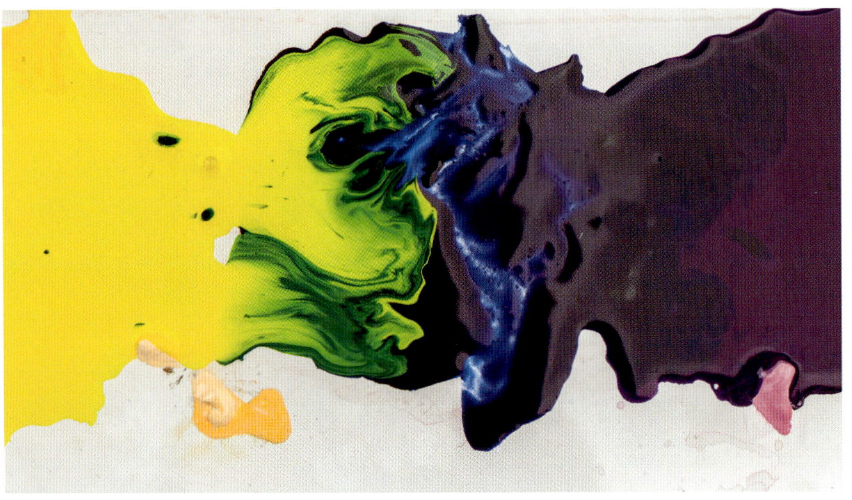

Friendly colour to ensure vibrancy

Here, ShinHan royal blue has been placed as a barrier between intense violet and cadmium lemon (both SAA paints). The blue works well with both, and ensures that the finished result is bright and clean.

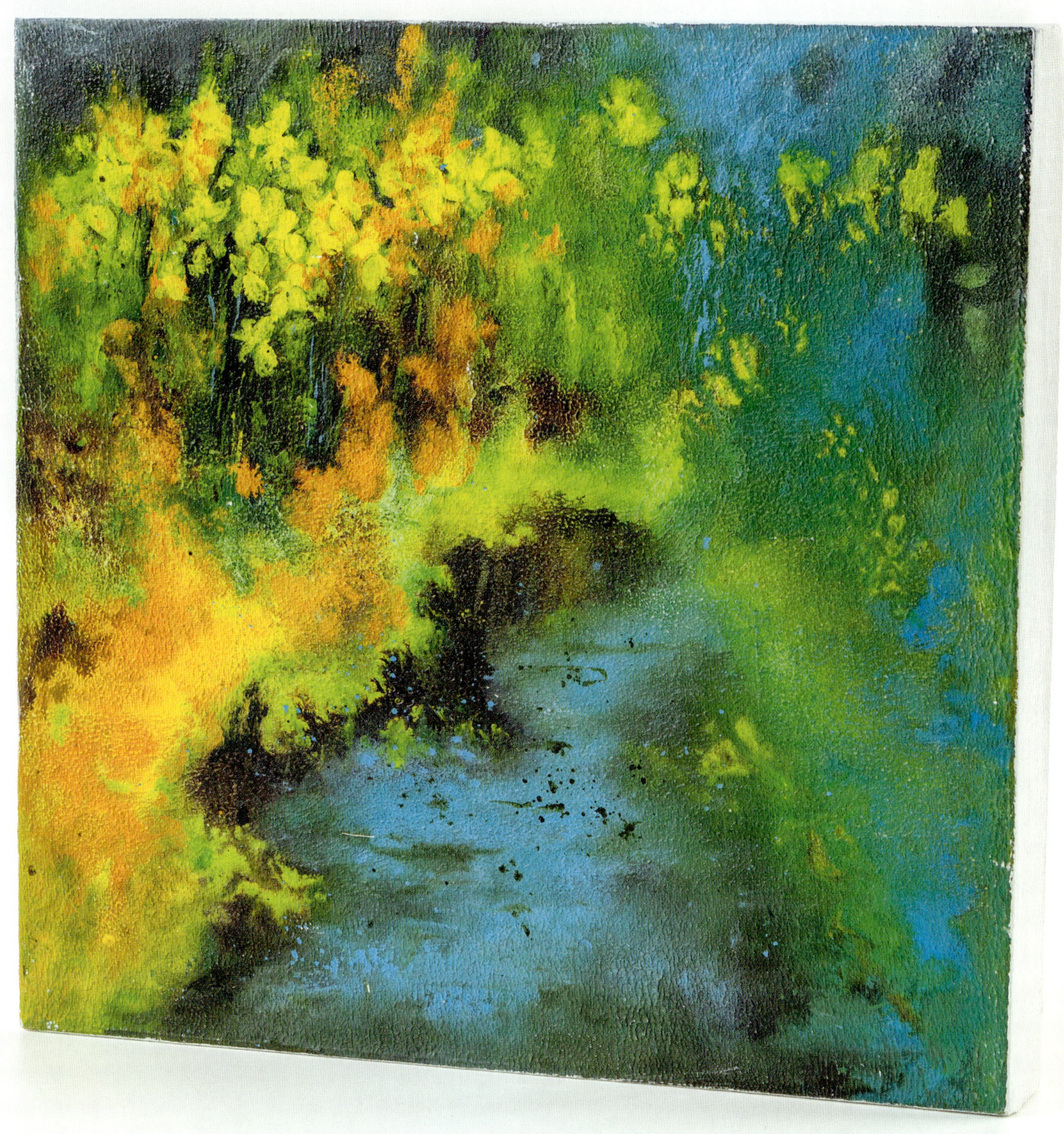

Yellow Irises by the Canal

30 x 30cm (11¾ x 11¾in)

*I used three really vibrant colours but a contrast of a dark indigo blue
and a brown were needed to balance the composition, create depth and
to make the bright colours stand out even more.*

swirling tide at porthmeor

Several techniques have been used to capture this atmospheric seascape showing a culmination of foam and bubbles swirling around the rocks as the tide is coming in.

The concept of texture was my starting point for this abstract piece. I wanted to produce a piece of work that includes many of the textures I associate with seascapes, along with the various blues and turquoises that represent the sea at different depths. The natural canvas, some of which I've left exposed, is also very fitting to the natural environment of this subject.

I also decided to use acrylic inks to ensure I could properly capture the vibrancy and brightness of a day at the beach.

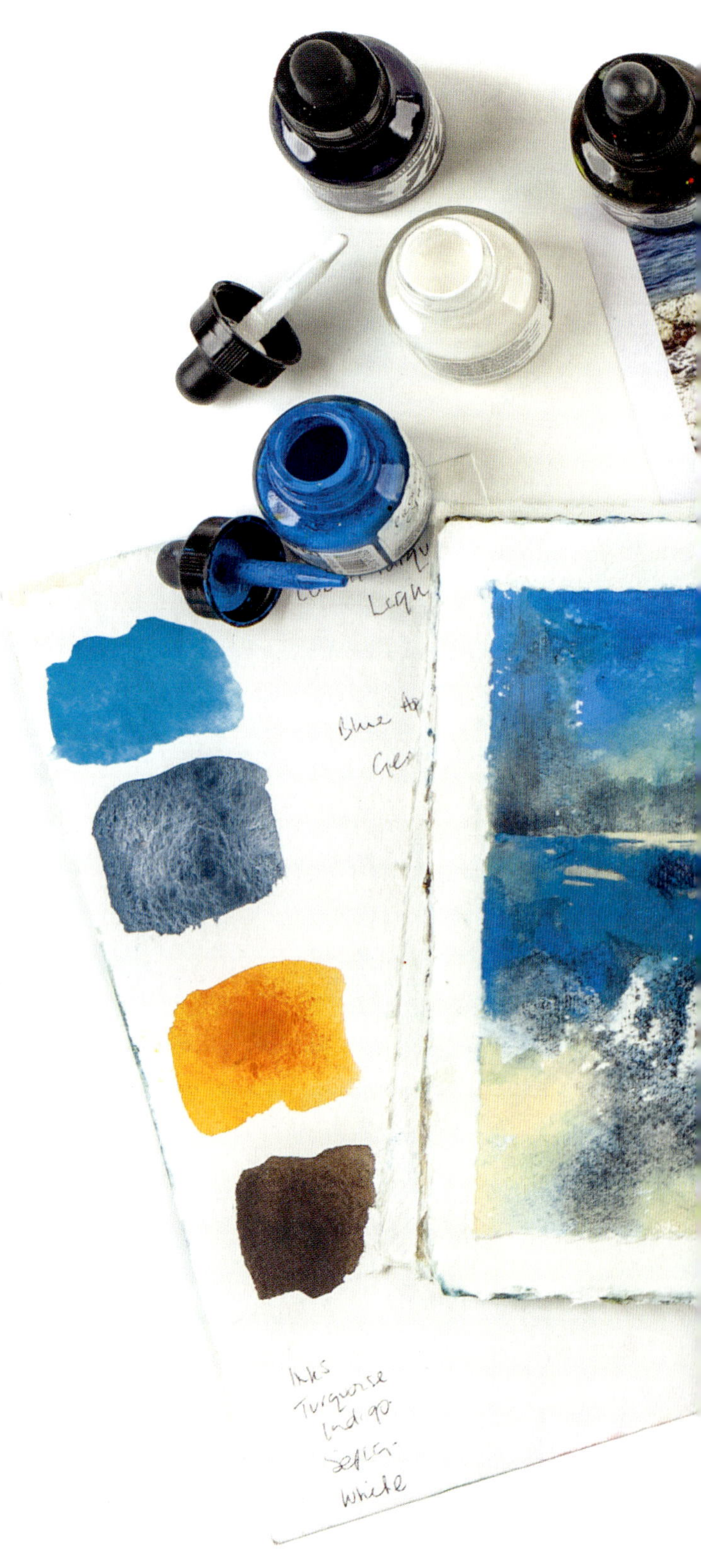

YOU WILL NEED

- **Block canvas** 40 x 40cm (15¾ x 15¾in)

- **Watercolour paints** Raw sienna (Daniel Smith), blue apatite genuine (Daniel Smith), vandyke brown (SAA); cobalt turquoise light (Winsor & Newton)

- **Inks** All FW acrylic: sepia, turquoise, white

- **Brushes** Four medium brushes (size 12), one large brush (size 16), fine brush (size 2 round), small brush (size 8), size 0 rigger

- **Other materials** Glass bead gel, crackle paste, transparent watercolour ground, coarse grain modelling paste, granulation medium, pipettes, two palette knives (one for smoothing out the pastes, and a second for spattering), old brush and white gouache

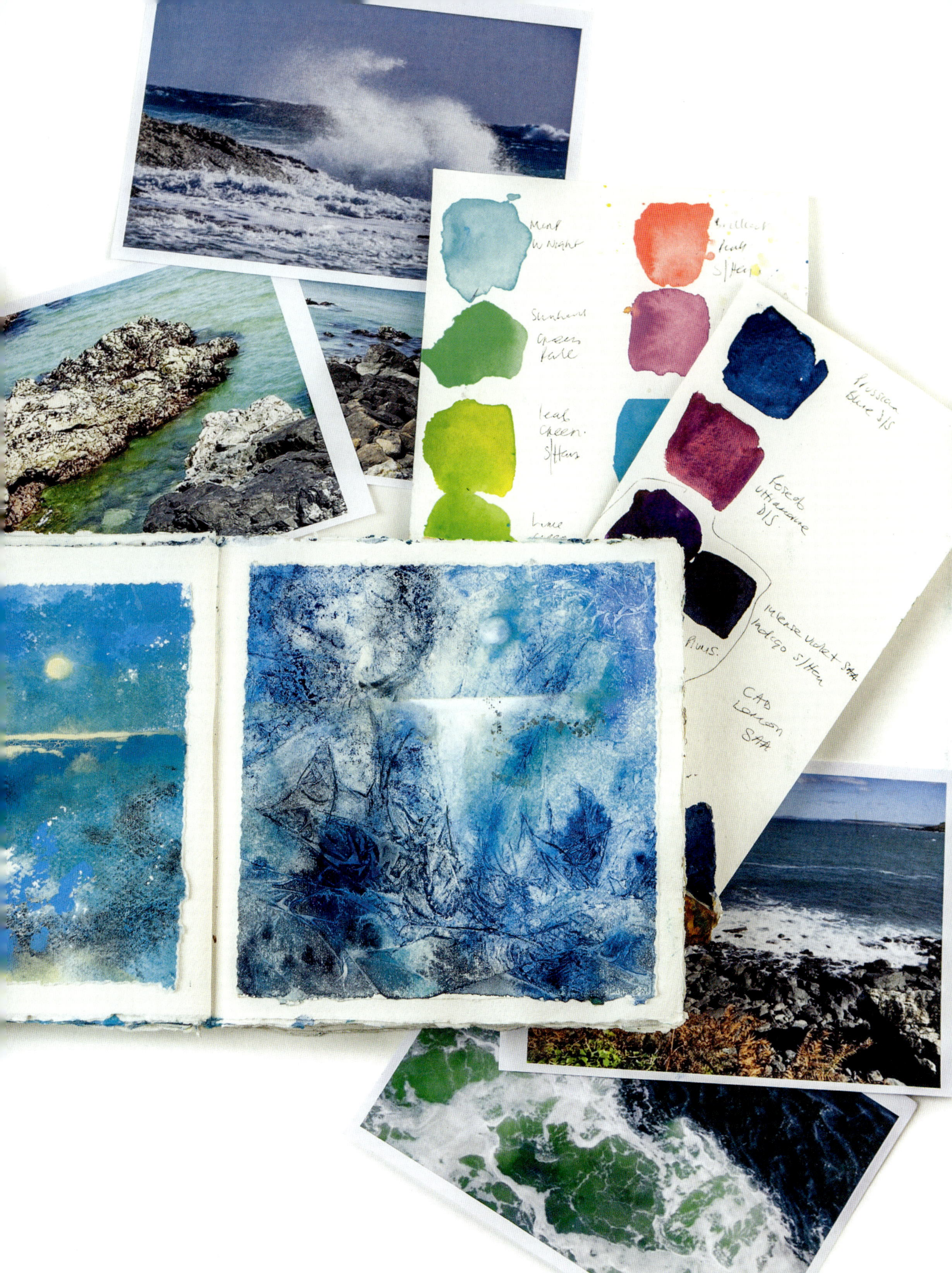

1 – **build texture**

- Apply transparent ground to the surface. While wet, apply crackle paste thickly. Aim to cover roughly three-quarters of the surface, leaving a gap in the centre for a mound of modelling paste later.

- Add glass bead gel around the crackle paste: we're trying to create the impression of bubbling foam around rocks, so bear this in mind as you apply the gel.

- Feather the edges with an old household brush.

- Switch back to a palette knife to apply coarse-grained modelling paste to the central area.

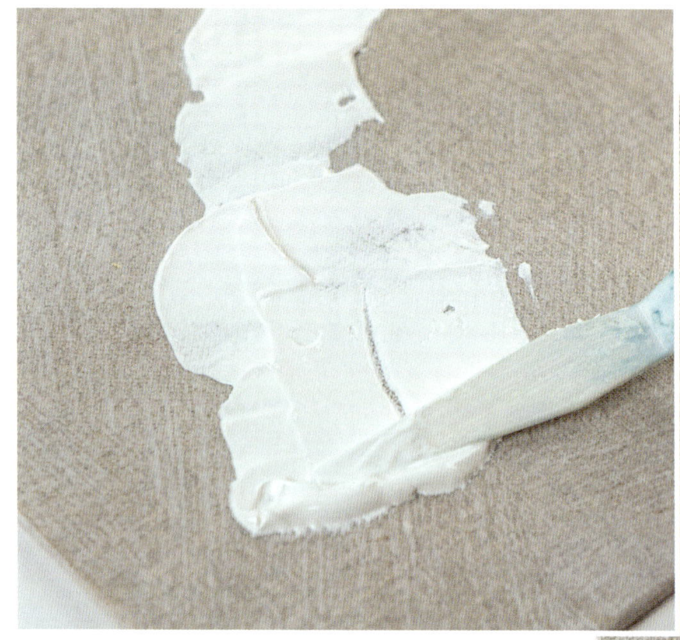

When applying the crackle paste, don't be tempted to try to smooth it out or refine it. In short, don't mess around with it too much.

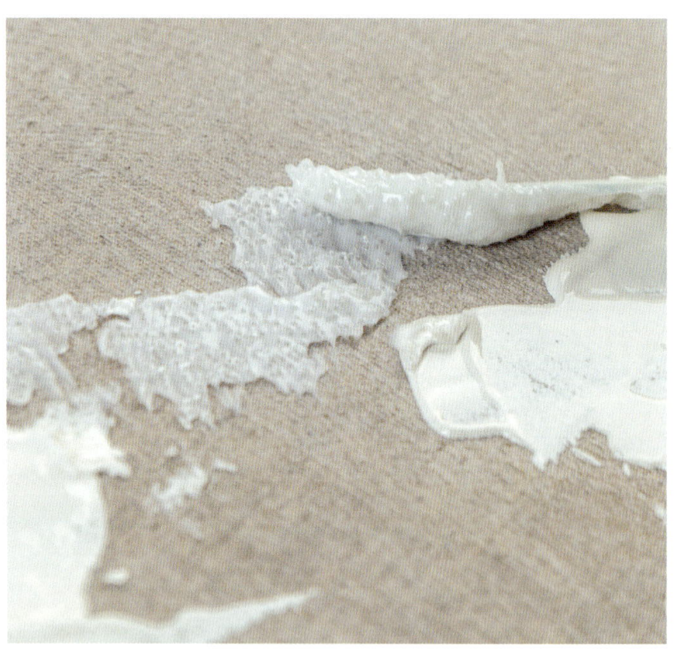

Adding glass bead gel. The combination of different textural effects helps to bring to mind the rocks above and below the surface of the water, as well as the water's surface itself.

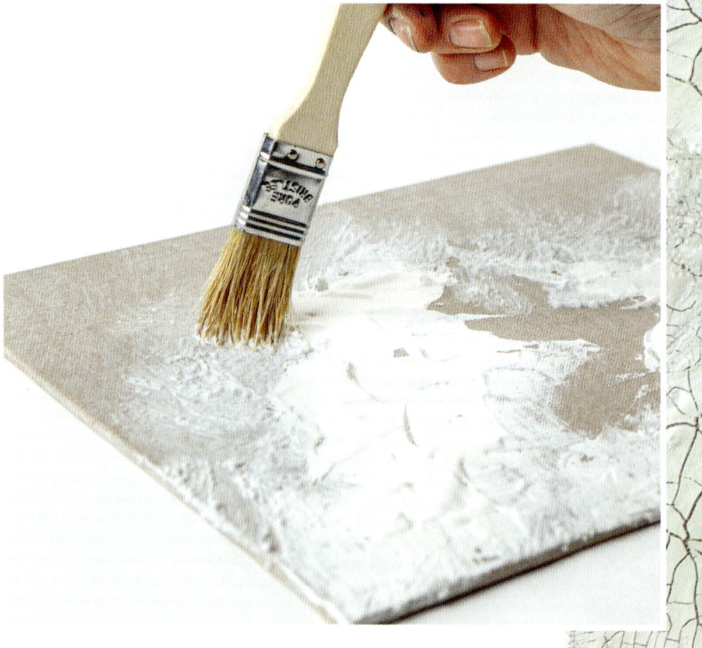

The technique of feathering simply involves brushing some of the texture mediums outwards, to prevent hard lines forming at the edges.

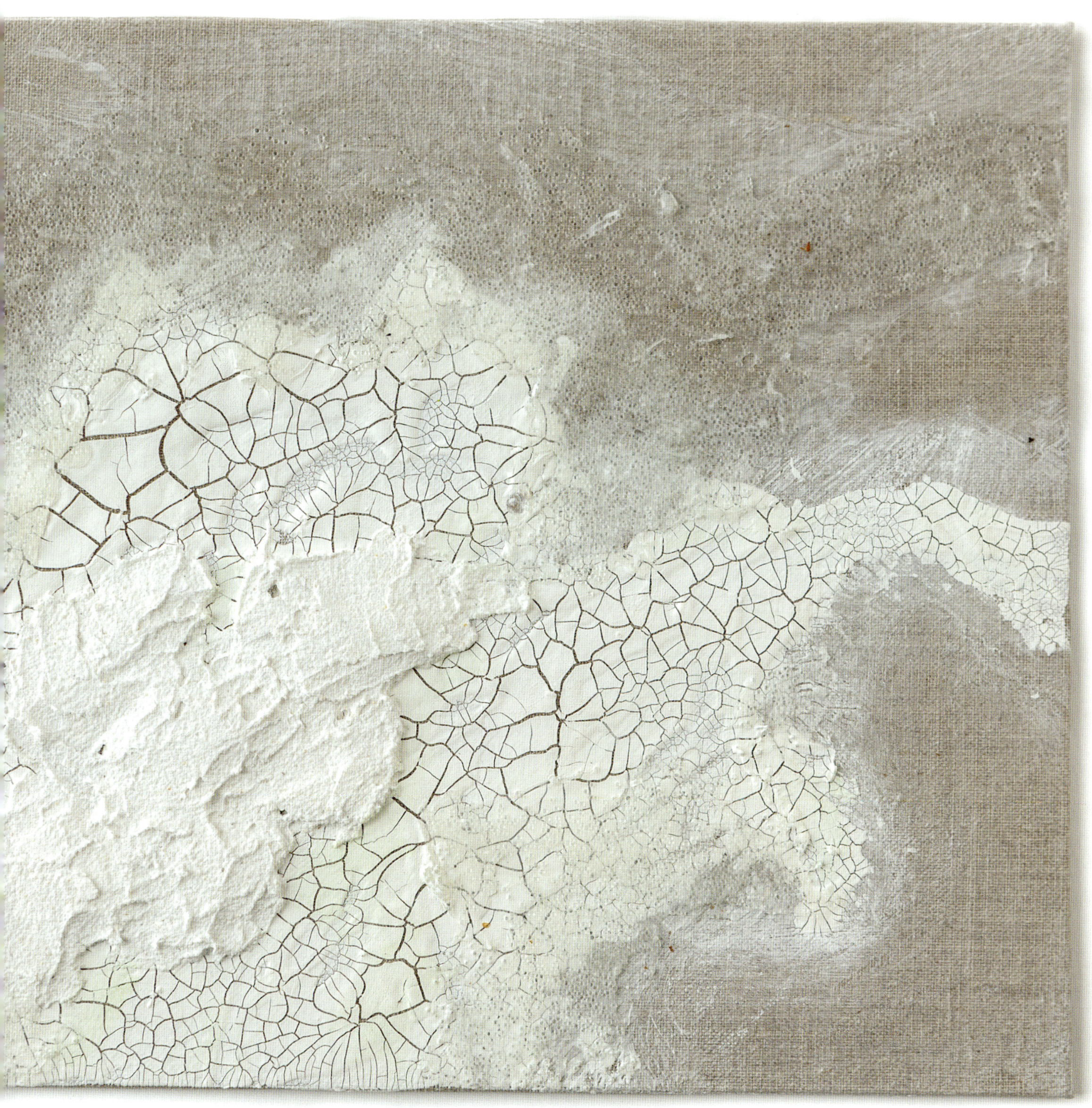

The painting at the end of this stage. Make sure all of the textural media have dried completely – not just on the surface – before moving on.

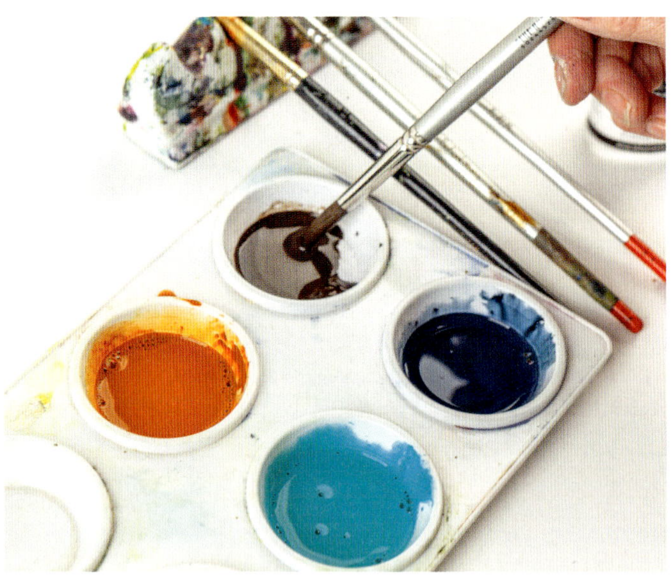

Prepare plenty of each of your paints in separate deep wells. This will ensure you have enough – it's frustrating to run out part-way through painting an area.

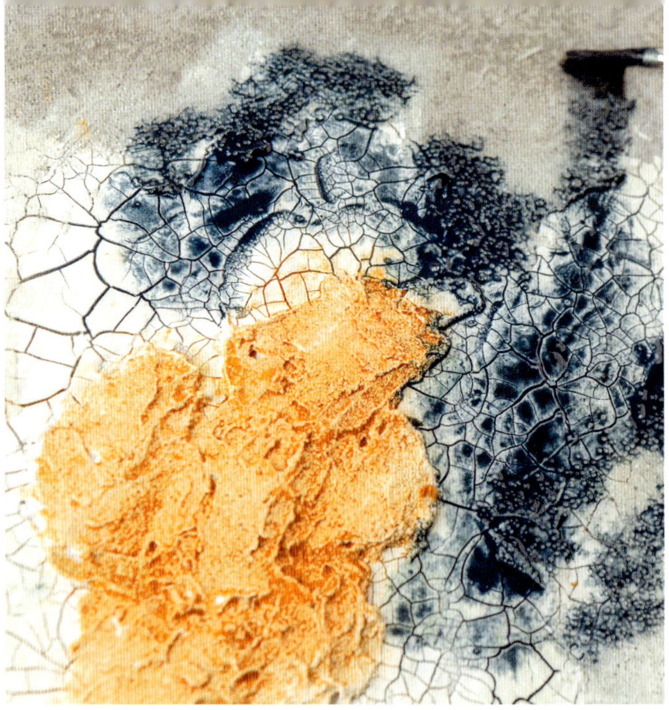

Pre-wetting the surface with clean water will help to ensure the fluid paint flows into the crevices, rather than just sitting on top.

2 – apply paint

• Mix up cobalt turquoise light, blue apatite genuine, raw sienna, vandyke brown. Use a different brush for each colour so you can work quickly and fluently simply by swapping brushes. It will also help to keep your colours clean.

• Wet the surface with plenty of clean water then start to build up a base layer of colour; building up rough areas in turn – use raw sienna for the rocks, and blue apatite genuine around it. Leave a few gaps, and avoid allowing them to merge at this stage.

• Working wet-in-wet, bring in cobalt turquoise light to vary the water area. Work the brush into the cracks and texture. Add vandyke brown at the base of the rocks.

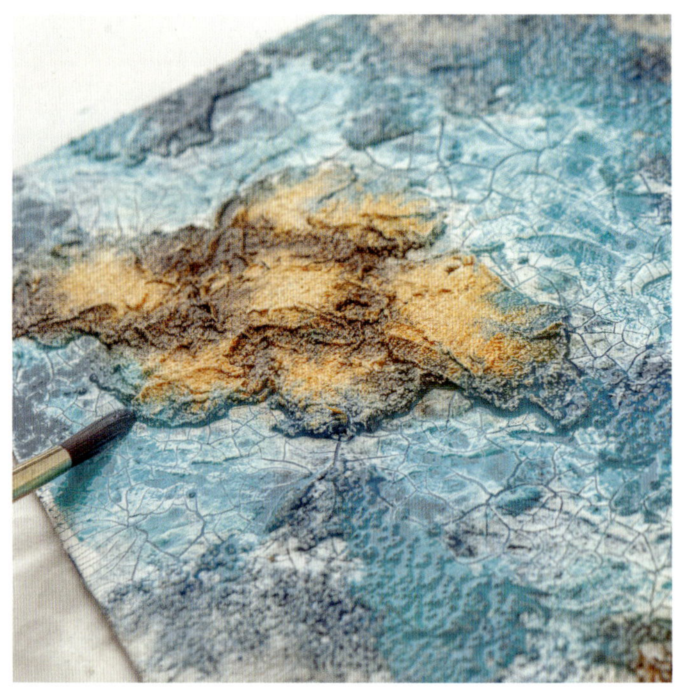

Working loosely creates an expressive, free feeling. In abstracting, there's a balance to be struck between representing what you see, and what you want the viewer to experience.

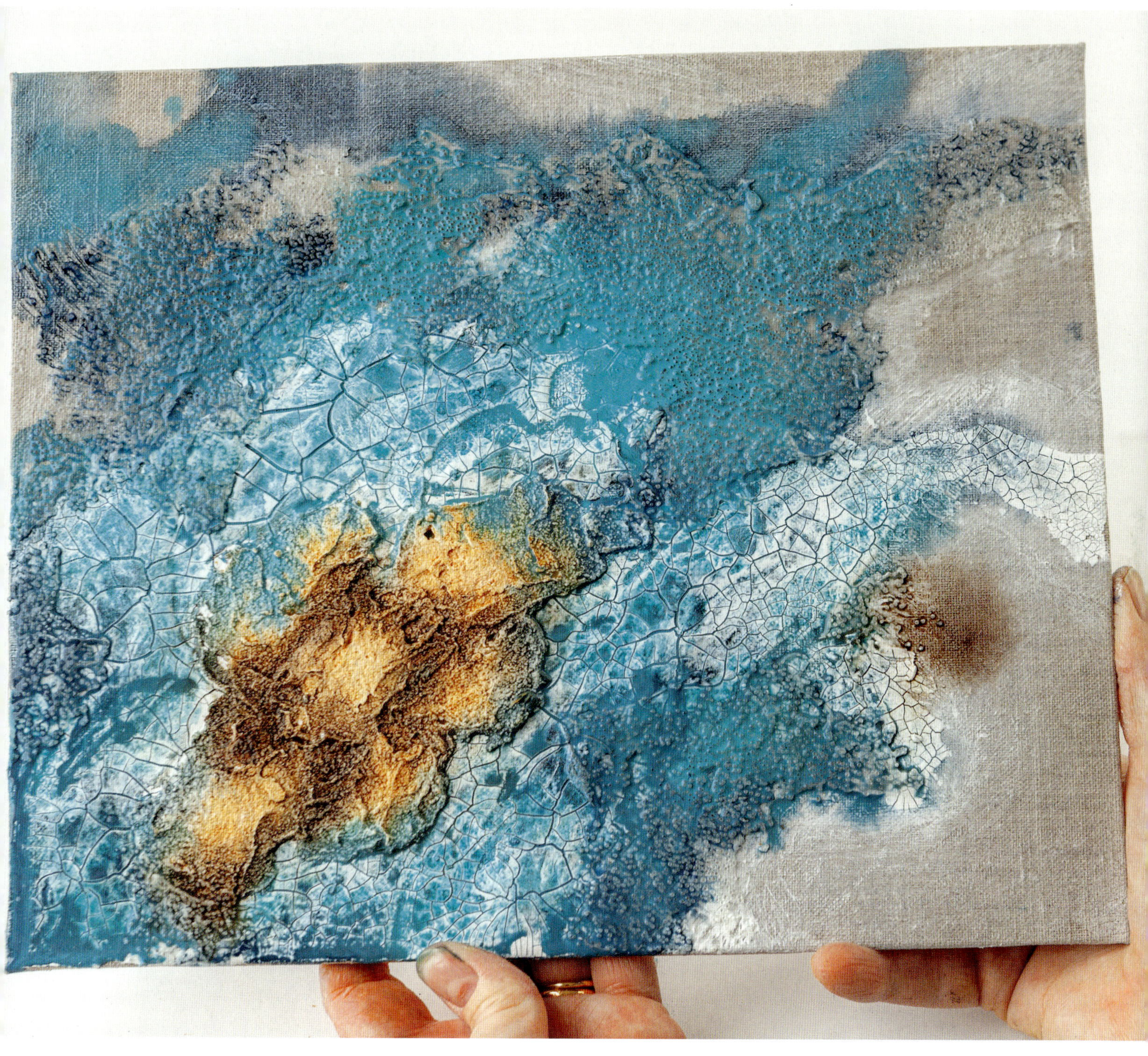

The painting at the end of this stage. We now need to wait for the paint to dry slightly, but not completely, before the next stage. Keep a close eye on the surface.

3 – add vibrancy and movement

- When the sheen has gone, but before the paint is completely dry, start to apply sepia and turquoise inks using the droppers. Add granulation fluid using a pipette, then tip and tilt the canvas to encourage the wet paint and ink to merge.

- Place the painting safely on the surface and allow the granulation fluid time to develop. Lift it out of the rocks with a brush, if necessary, to ensure you keep this area clean and light.

- Add sepia at the base of the rocks, again adding granulation fluid for variety.

- Adjust and lift out paint and ink as you feel fit, using curving strokes of the brush to blend away the paint and suggest breaking waves.

- Add turquoise ink, using the dropper to draw marks and suggest movement.

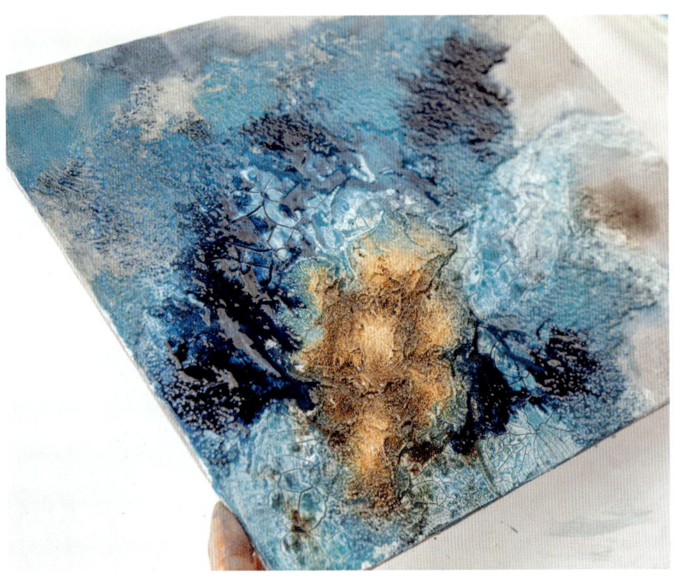

As it's a rigid surface, canvas board is well suited to the technique of tipping and tilting to allow wet paint to flow – unlike paper, there is no chance of it bowing or pooling.

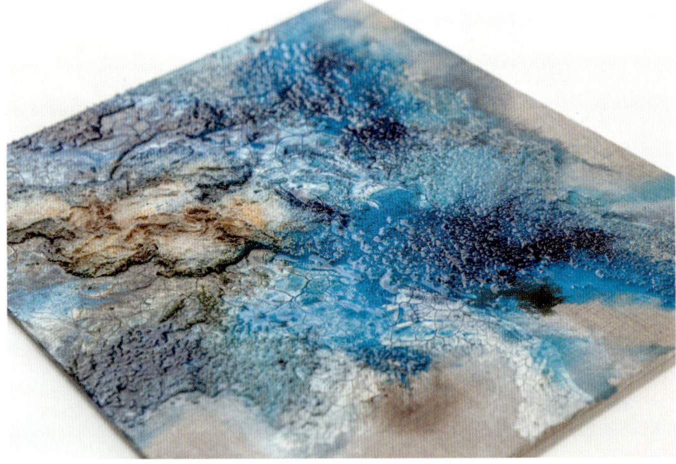

Note that clear spaces are left on the canvas. Don't be afraid of leaving bare canvas showing in your abstract work.

Curved strokes add energy and direction to the painting. You'll need to work out where they are best placed in your particular composition – try to avoid being too literal and obvious in painting waves, and instead concentrate simply on the movement of the brush on the canvas.

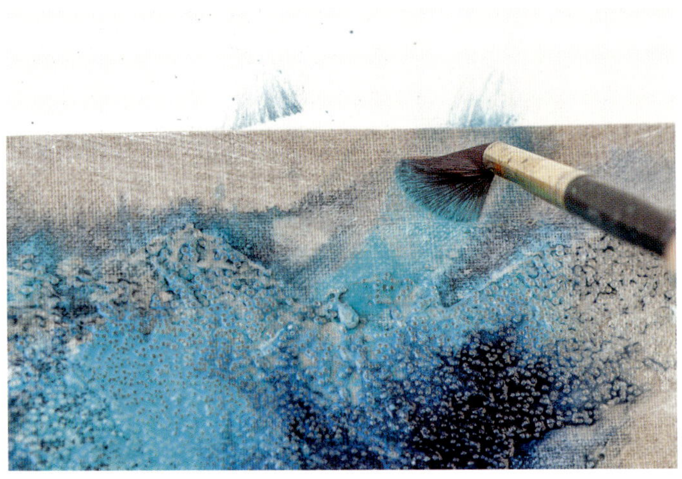

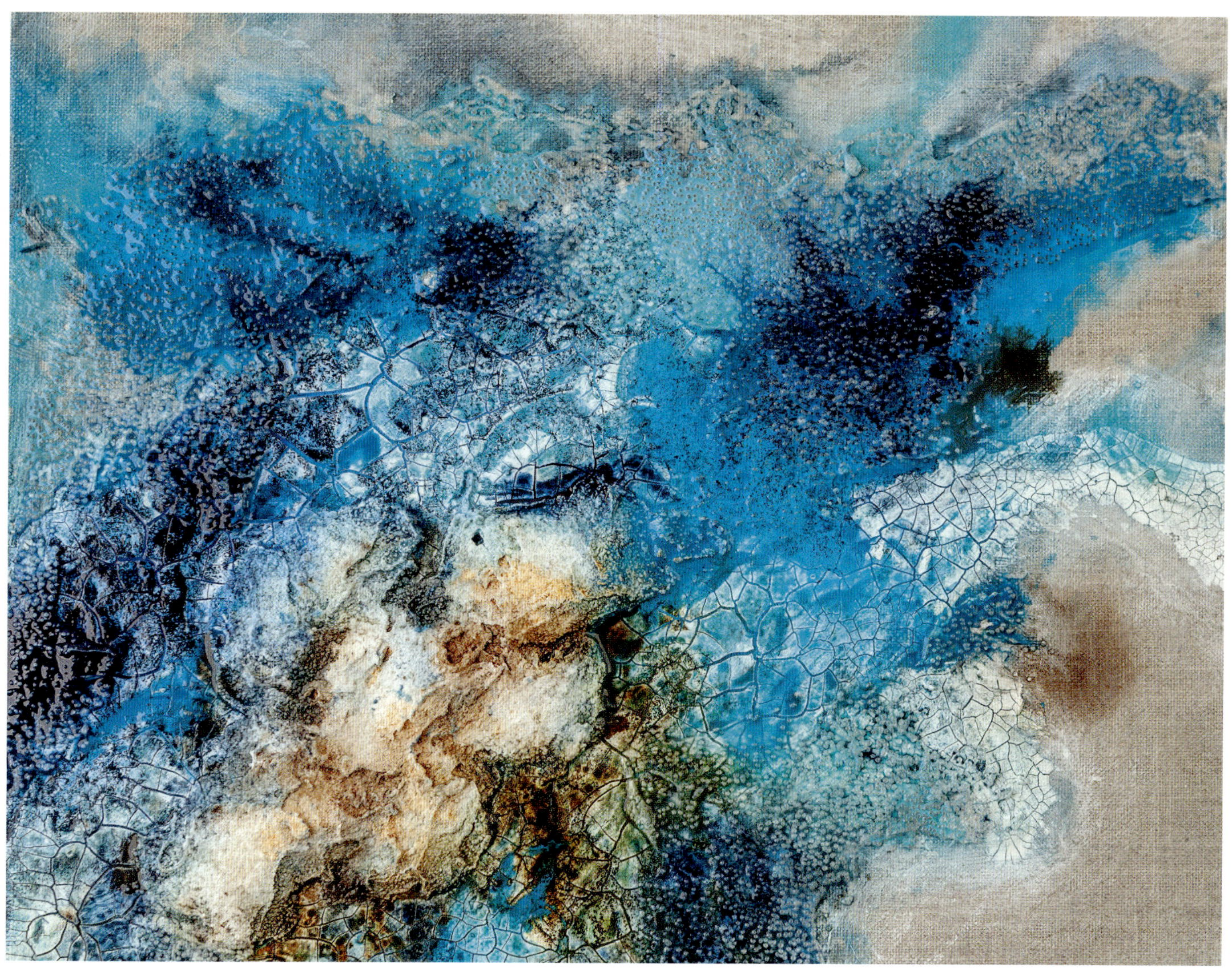

The painting at the end of this stage.

4 – adjust the tones

- Allow the painting to dry a little, then add white ink – don't apply it across the whole surface in one go. Instead, work a small section at a time. Use a small brush to encourage the ink to blend and bleed.

- Lift out a little paint from the crackle-paste areas using a dry brush or kitchen paper. This highlights these areas and re-establishes them.

- Load a palette knife with white and/or blue ink, and flick it onto the surface to spatter a few areas and add highlights.

- Using a fine rigger brush, re-establish the dark areas with vandyke brown. Reinforce the shapes suggested by the modelling paste.

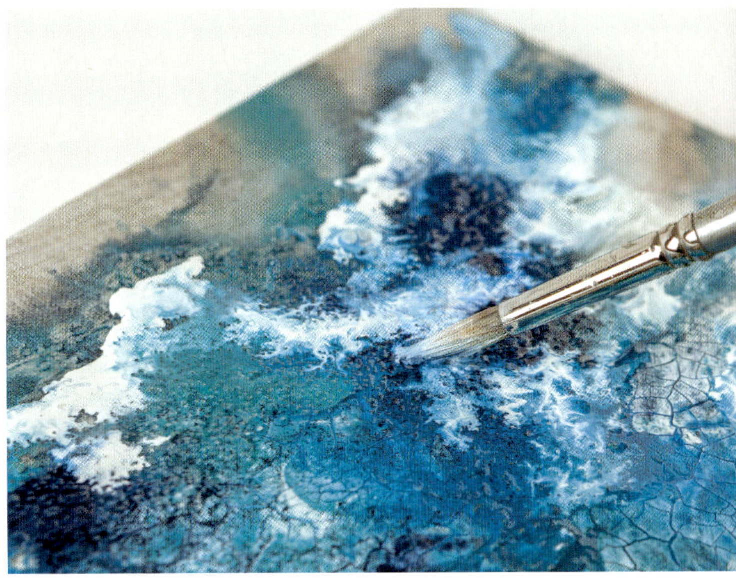

Adding and working with the ink a small section at a time takes away any pressure and urgency. It will also lead to a variety of textures being created, as the ink will react differently with areas that have dried more or dried less than others.

Spattering is a great technique for suggesting motion. Dip the palette knife in your prepared paint or ink (or use a brush to load the knife), then hold it in place over the painting. Use your finger to tension the knife, then let go to release a fine, semi-random spray across the picture.

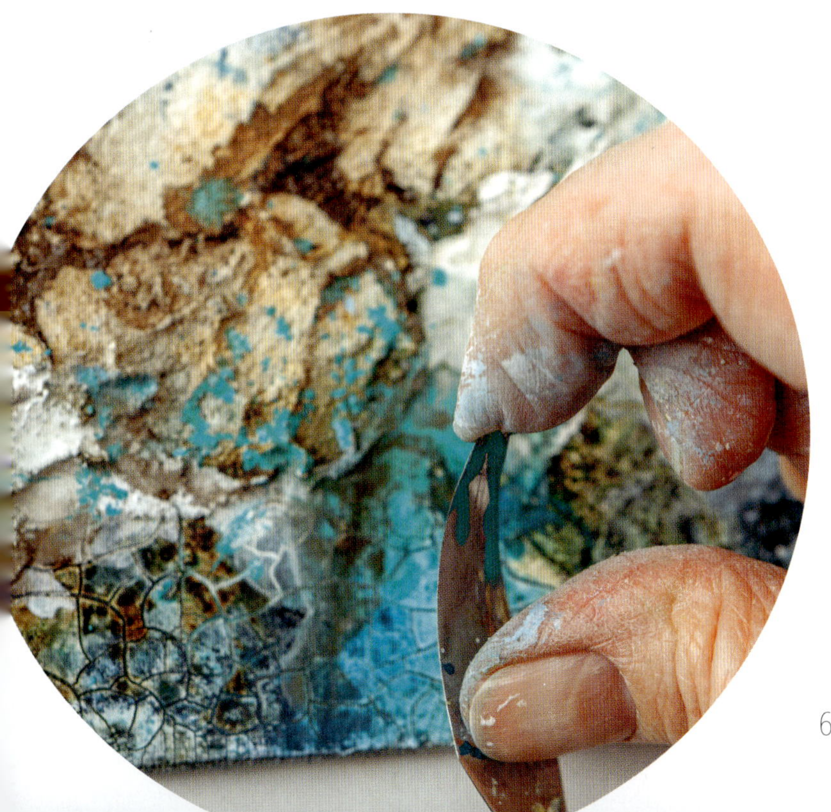

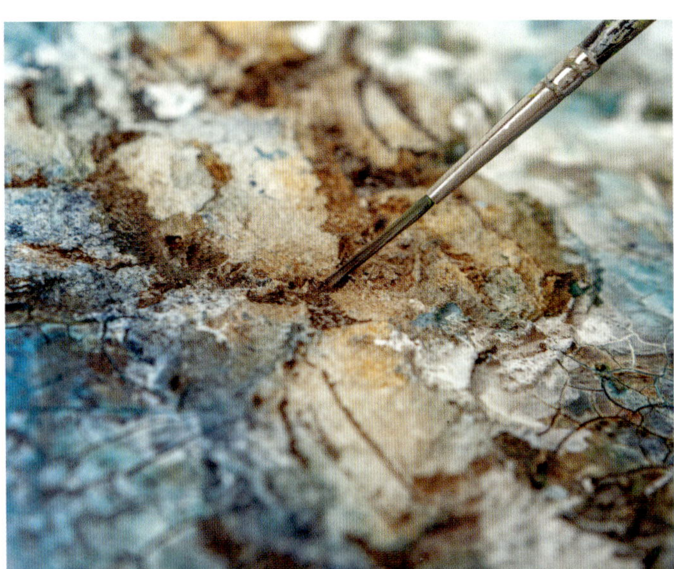

To get a sense of movement in the water, it's important to have contrasting areas that suggest stillness and solidity, even within an abstract painting. Adding texture and detail into and around the rocks draws the viewer's eye and helps anchor the picture, even if they're not as fully rendered as in a representational painting.

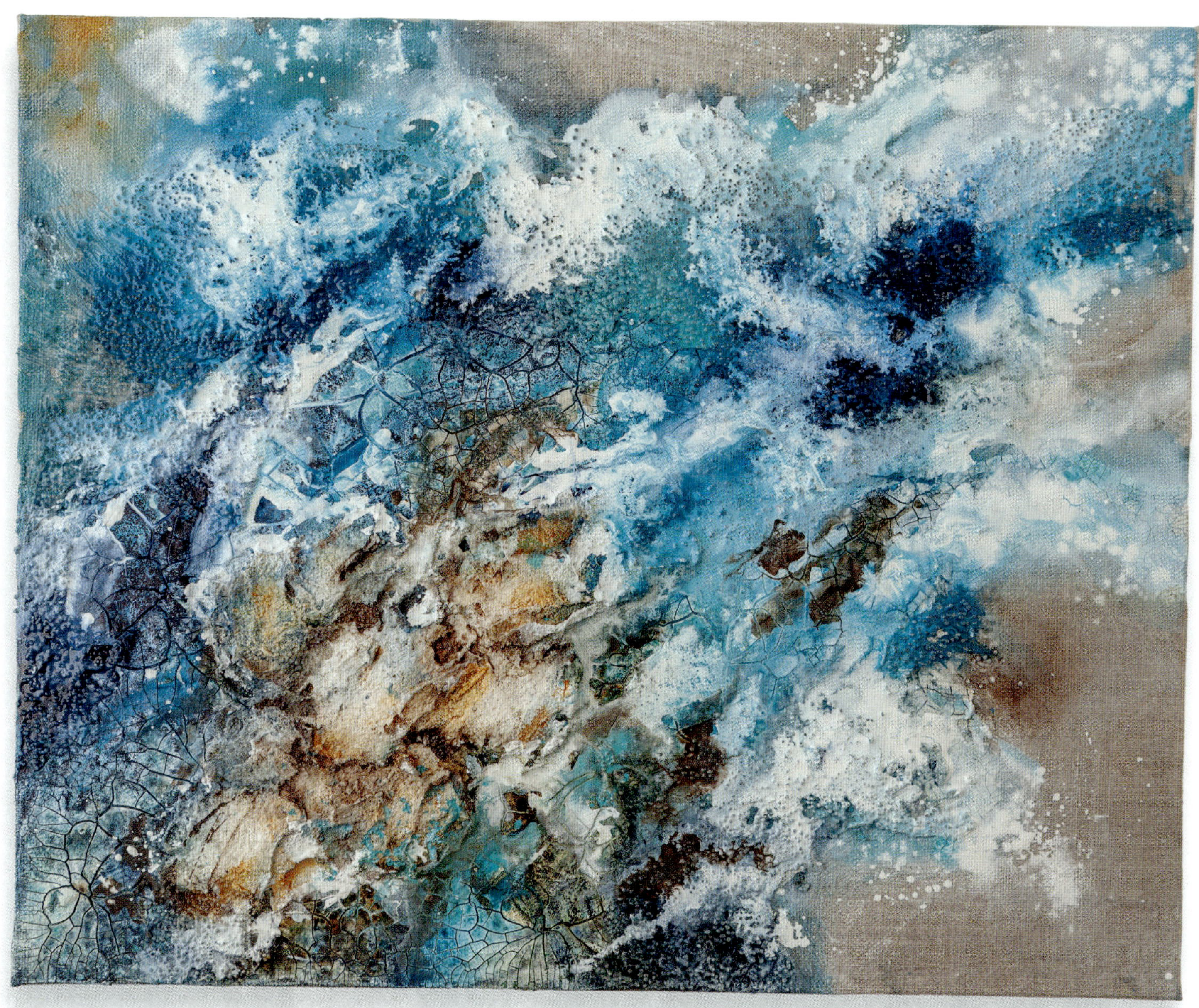

The painting at the end of this stage. You might wish, as I did here, to use a small brush to add some additional paint to suggest submerged rocks around the main group. This helps to integrate the textured area, by letting the eye glide across similar tones.

5 – finishing touches

- Pick up a little white gouche on your finger, wipe off the excess, then gently brush it over the glass bead areas to pick them out.

- It's easy to over-develop any painting, and that's doubly true of abstracts. Consider carefully what you want to add or minimize and place these last marks carefully.

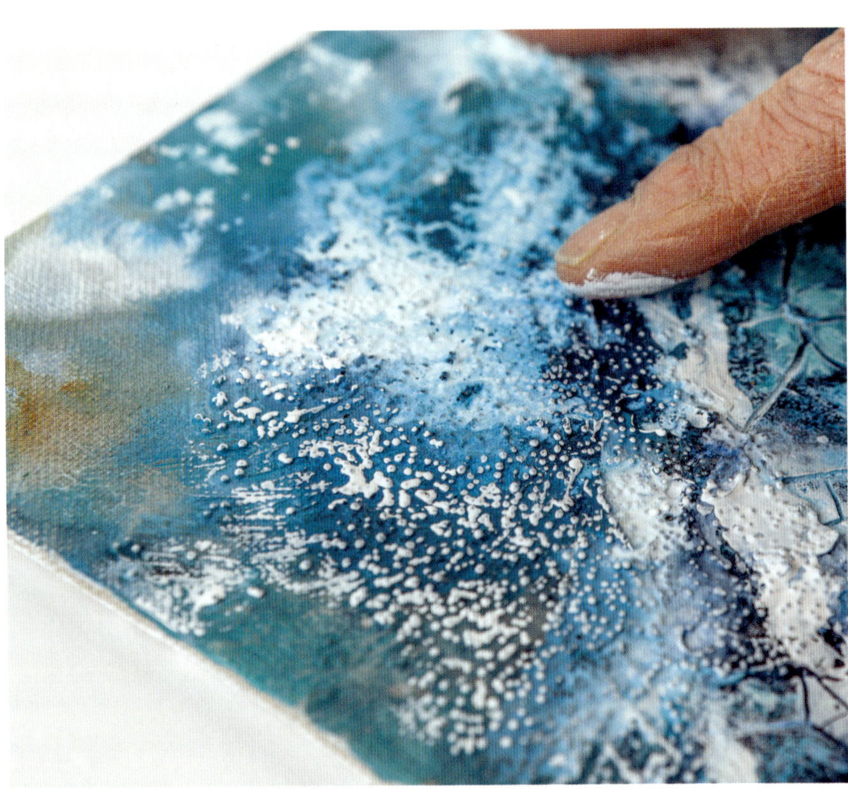

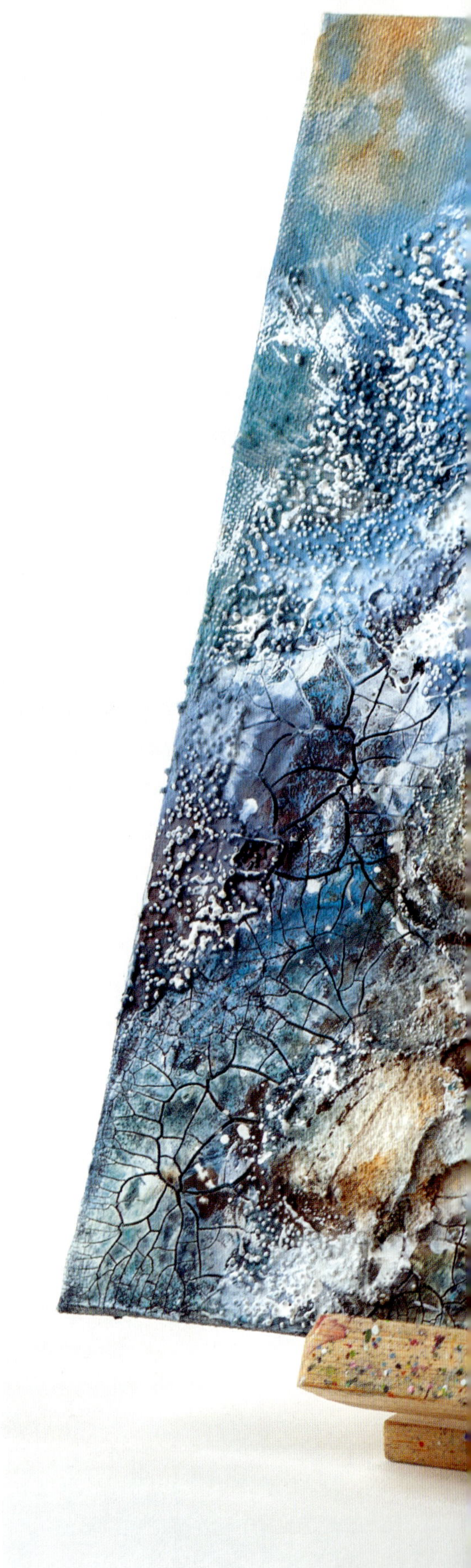

The texture and rigidity of canvas, together with the various textural mediums we've added, will allow you to come to grips with watercolours in a free and creative way – quite literally, it's at your fingertips!

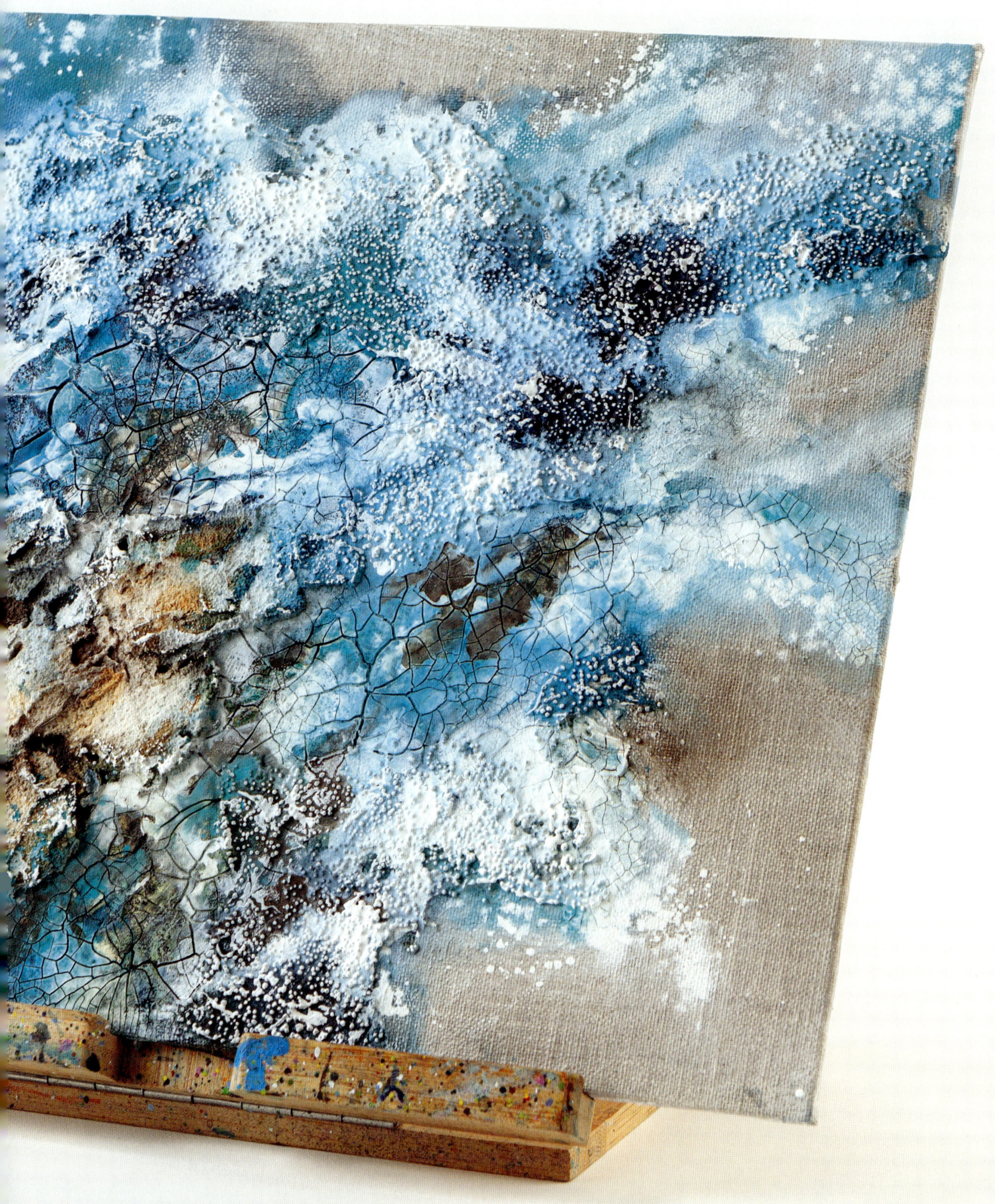

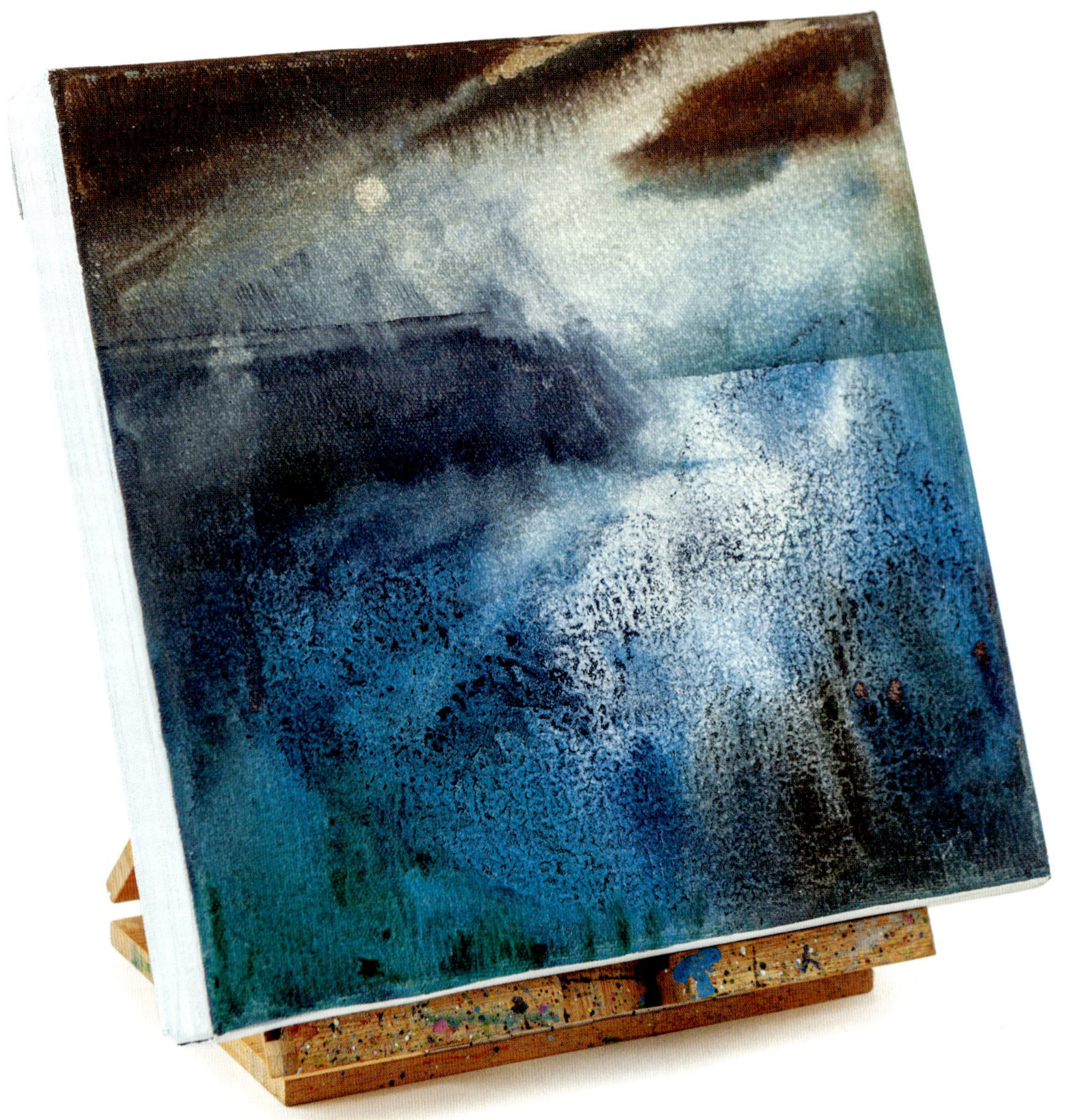

Storm over Smeaton's Pier

25 x 25cm (10 x 10in)

I've tried to create a sense of anticipation in this painting, which uses many of the same techniques as the preceding project, but the texture is created through granulation on the canvas rather than heavy use of additional surface mediums. Wanting to evoke a sense of atmosphere and impending rain, I also ensured a glimmer of light remained, where the sun is trying to emerge from behind the dark clouds – a glimmer of hope that it will turn out to be a nice day after all. This creates a sense of tension and interest.

There's a similar little bit of mystery around the base of the pier, where the light is playing across the sea and the sky. To achieve this effect and made it look like the light was sparkling on the sea, I used granulating blues and greens which separated to give speckled results. I also added a touch of sepia and indigo ink to create depth and to balance the painting in the foreground with the heavy sky. Strong diagonal brush strokes, using a flat brush, were used to suggest either the rain or the rays from the sun – it's up to the viewer to interpret which it is.

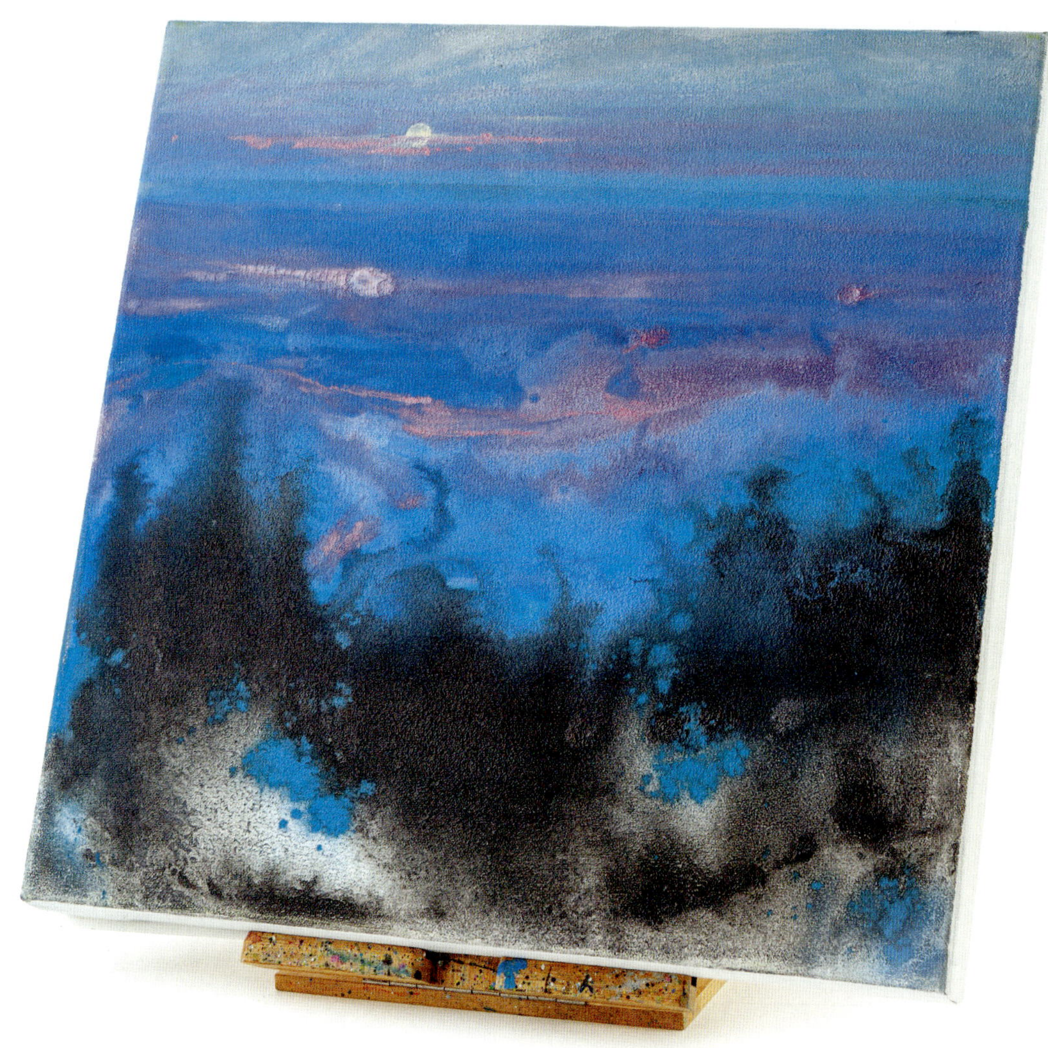

Porthmeor Sunset

40 x 40cm (15¾ x 15¾in)

This was inspired by one of the many St Ives sunsets that I have witnessed. The light there is amazing and extra special. The sky turned a vibrant pink and turquoise as the sun went down. I added some lunar black and sandstone paint to the bottom area to suggest living organisms and seaweeds and other plants.

In sharp contrast to the very textured, moving, swirling sea on the previous page, there are no hard edges or movement in this painting. Instead, I've concentrated almost entirely on evoking a calm, peaceful atmosphere in this artwork. I've tried to create a slightly enigmatic finished piece, encouraging the viewer to question how these colours can appear in the sea – one of nature's secrets.

When painting in an abstract way, it is freeing to realize that there are no rules – you can use whatever colours (and techniques) you wish to evoke the impression you want to instill in the viewer.

deeper into abstraction

There are many talented artists who paint in a realistic style, where precise detail is painted in a painstaking, slow process to capture an accurate representation of the subject. While I can appreciate just what an amazing talent this is, I know it's not how I wish to paint. I like to see art that intrigues, involves and challenges the viewer; asking them to engage and interpret rather than presenting things exactly as they appear.

In abstract art, techniques, colour and brushwork create something with life, atmosphere and character. Many artists, especially watercolourists, gradually drift into painting in a looser style. This sometimes happens by accident, by becoming more prolific and gaining confidence, or by choice. I have taught many students over the years who have said to me, 'I want to loosen up; I always end up adding too much detail.' It is hard. I used to think that when a painting is done in what appears to be a casual, random way, it would be so easy to emulate, but it isn't. You really have to say 'stop' to yourself just before you think you have finished. You have to resist the temptation to add too much detail and start fiddling.

Just how far do you have to go before a semi-realistic, or semi-abstract, painting becomes an abstract piece of art? That's quite difficult to say, as opinion varies widely on the subject. Some critics say that an abstract piece should be completely unrecognisable and bear no resemblance to anything; others disagree. My own view, and also my personal preference, is a very loose semi-abstract style. I like to know what I'm looking at, but I like to decide for myself what the composition, marks, colours and shapes are telling me. So this is what I aim to do. Sometimes it works and sometimes it doesn't – but if I'm left with a painting that I really like, that's a success to me.

Fly Away
40 x 47cm (15¾ x 18½in)

The dandelion here is fairly representational although there's not much detail, but the random, more abstract background of paint and inks contrasts beautifully, loosening up the whole composition and giving an overall abstract impression.

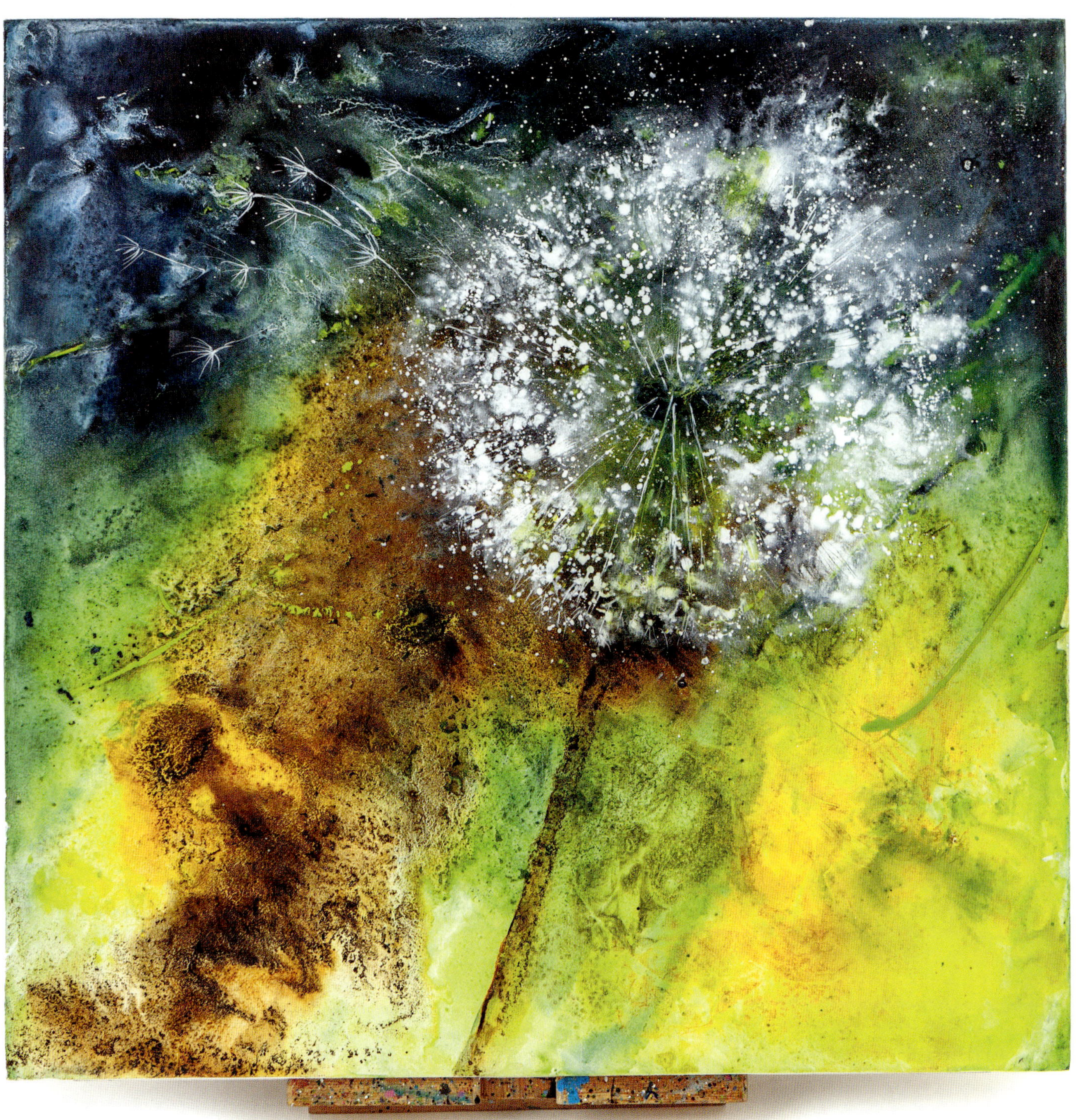

Semi-realism

The paintings shown here are both of a clump of trees, affectionately called 'the nearly-there trees' by holidaymakers making their way down to the south of England. They are positioned on a hill near Lifton, on the border between Devon and Cornwall. Opposite, I've painted them in a semi-realistic (also known as semi-abstract) style. This is basically painting a subject in a stylized way that neverthless remains recognisable.

This is a good – and simple – way into abstraction. Simply by using bigger brushes and leaving out fine details, you cannot help but simplify and loosen up your work, putting you on course towards a more abstract style.

Over time, working in this way will build your confidence, so that you will feel comfortable saying: 'I quite like that and yet there's not much detail to say what it is.' In semi-realism, it's your interpretation of what you saw, rather than realism, that counts.

There are different degrees of semi-realism. In the painting opposite, of the same subject, I decided to highlight the trees more and created a halo around them to give them prominence. I decided to lean it slightly more towards abstraction by adding some shapes in the foreground using ink. Adding subtly different elements has given the viewer so much more to look at and think about than the straightforward version below. If they didn't know the area, the viewer could, perhaps, assume that the trees stood above some cliffs. Another interpretation might be that, because the foreground is painted pink, there are flowers blooming on the grassy bank below the trees. This is the amazing thing about semi-abstract work, it starts to get the viewer involved, encouraging them to make their own mind up about the scene.

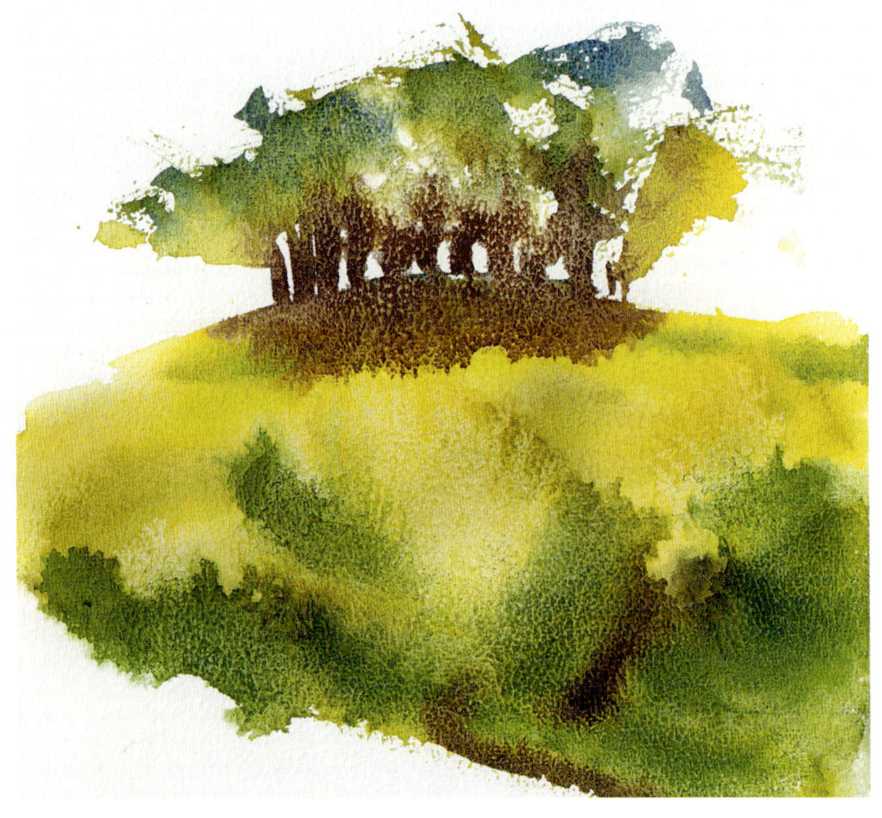

More realistic version of the nearly-there trees

20 x 20cm (8 x 8in)

There are no intricate details in this semi-realist take on the subject, as I used a big brush and made bold marks using only three colours. You can, however, tell exactly what they are meant to be because the key elements of colour and shape are immediately familiar.

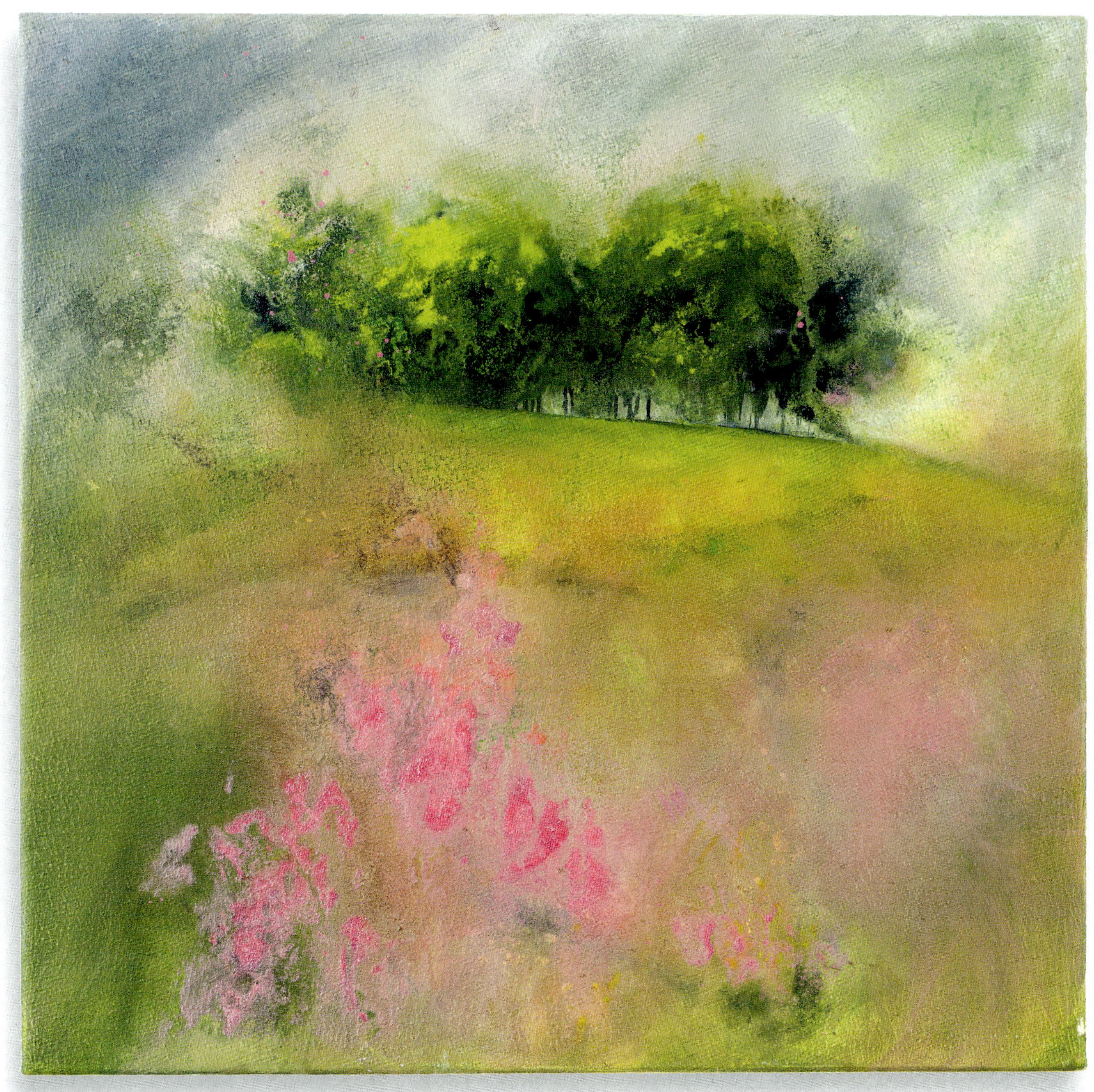

More abstract version of the nearly-there trees

40 x 40cm (15¾ x 15¾in)

I love how simple decisions in colour and placement make this take on the subject different to any other that I've seen. Abstraction gives you more freedom to create.

Abstracting through mark-making

Sometimes I can't help but respond to an inspirational subject
or exciting experience by laying down some gestural marks.
These might be lines, dots, dashes, circles, squiggles or anything
else I feel like doing. I often use abstract mark-making in my
sketchbook as an immediate response to what is before me when
out and about; and I also use it when I'm sitting in my studio
and an idea comes into my head and I start playing around – as
I do with most of my paintings. To make this more approachable,
you might think of it simply as doodling with paint: it should be
spontaneous and fun. See page 114 for an exercise in how this
sort of mark-making can be used to deliberately introduce a
random element to your work.

Try different ways of making marks to see what works for you.
Strong directional mark-making strokes, using big brushes and
a sweeping arm movement, can add a lot of movement and
dynamism to a piece of work. You might also try working quickly
and without forward planning, letting your hand, wrist and arm
take the lead, instead of your head. Loose, non-representational
mark-making in this way is really liberating. It creates spontaneity,
and because it's intimately connected to your physical form,
it creates very personal marks. The hardest part is leaving it
alone and not fiddling. Sometimes, I keep this sort of painting
for myself, as a reference to what I had in mind and as a private
response to my thoughts. At other times, if I think they're good
enough, I will exhibit them.

Splashy Puddle

30 x 20cm (11¾ x 8in)

*The inspiration for the painting opposite was captured in my
imagination when my husband and I were out walking on a
rainy day. A car raced past us, through a deep puddle, and
the rainwater just swished up in the air – we laughed so much,
because we got drenched. It's memories like this that you can
capture by using just a few strokes with mark-making.*

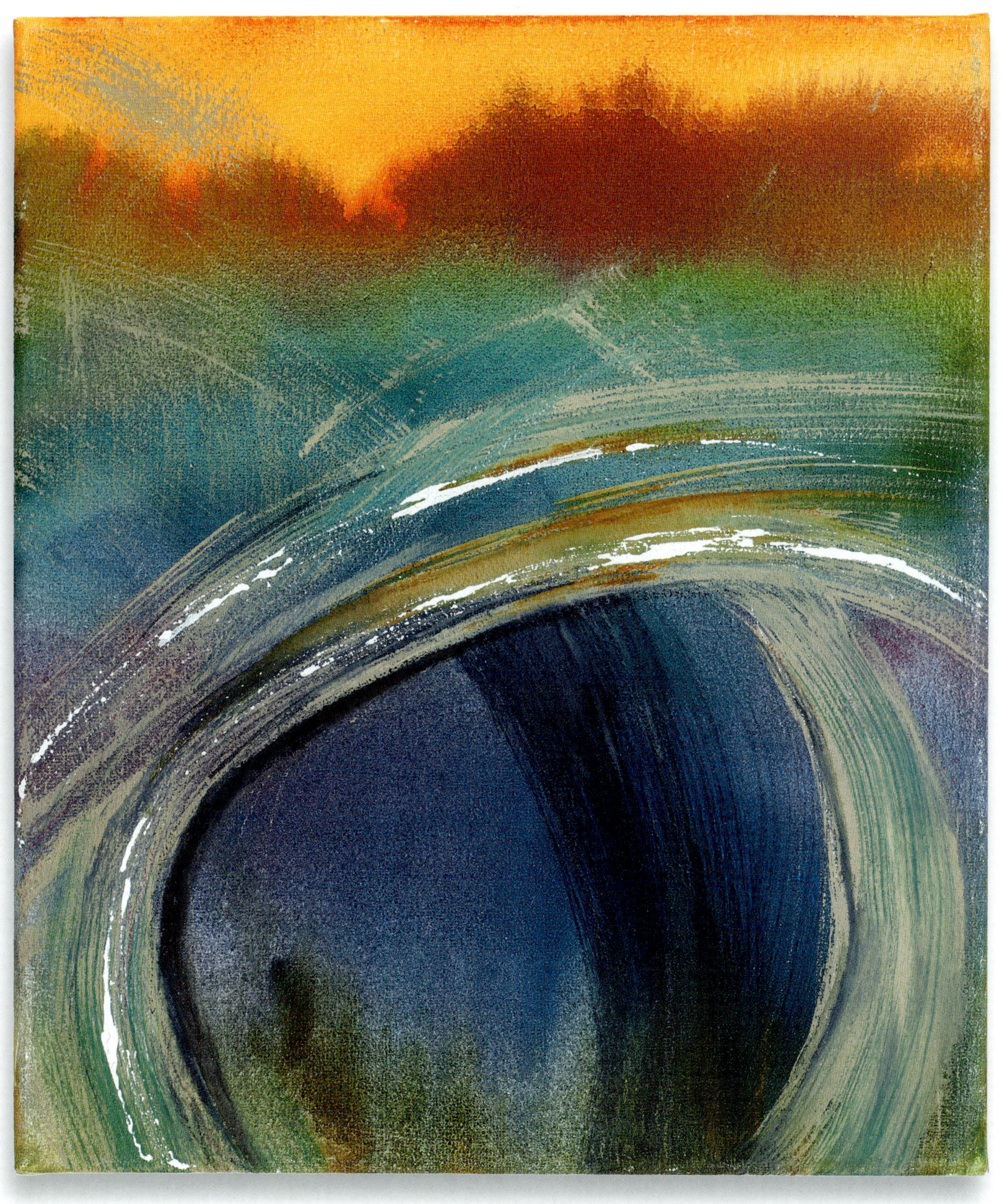

Abstracting through colour choice

Representational colours give a realistic approach to a subject, so if you're trying to loosen up and want your work to take on a more abstract style, using non-representational colours is another good route to take on your journey. I always try and add a little touch of random colour, here or there, to make my work more interesting. If painting rocks, for example, I often add a touch of turquoise or pink. This unexpected touch gives a more unusual and contemporary effect to the painting.

Adding a touch of colour from something else in the painting to an area that does not have that colour helps to tie everything together – this is sometimes important if you want the elements of your composition to work well together: the flash of familiar colour leads the viewer's eyes to the new area. I like to add some of the flower colour into any leaves I'm painting, for example. I also stamp over foliage using a leaf coated in an opaque lime green or yellow, which is a good way to add a little more light and texture into the painting.

It's a good idea to play around in your sketchbook with colour combinations – as noted earlier, I keep a sketchbook in which I experiment just with paint colours. Try reserving one sketchbook for this: you'll find it very useful, as you will be able to flick through it and see what particular combination of colours really jumps out at you on any particular day.

The painting opposite was from my imagination – it's a variation on the technique-led painting idea (see page 28), in which using non-representational colours was the 'technique'. I tried to capture a deep, red, night sky with a golden moon and distant trees reflecting on some water. The unusual palette resulted in a striking, attractive painting.

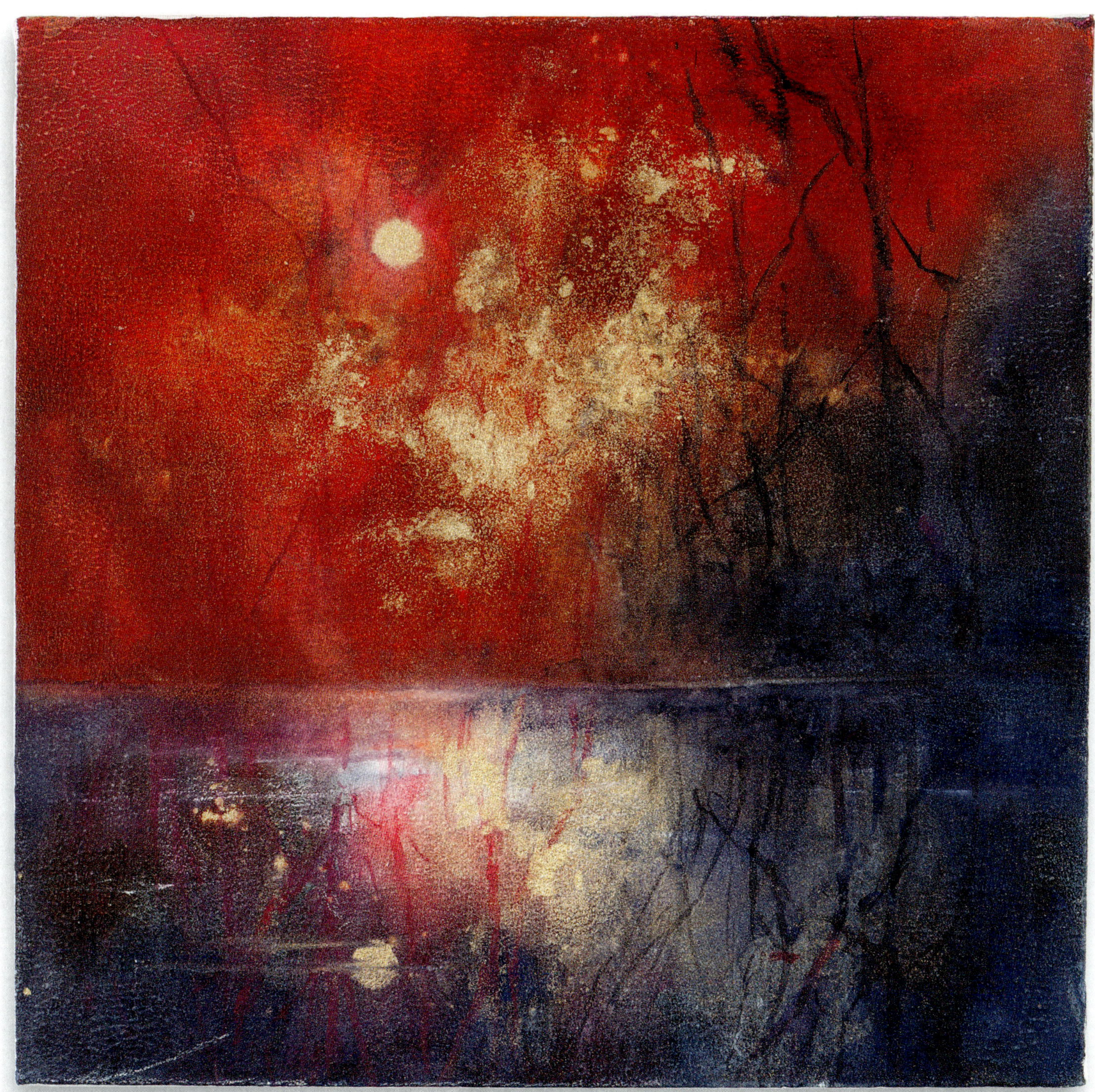

Red Sky at Night

30 x 30cm (11¾ x 11¾in)

I used a deep burgundy red to cover the whole of the sky. The addition of the metallic gold helped me to achieve the opulent, lush effect that I wanted – much more interesting than painting a red sky in a strictly representational style.

Using photographs

Not only do I work from my imagination and sketchbooks, I also work from photographs. For me these are a back-up to feed whatever information you may have absorbed whilst out sketching or what's in your imagination.

Over the following pages, I show three different approaches to abstracting the same subject from a photograph: a foxglove.

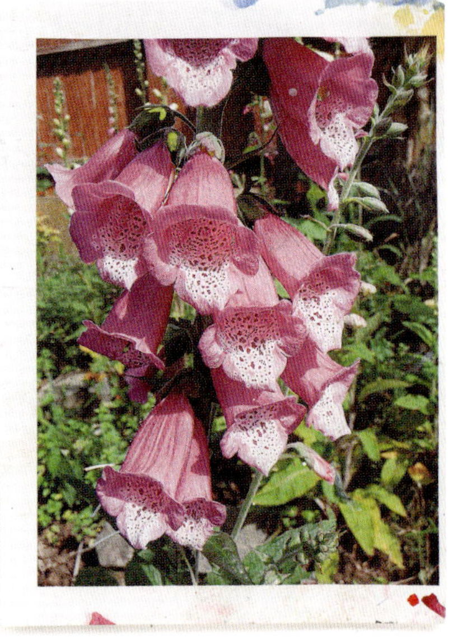

Source photograph

EXERCISE: Take just the critical parts

When trying to paint in a more abstract style, you need to pick out the main elements from the photograph, then represent them on the canvas with as little detail as you can.

To do this, study the photograph and identify the shapes, forms, colours and movements you can see. Here, the photograph is mainly green leaves and surrounding foliage, but it's the foxglove flower heads that I want to focus upon. To ensure they take centre stage, I make a note that the pink should be made more of. In the finished painting opposite, you'll see that the pink area covers the majority of the canvas surface, and that I've also used line and shape to develop and draw attention to the flower heads, while leaving the greens soft and unresolved.

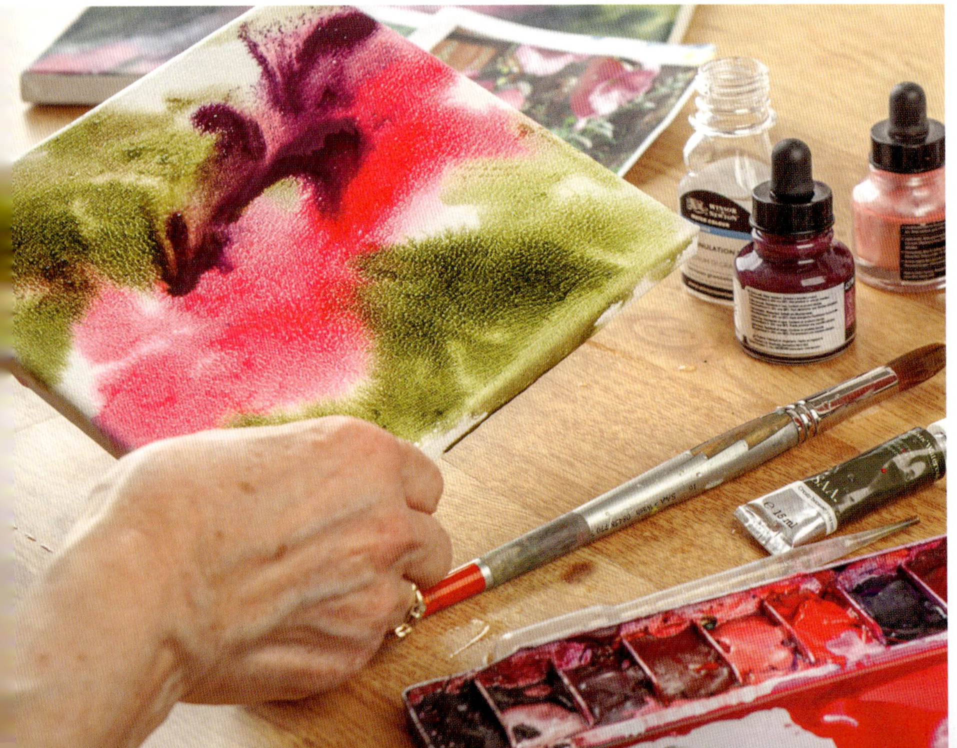

The best way to identify the main shapes – those that really matter – is to half-close your eyes and start painting in the areas of your reference photograph that stand out when viewing in this way.

The light on the end of the bell-shaped petals stood out to me, along with the shadows behind the part of the petal that curled back – so these were the parts on which I focussed.

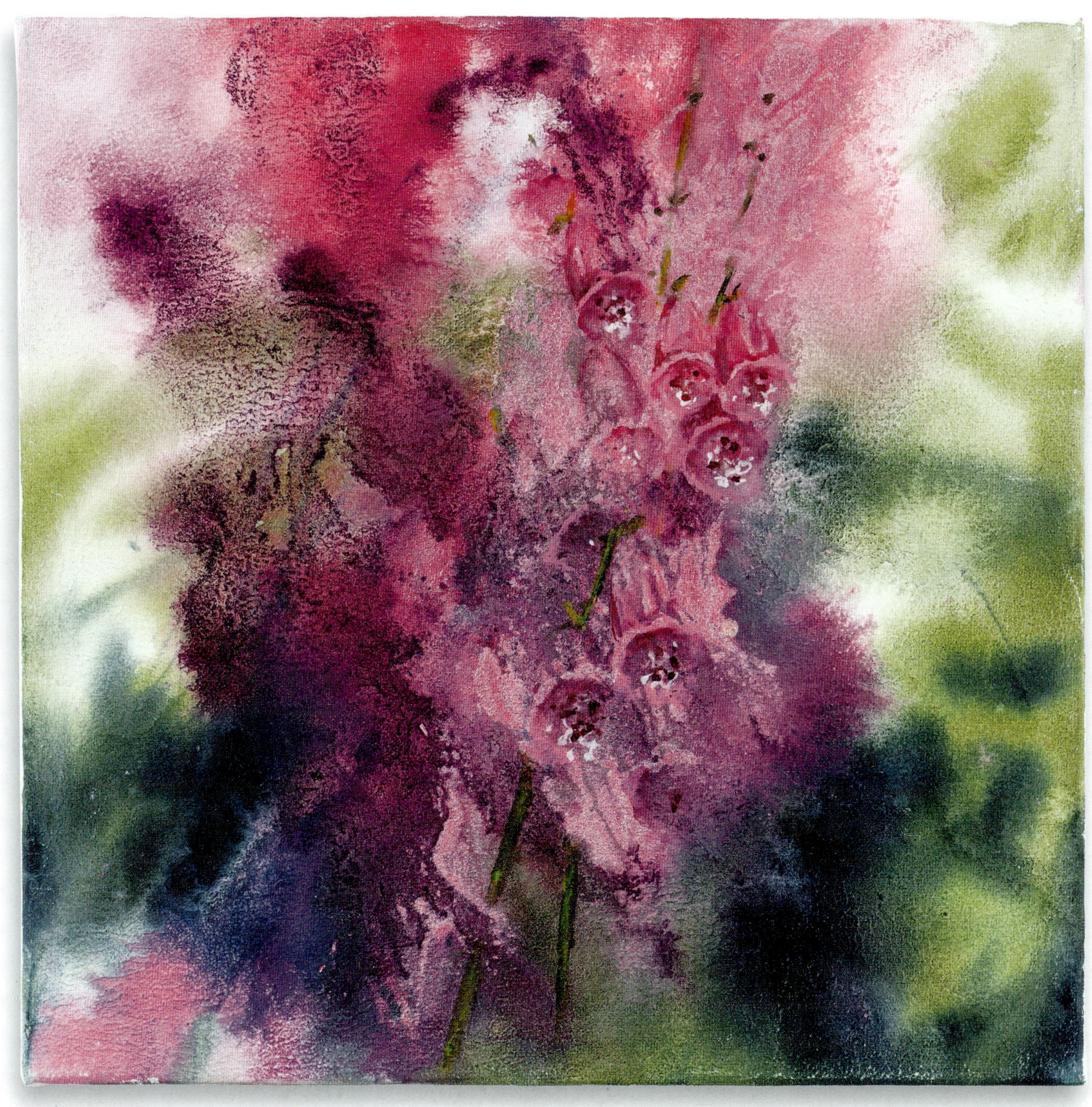

Foxglove 1
30 x 30cm (11¾ x 11¾in)

EXERCISE: Experimenting with techniques

I try out lots of different techniques and record them in my sketchbooks. When I approach a new subject, I often flick through and see how particular techniques might bring out the nature of the subject. Here I'm using plastic food wrap to create texture suggestive of foliage.

The colours and shapes I'm concentrating on remain the same as in the previous exercise – compare the results. Which evokes the photograph more? Which do you prefer? Once you've got the key elements of the photograph fixed in your mind, you can keep building your skills by trying this exercise again with more techniques.

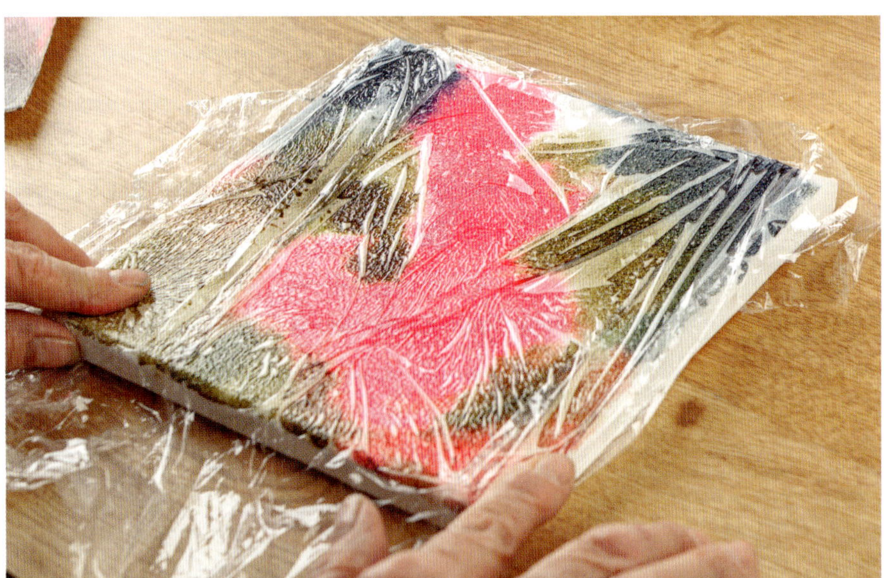

Placing plastic food wrap over wet paint is a fairly well-known technique in watercolour circles, but there's a reason for that – it's very effective in producing an interesting semi-random background. The process works just as well on canvas as on watercolour paper, and simply involves laying down clean food wrap over the wet paint. Where the wrap touches the surface, the paint gathers. You can leave it purely random, or use your fingers to adjust and direct the wrap, then leave it to dry.

Note that the paint will take longer to dry, so don't rush. Leave it overnight, then carefully lift away the wrap to reveal the results.

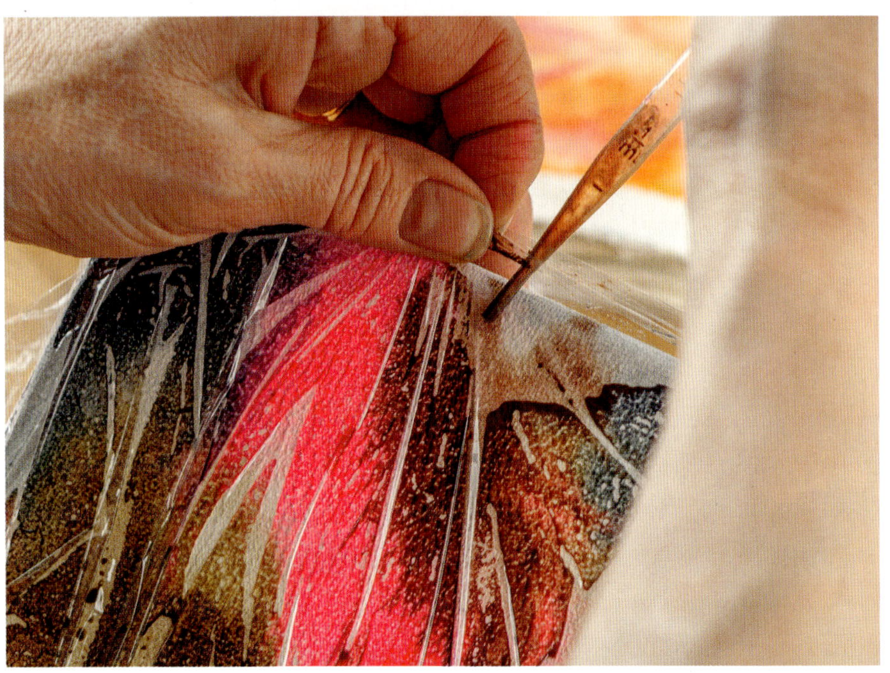

A twist I've added to the technique is to cut small holes into the plastic food wrap once applied, and then to 'inject' more paint, granulation medium, inks – or all three! – directly onto the wet surface using a pipette. The additional paint, ink or medium will travel along the folds and reach other parts of the painting. This gives you more control over the effect, but retains an element of randomness.

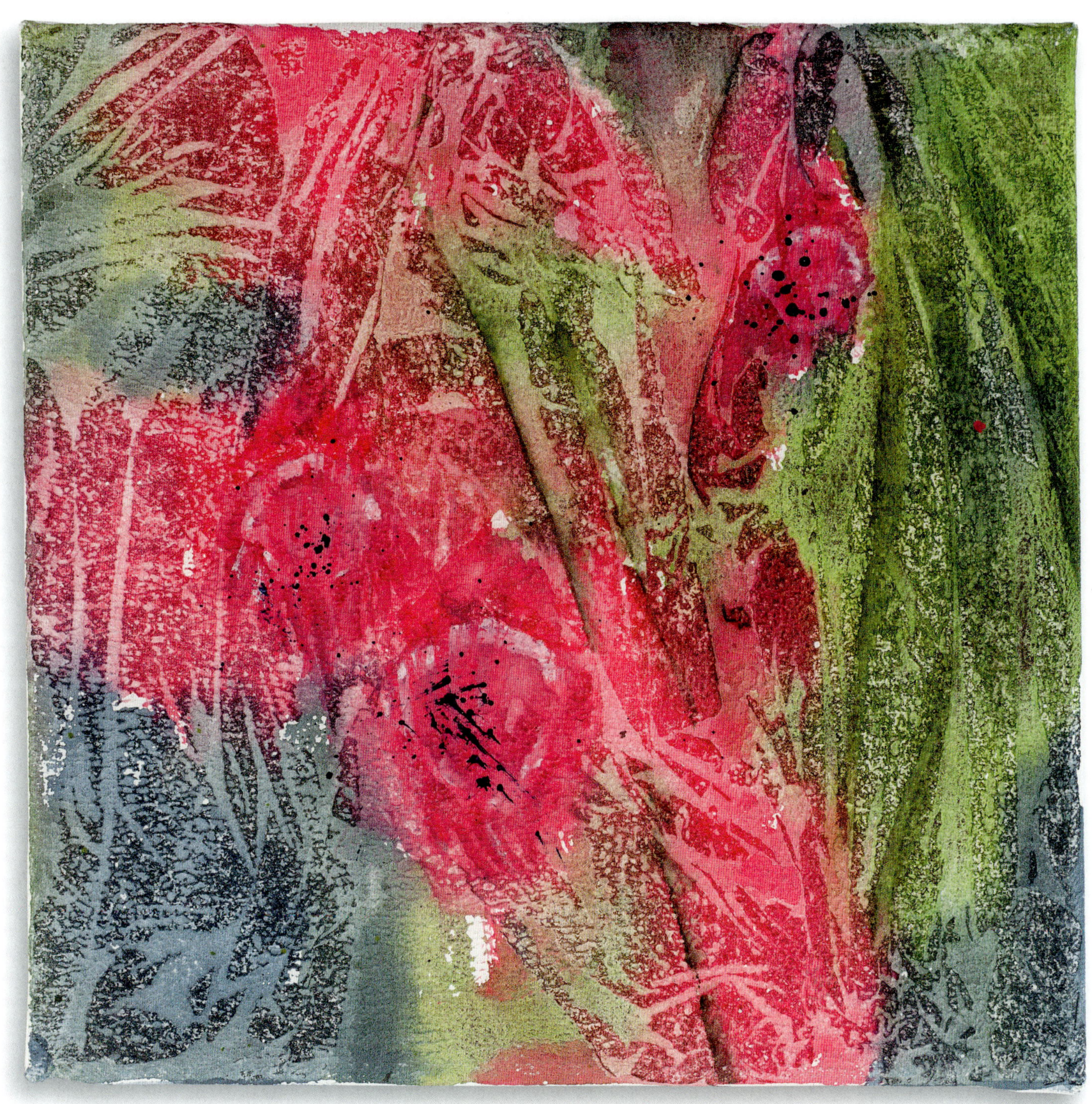

Foxglove 2
20 x 20cm (8 x 8in)

EXERCISE: Foxglove collage

Replicating some of the characteristics of the subject can be an enjoyable way to experiment with different techniques. Here, I wanted to focus on the speckles inside the bell-shaped flower heads of foxgloves. To emulate these and make them really stand out, I used the little circles left over from using a hole punch with a sheet of cartridge paper – never think that something isn't worth trying, just because it's simple. Adding this raised layer emphasized the black speckles and white mottled background, making them really stand out.

Once the glue had dried, the remainder of the painting was done in a more traditional way – differentiating it from the foxglove paintings on the previous pages, where in both cases the whole painting was abstracted. This simple loose interpretation, with just a touch of added interest, is my favourite of the three.

It's always good to remember that, no matter how simple a method of adding interest is, it is sometime all that is needed.

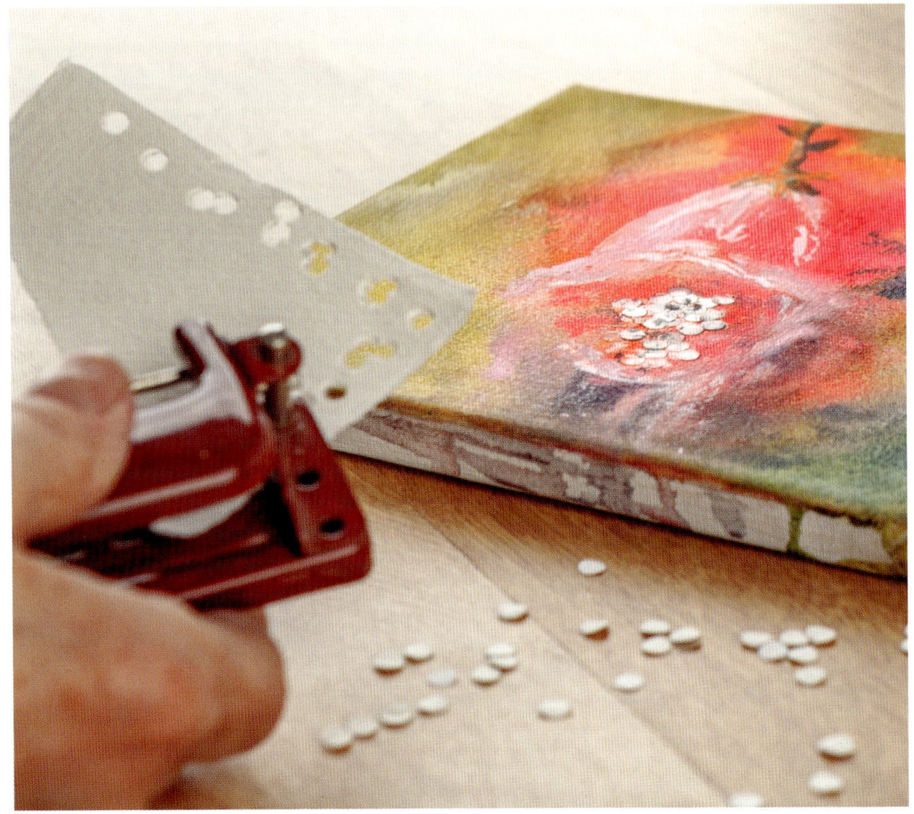

Here I'm attaching punched paper holes with white glue (Mod Podge). Collage is a fun, approachable technique that complements canvas really beautifully.

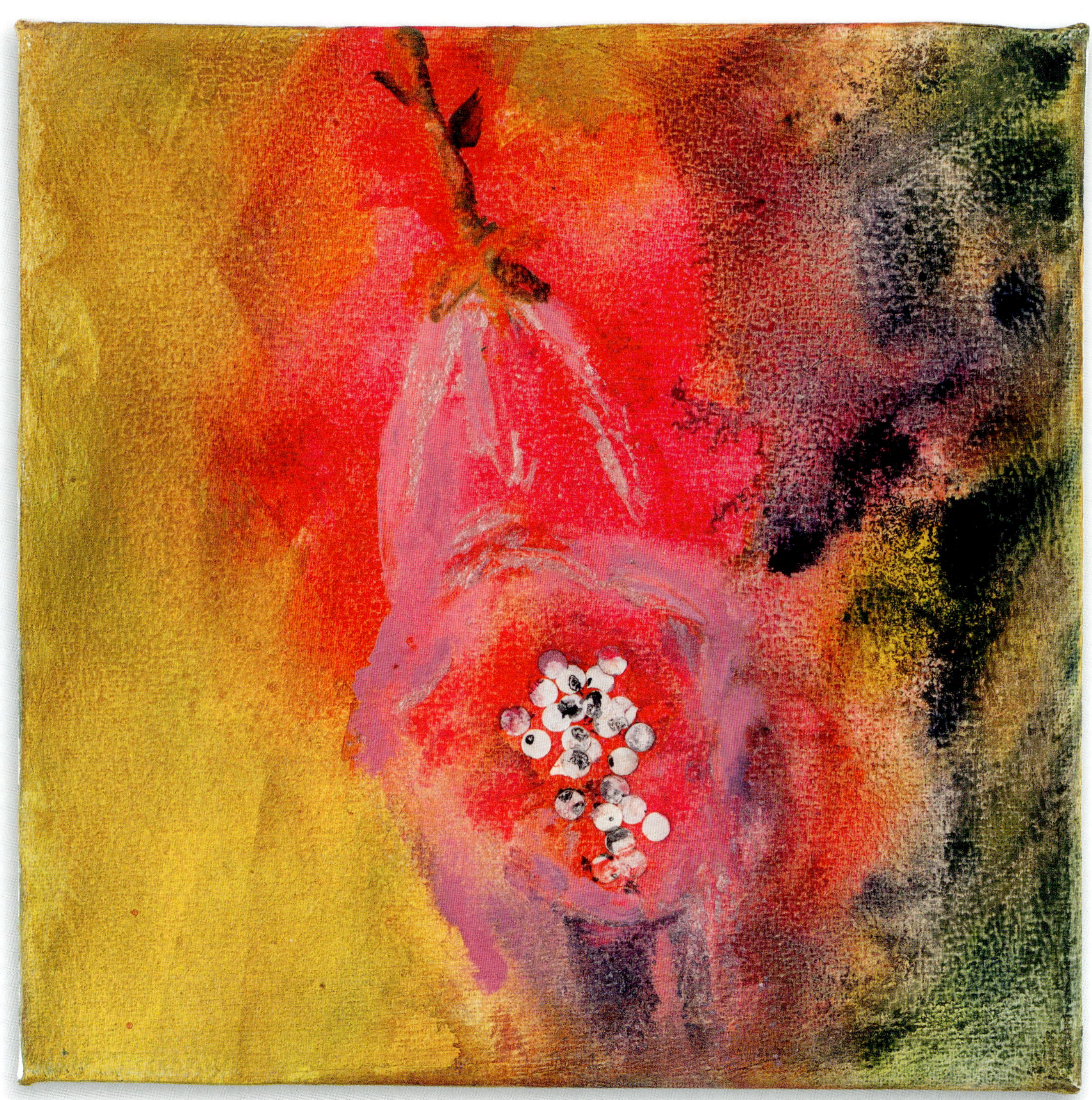

Foxglove 3
20 x 20cm (8 x 8in)

How much to give

We all have different preferences and tastes when it comes to what paintings we find attractive. It's the same for many things in life, be it clothes, furnishings, cars, music, or even our personal appearance! We are all different – and that's wonderful. It means that there is no right or wrong way to perceive art, there's no law stating how a subject should be conveyed. The viewer will make up their own mind when looking at an artist's work to see if it appeals to them.

Artwork that's not painted in a realistic style may receive criticism from some of the many realism fans out there, but this doesn't mean that what you have created, in whatever style is your preference, is wrong. Rather, it shows how narrow-minded some people are if they dismiss other forms of art without giving it just a little bit of thought.

My personal preference is to try and give enough detail in my work to engage the viewer, but also to leave enough open for them to interpret the painting in their own way. I like to be able to tell what my subject is but paint it in an atmospheric, unusual semi-abstract style. I've tried to demonstrate what I mean in the two paintings opposite. Both backgrounds are more or less identical – so could be perceived as sea or sky, but, by placing a bird on one of the panels and a fish on the other, our brains automatically know which is which.

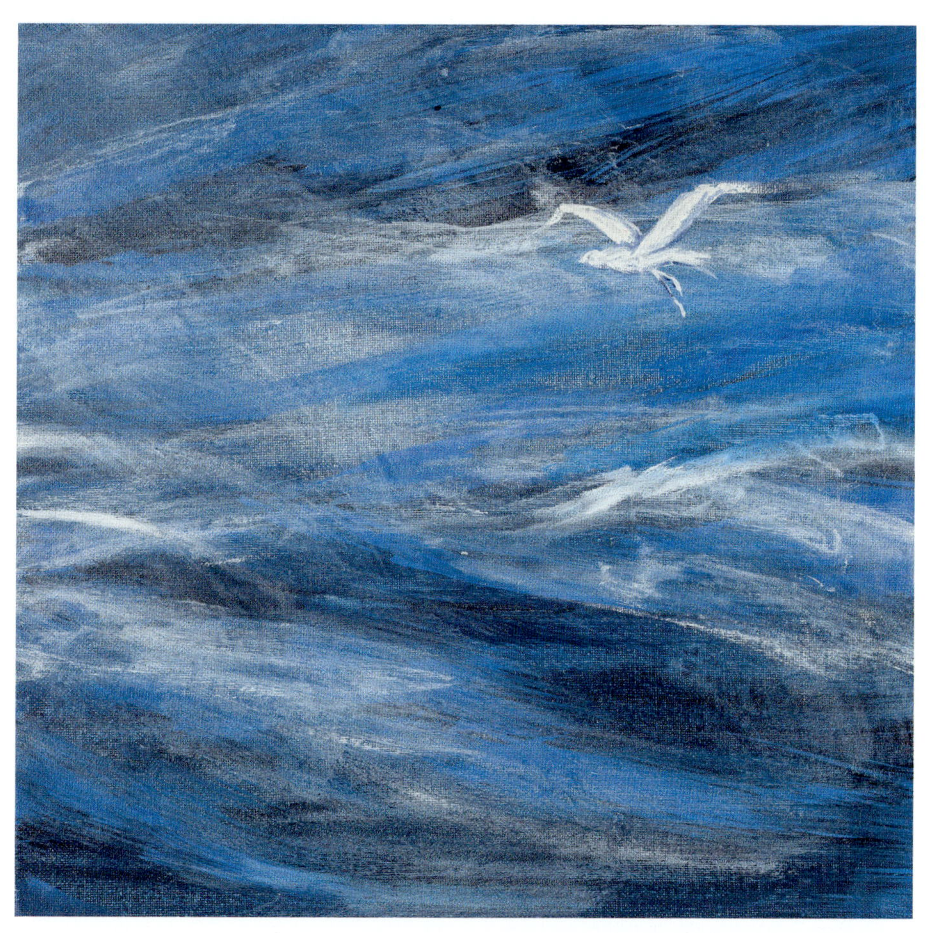

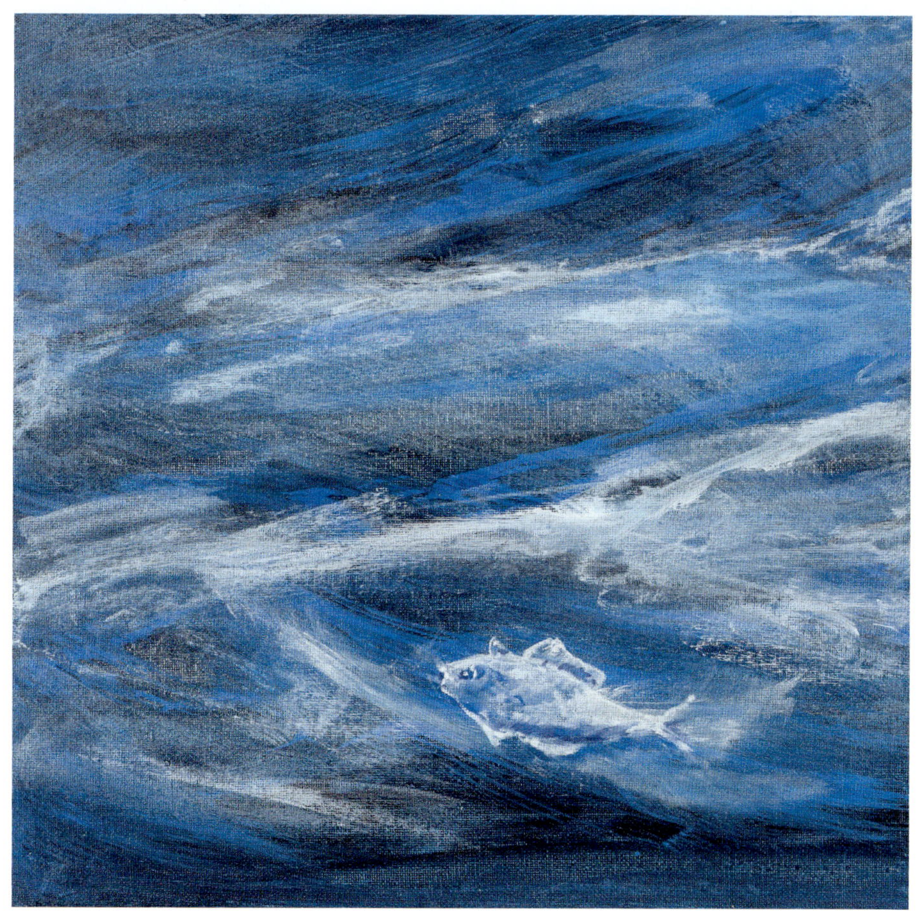

EXERCISE: Simple poppy

By giving the viewer only a certain amount of information – either using colour or shapes – the artist is prompting and aiding them to decide what the subject is; particularly so when there is only a very small amount of detail relevant to the subject matter.

The poppy painting opposite was created simply by letting two colours (red and pink) merge on the canvas before adding a dribble of black ink.

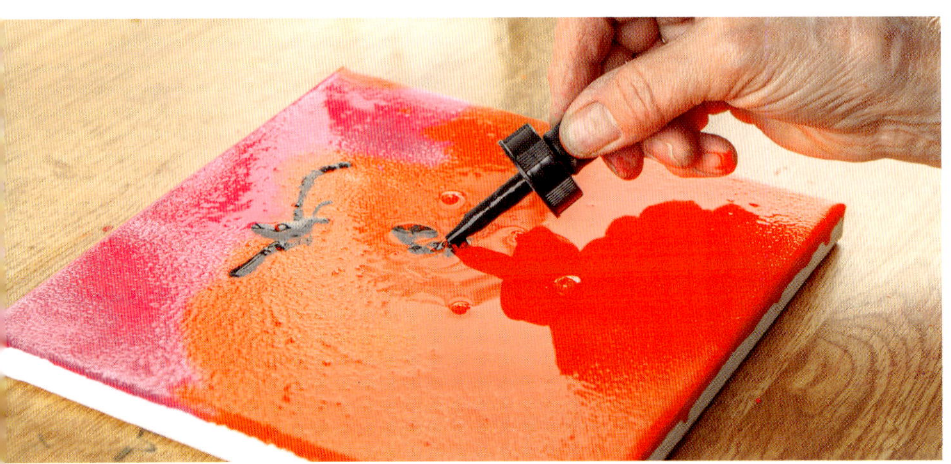

With just areas of pink and red in place, the image is almost purely abstract. Look how little ink needs to be added to draw the viewer's eye and create contrast.

I used the dropper to draw directly into the wet paint, being careful not to create too many lines – this would have 'resolved' the painting too much and lost the appealing sense of brightness.

I tilted the canvas to guide the ink in the direction I wanted it to go and this formed a suggestion of the outline of the flower and the round centres.

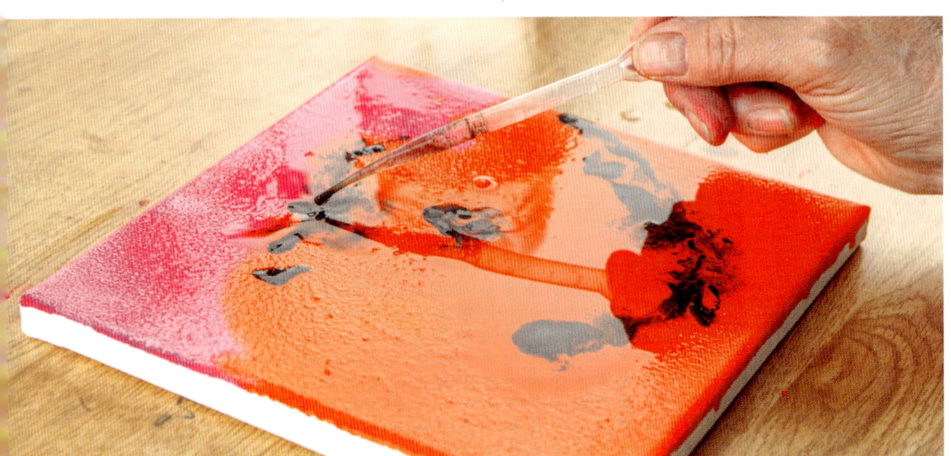

While the paint and ink remained wet, I added granulation fluid to help the two different media to combine and merge. I applied it more generously where I wanted the ink lines to break up more, and was more sparing where I wanted more definite marks to remain.

Granulation fluid is wonderful for suggesting natural textures, and for this poppy it's got just the right balance of softness and suggested visual texture.

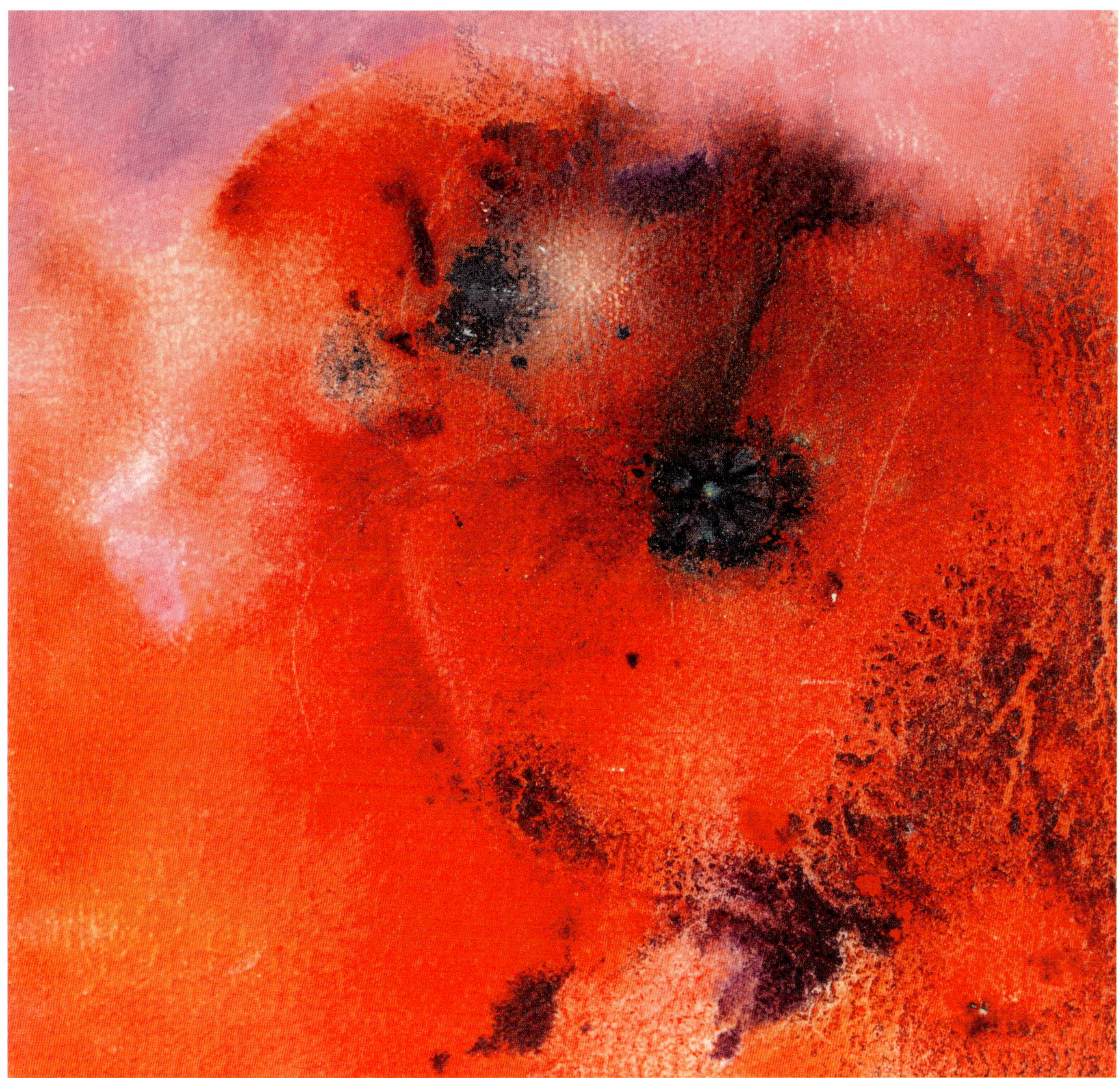

Poppy Fusion

20 x 20cm (8 x 8in)

Once dry, a few additional details were added to the poppy centres to help guide the viewer – but note that the shape of the petals is only hinted at very loosely. Leaving some work for the viewer to do in resolving what's in front of them is engaging and rewarding for them.

EXERCISE: Minimal detail

When summer is over and autumn begins to set in, the poppy seedheads are often seen blowing in the wind before the harshness of winter arrives. At this time, lots of plants die back after going to seed, but the dried poppy head withstands the winter weather, its hard casing remaining strong and sturdy for most of the season.

In the painting opposite, I've used wintry colours for the seedhead and a background suggesting a heavy grey sky. Only a few details were added to say what was needed to be said really.

Identifying what these details are is key to a successful result: say just enough to get your idea across.

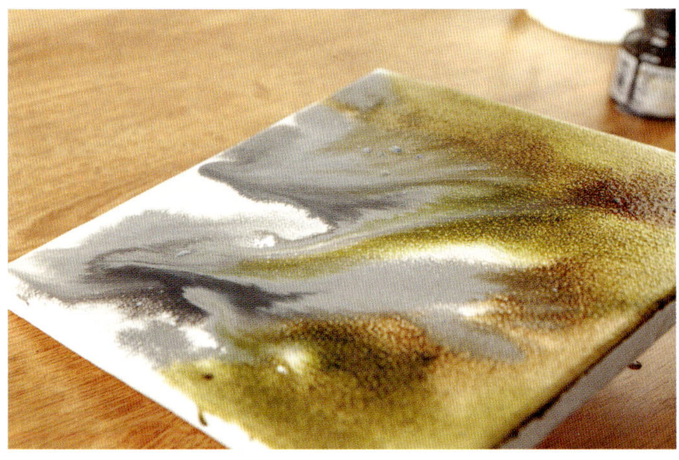

Granulation fluid was used for a mottled finish. It was applied mostly in the lower half, so the top 'sky' was left clean and clear. The suggested texture lower down draws the eye and suggests to the viwer that this area is the foreground. The muted colours were chosen to suggest the grey skies and fading greenery of autumn.

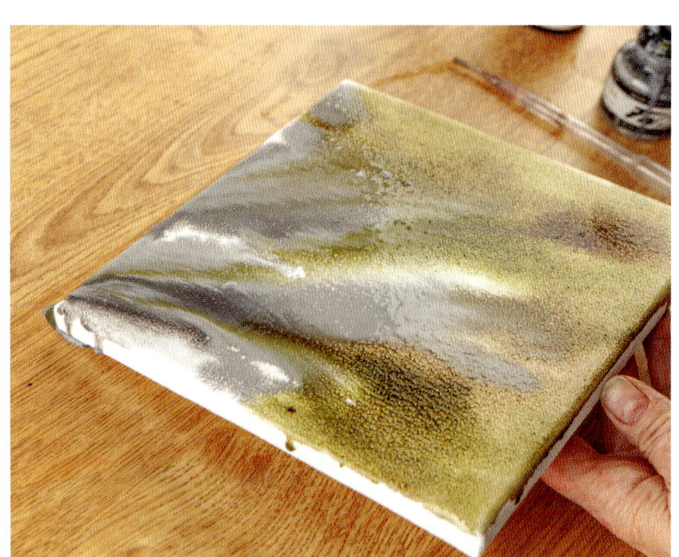

While the canvas was wet, I tipped and tilted it to encourage the areas to mix and merge. This ensured no hard lines were created. As the final marks would be subtle, I didn't want things to interfere with the poppy 'reading out' from the background.

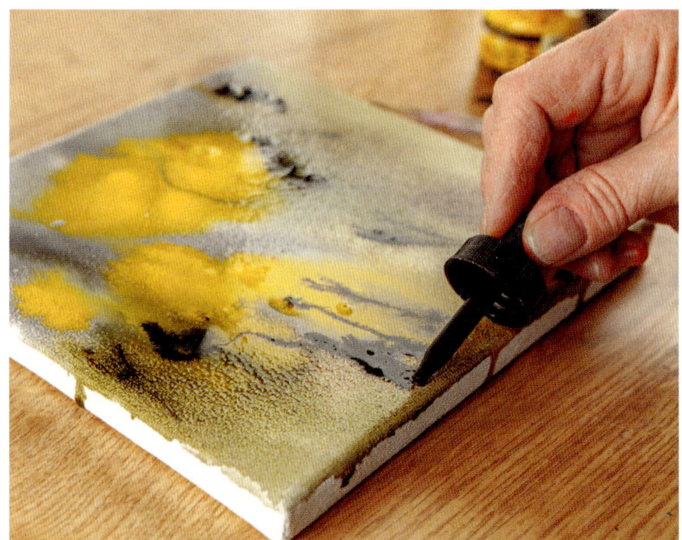

With the background ready, I now dropped in inks – yellow and sepia – to add more definite marks and structure. I drew with the dropper directly on the surface to hint at the idea of growing stems. As the paint dried, the marks made with the ink became clearer until, as you can see opposite, I was able to hint at a lone seedhead, rendering it more clearly. Note that even this is not drawn out fully – the shape is left to be resolved in the mind of the viewer.

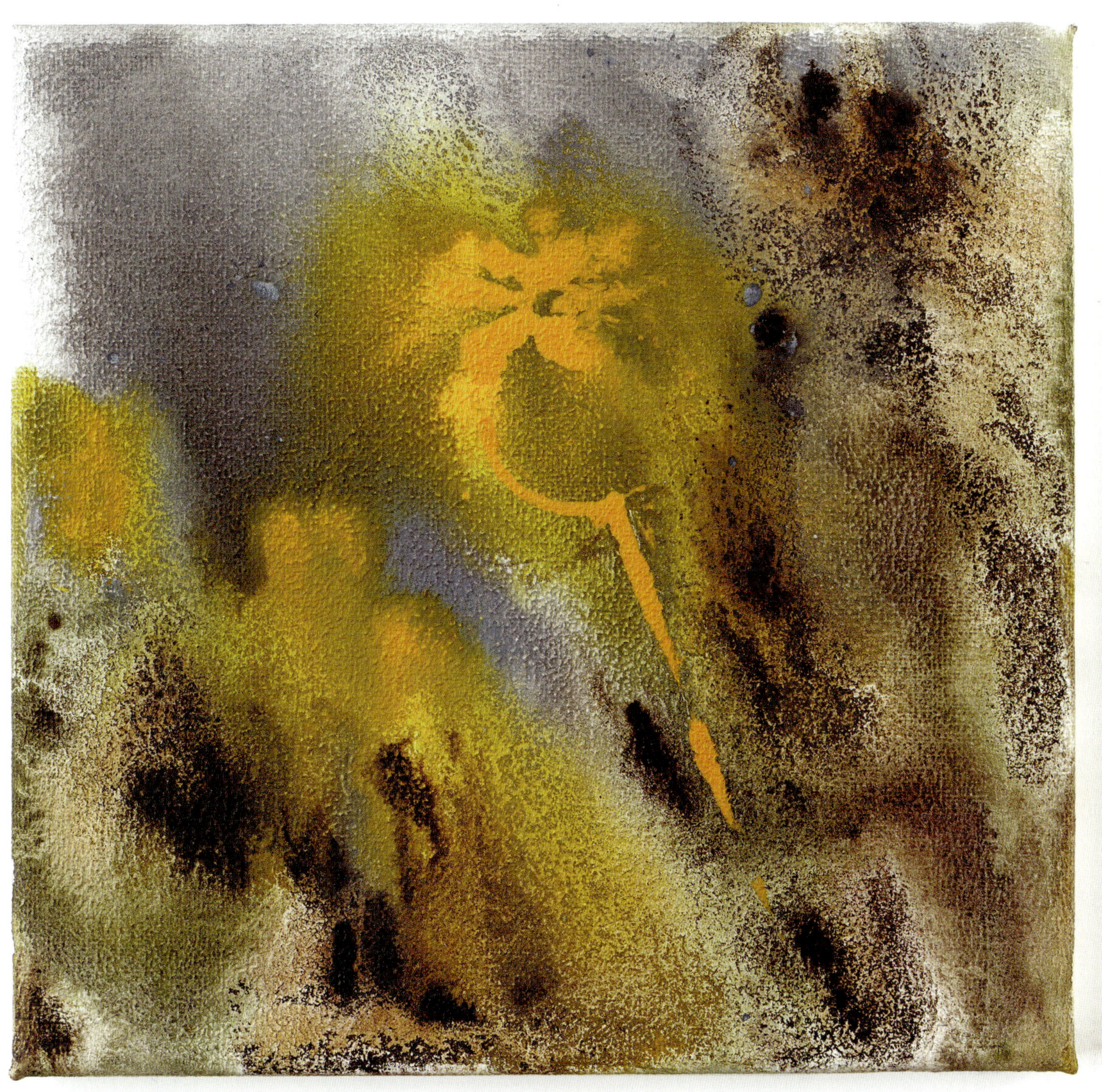

Dried Seedhead
20 x 20cm (8 x 8in)

magical honesty

My favourite seedheads are from the honesty plant, *Lunaria annua*. It bears clusters of small, purple flowers in late spring and early summer, followed by flat, round, silvery seed pods. These pods have several layers of a paper-thin covering and, if you rub them between your fingers, the outer layers come off to reveal a silvery disc in the centre. I like the outer coverings just as much as the main pod – they are actually more textured and interesting, with some of them taking on a purple hue. In winter you can see them blowing in the breeze, and, as some have lost their outer casings, they really catch the light. When most other plants have died back and gone to seed, they leave some really interesting, textured, scraggy stalks and leaves; very often battered by the fierce winter winds and temperatures. Seeing these 'remnants of winter' never fails to get my creative juices flowing. I've painted them literally hundreds of times in many, many ways.

In this project I've tried to capture the textures by using gauze, skeleton leaves and real seedheads adhered to the canvas to give a three-dimensional effect. I also decided to use non-representational colours to steer more into the abstract direction.

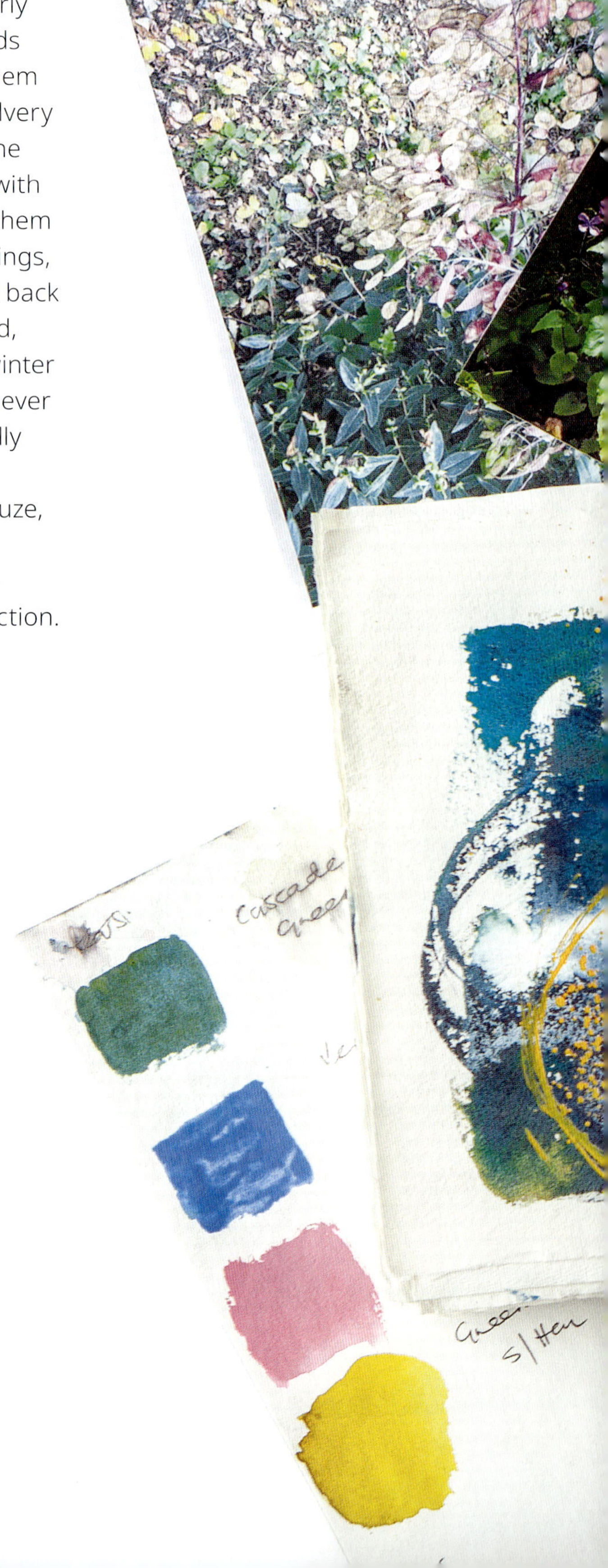

YOU WILL NEED

- **Block canvas** 40 x 40cm (15¾ x 15¾in)

- **Watercolour paints** Cascade green (Daniel Smith), verditer blue (ShinHan), pink peony (White Knights), greenish yellow (ShinHan), vandyke brown (SAA), jaune brilliant (ShinHan)

- **Inks** All FW acrylic: burnt umber, indigo, white

- **Brushes** Three medium brushes (size 12), one large brush (size 16), one very large brush (size 20), fine brush (size 2 round), small brush (size 8), 25mm (1in) rake brush, size 0 rigger

- **Other materials** White glue (Mod Podge) and tweezers, white gouache, baking parchment, white watercolour ground, foam roller; found materials: twine, skeleton leaves, split peas, honesty seeds and honesty seedheads

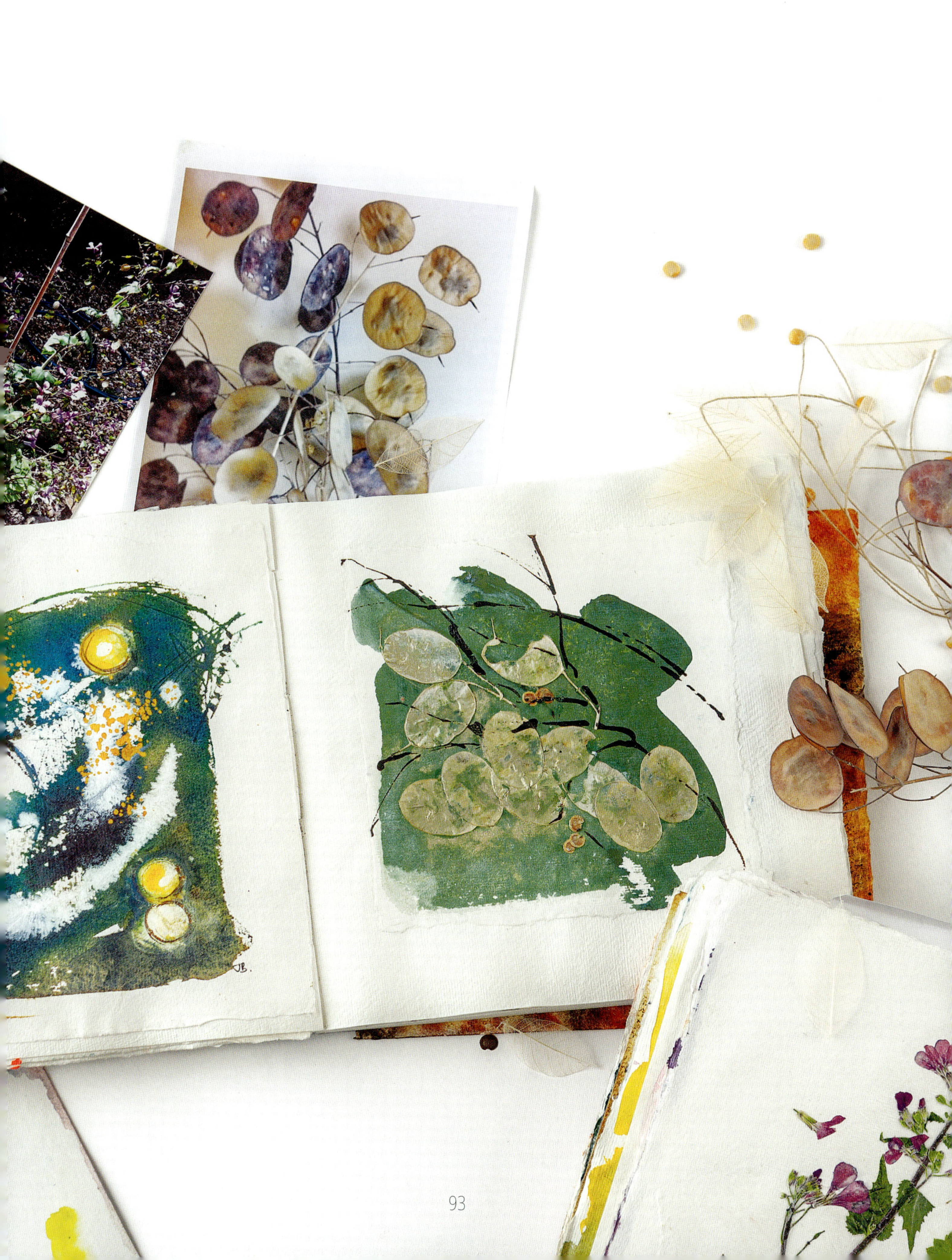

1 – establishing texture

• Place some baking parchment/greaseproof paper down and use an old brush to apply white glue to the found materials. You can then glue the pieces directly onto your prepared canvas, as we'll be working over the whole surface with watercolour ground, but it's easier to arrange and apply the pieces this way.

• Re-arrange the found pieces until you are happy with the composition, then allow the glue to dry. Once dry, start to paint over the whole surface with white watercolour ground.

• Swap to the foam roller to create a smooth, clean surface over the whole canvas (this helps to ensure there's no obvious break or line around areas bare of found materials, like the top right corner), then leave to dry overnight.

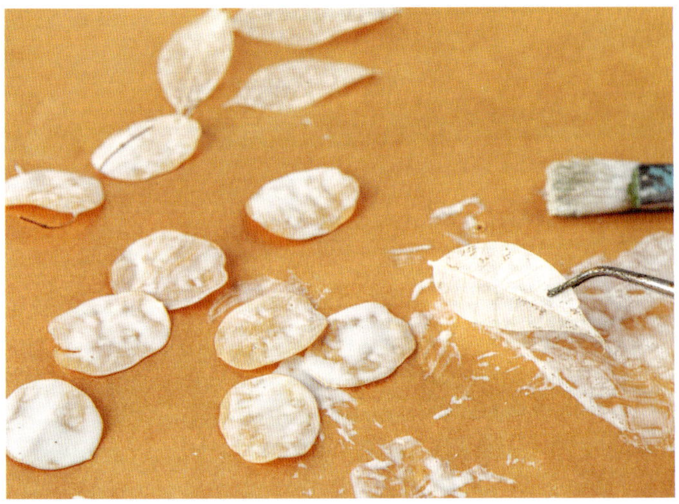

Pick the pieces up with a pair of tweezers, and apply them to the canvas.

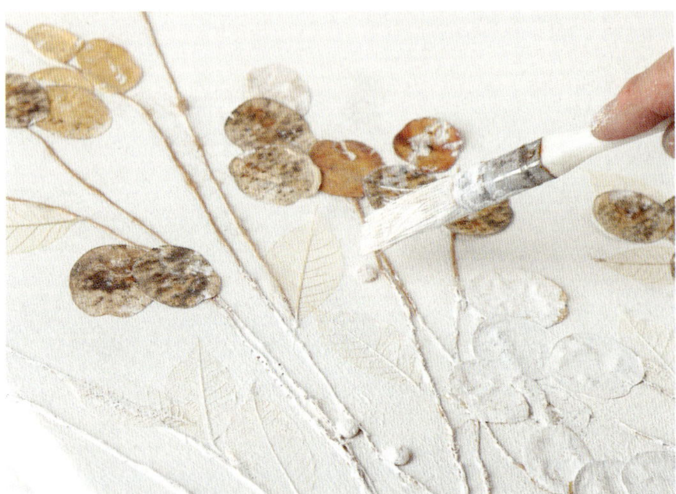

Work the ground right over and around the found materials; both to ensure that they'll be paintable, and to help secure them to the surface.

When using a foam roller, make sure all the nooks and crannies are covered.

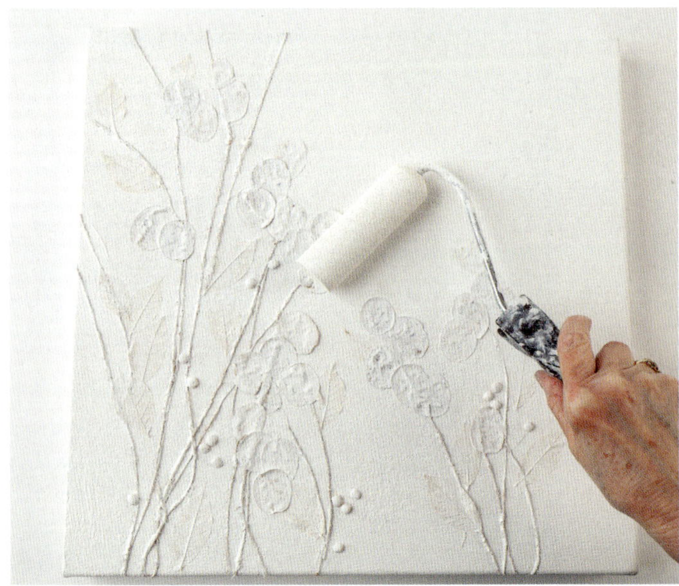

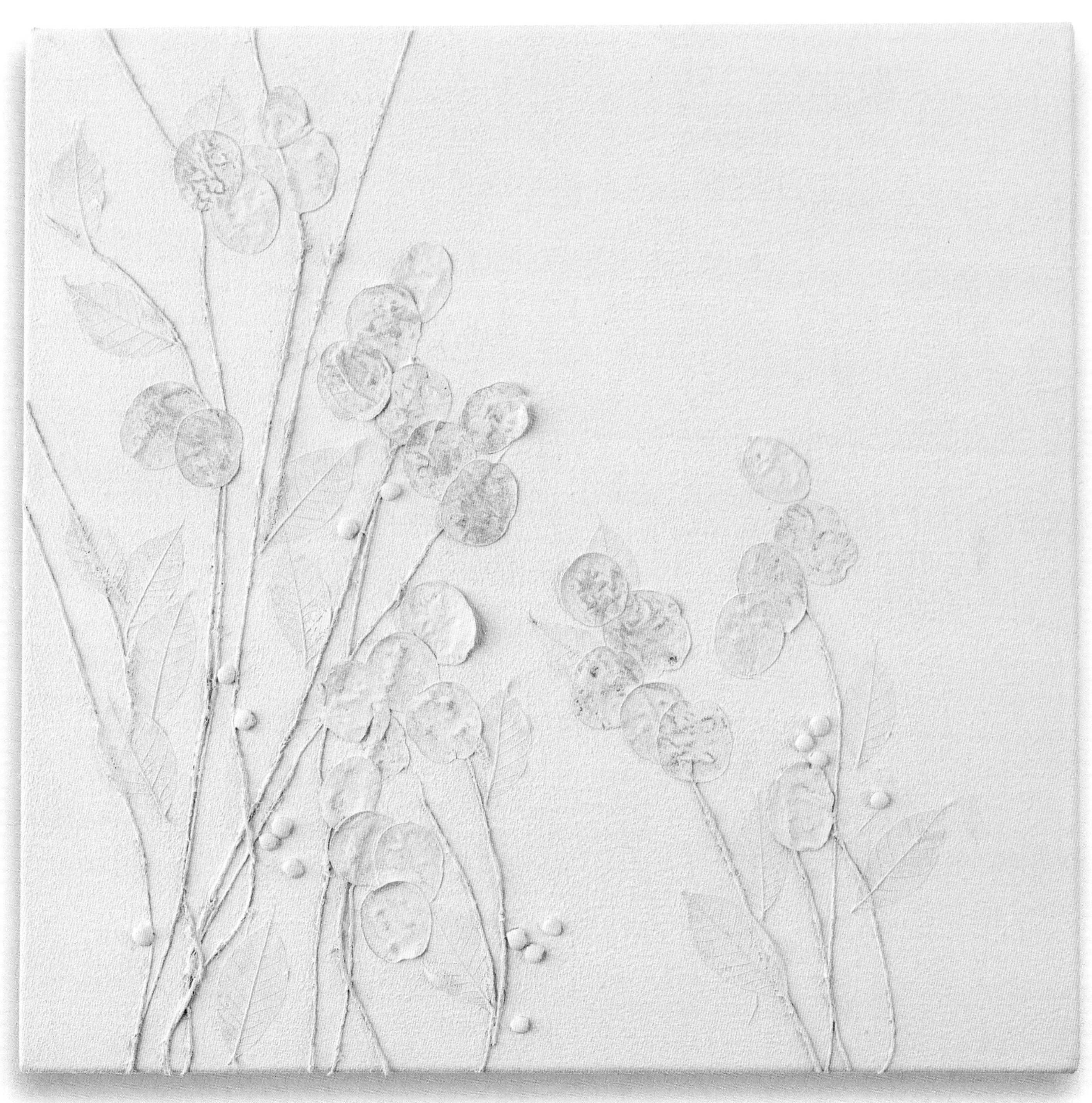

The painting at the end of this stage. All the preparation is finished. Once dry, the paint and ink can be added to create the magical effects. Time spent early on will pay off later.

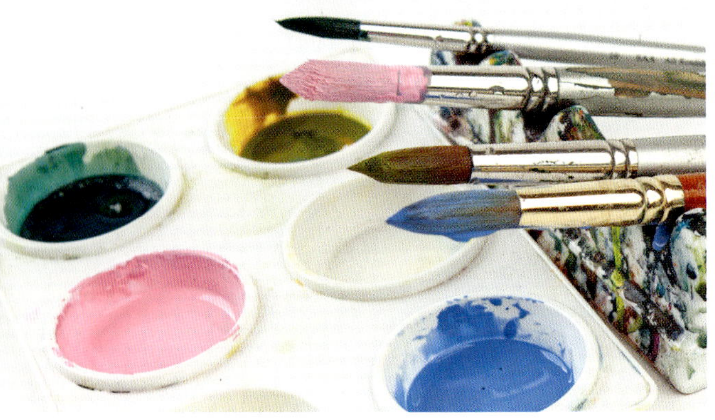

Why use a size 16 for the pink? Simple: for covering larger areas, you should use larger brushes.

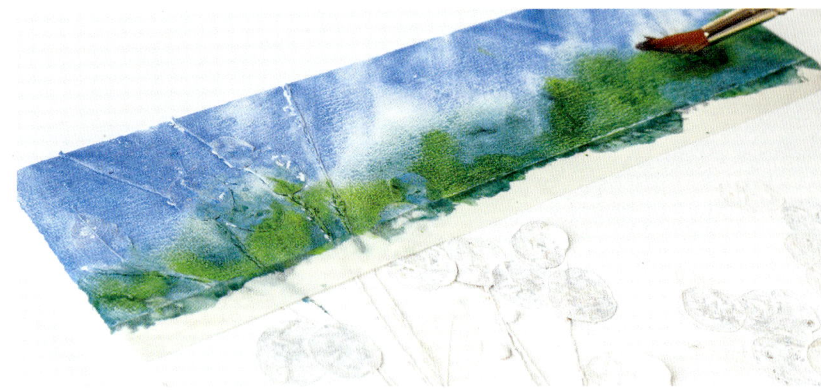

When painting down to the masking tape on the horizon line, don't worry about working over or around the attached found materials. We'll paint over these again later.

2 – adding colour

- Prepare your paint, with a different brush for each: cascade green, verditer blue, pink peony, greenish yellow. Use a larger brush (I'm using a size 16) for the pink, and medium (size 12) for the others.

- Apply a strip of masking tape 10cm (4in) down from the top to suggest a horizon line, then prop the painting up on the roll of masking tape to set it at a slight angle. Wet the canvas surface above the masking line with a very large brush and clean water, then apply verditer blue, working down from the top.

- Next, work up from the horizon line with cascade green, blend it upwards into the blue with clean water, and add greenish yellow wet in wet.

- Remove the masking tape at this point, then continue wetting the surface right down to the bottom (make sure to wet over the sides, too), then paint up from the middle of the canvas with pink.

- Wait a while for the water to dry a little, then add more pink below the band. This will look stronger and darker than the pink applied on the wetter surface.

- Apply some cascade green and hints of greenish yellow to the bottom of the painting, wet in wet; particularly around the corners. This helps to keep the eye in the painting, and also ensures the bottom of the composition has something in common with the top.

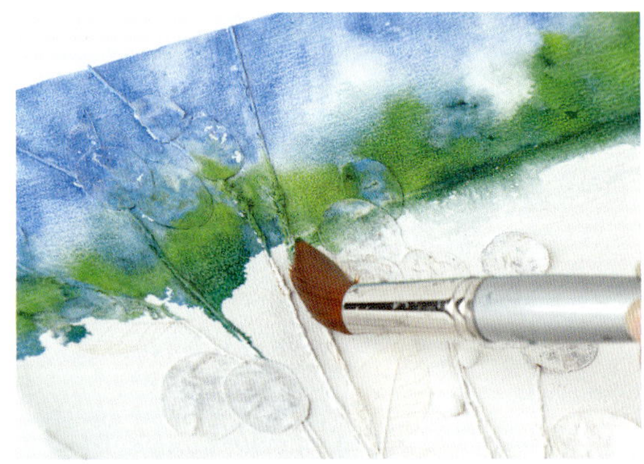

Owing to the texture of the canvas surface, it's almost inevitable that the paint will creep underneath the masking tape. Don't worry about this; just use a very large damp brush to soften the line and let the still-wet green bleed down.

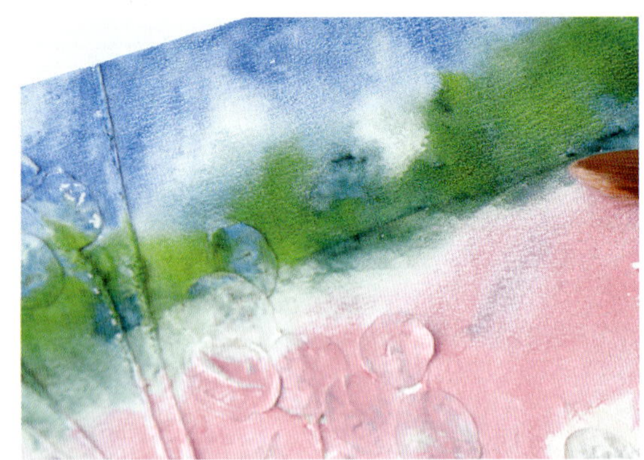

When adding the pink, don't paint down from the green, or you'll muddy the mix. Instead, paint the pink in a band a little way below the horizon, then work a small amounts upwards into the green.

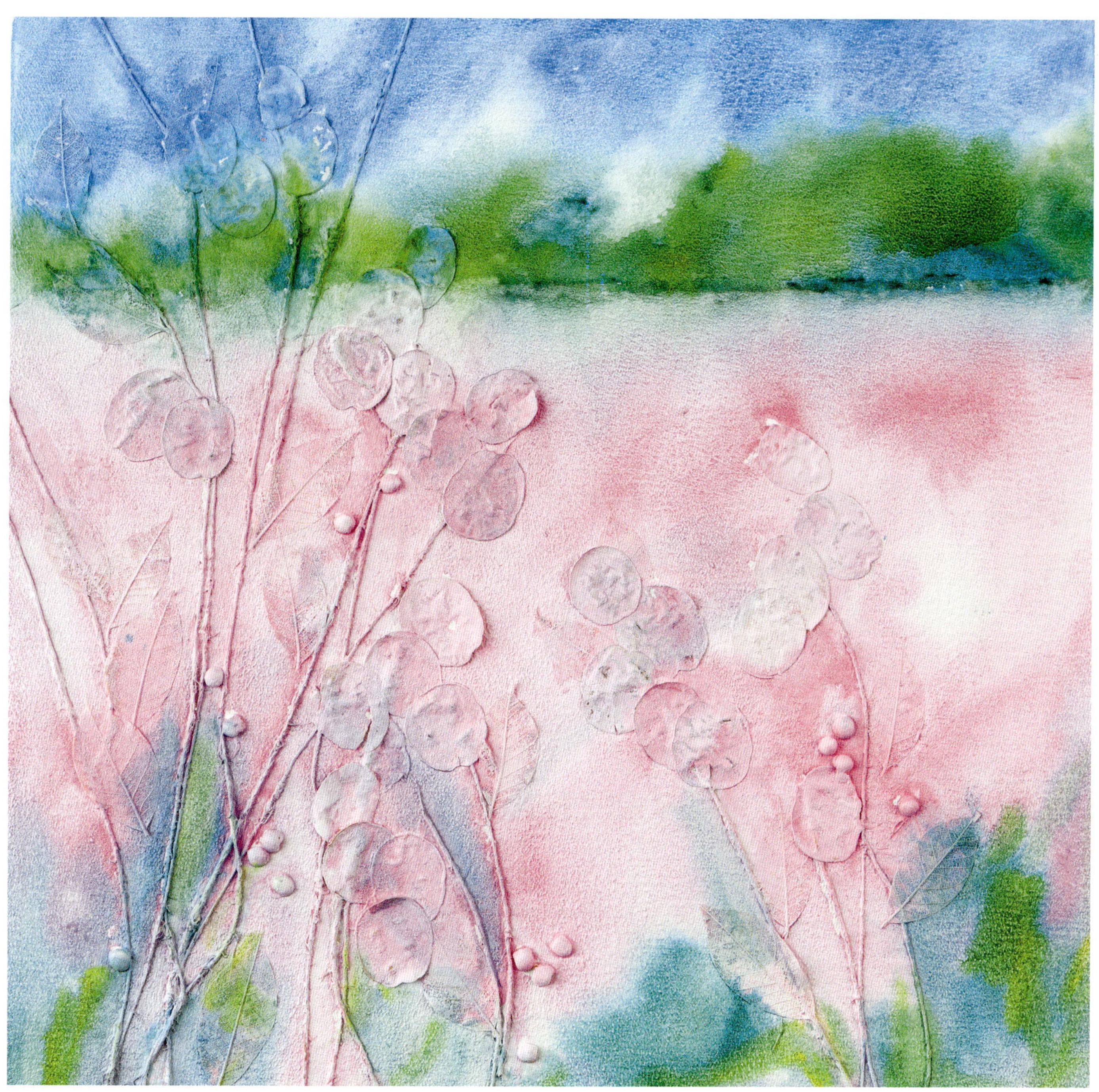

The painting at the end of this stage. Canvas is less absorbent than paper, so it's easy to move the paint around; particularly while still wet. Before moving on, spend some time deciding whether you want to adjust anything. If so, use a clean damp brush to lift out areas.

3 – inks and adjustment

• Use the burnt umber dropper to apply ink here and there across the found materials. Apply granulation fluid with a pipette, then pick up the painting and tip and tilt it to help direct the flow.

• Add some indigo ink in the same way while the burnt umber is wet. You're aiming to emphasize some of the elements, not to outline every single one.

• Allow the painting to dry, then re-establish any areas that you think need strengthening. Watercolours always dry lighter than they appear while wet, and the effect is particularly noticeable on canvas. Be aware that it's easy to lift off or remove watercolour paint from canvas when glazing like this – that's why it's important to use Aqua Fix in the mix: this helps the paint to adhere and resist being removed.

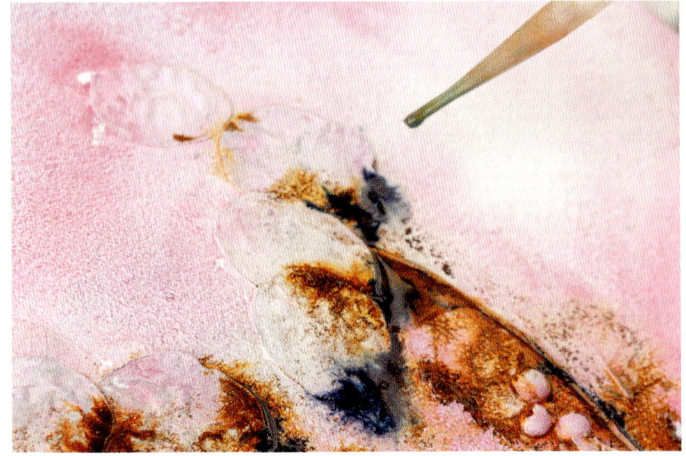

The granulation fluid will start to take effect immediately, but you won't see the full effect until the painting dries. Compare this picture to the dry version opposite to see how the effect develops.

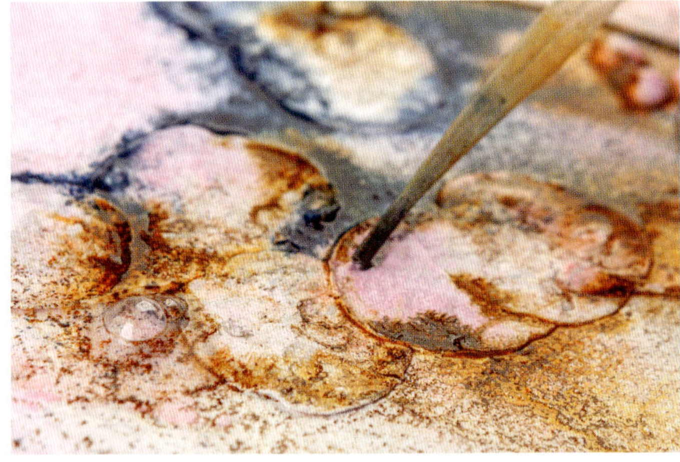

When adding inks, do consider what needs to be added where; there's no need to copy this exactly – rather you should interpret and adapt to what's happening on your canvas. You don't want to completely cover the pink area, for example, just for the sake of it.

Here, I'm using a large 50mm (2in) flat brush to strengthen the pink. I'm using a flat brush, because the blade of the brush enables me to work right up to the horizon line cleanly.

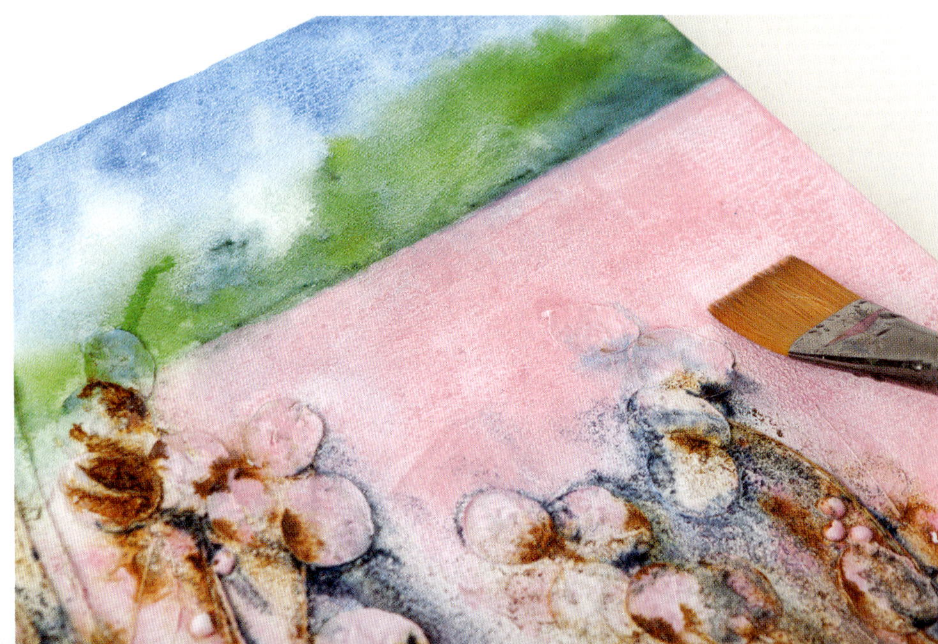

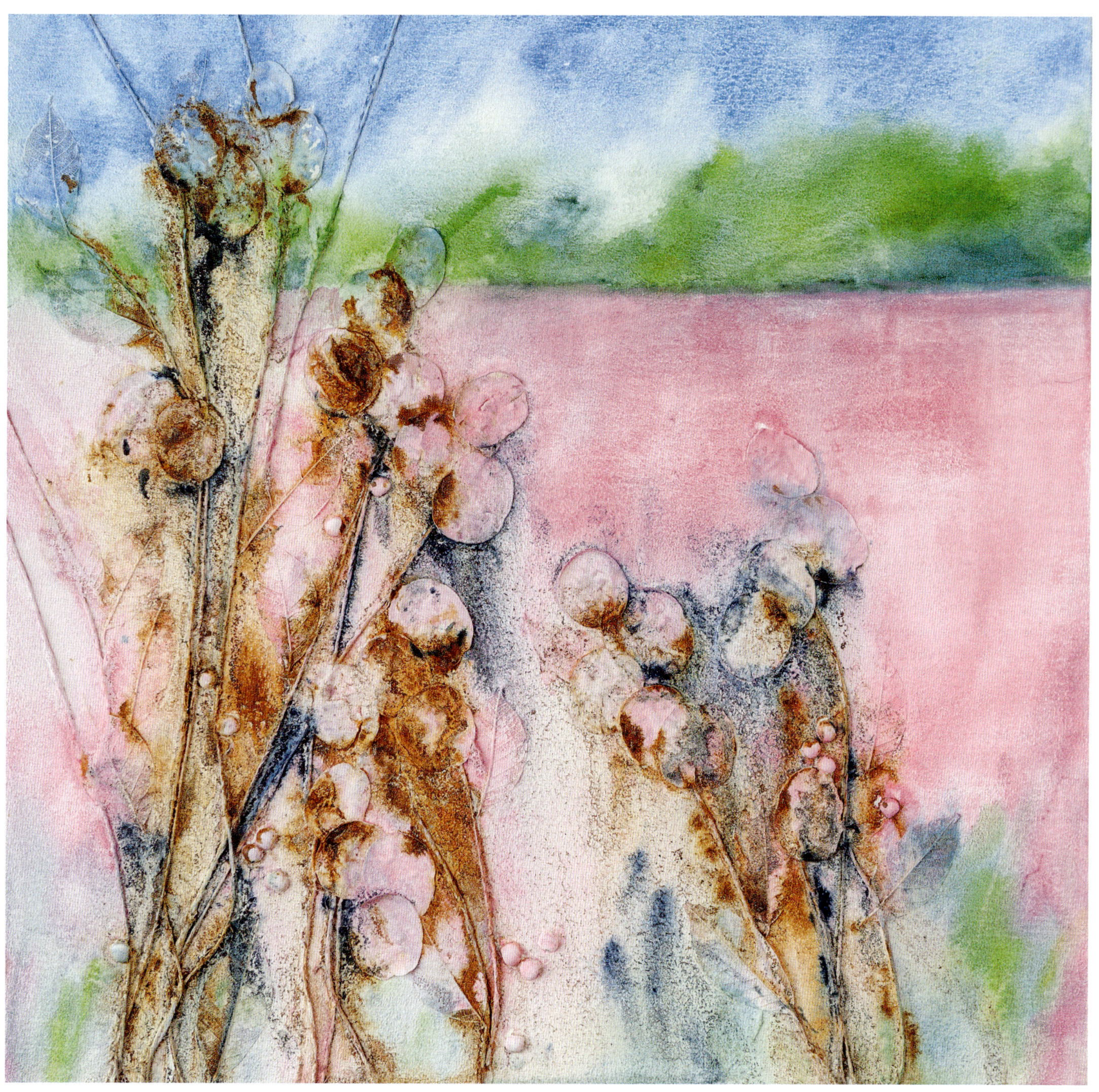

The painting at the end of this stage.

4 – lights and details

- Use a fine brush (such as a size 2 round) to apply vandyke brown to the stems in a hit-and-miss fashion, and pick out some subtle details on the skeleton leaves, too. Hint at the found materials rather than outlining them by applying the paint and immediately blending it away into the background with a clean damp brush. You can use different colours for this – verditer blue is great for the lighter areas.

- Paint the split peas with brown; aiming for a bold effect. Paint the canvas below them, as well. This helps to integrate them with the rest of the painting and create strong tones to contrast with the white also added in this stage.

- Pick up undiluted white gouache on a small brush (size 8 round) and use a dry brush technique to just skim over the surface of some of the honesty seedheads, particularly on the left-hand sides. Use a damp brush to gently blend the colour over to the right-hand sides.

- Break up the lines of the stems with a few marks of vandyke brown to suggest side branches, and add some dark details to the honesty seedheads.

- Switch to some white acrylic ink and pick out the little points that come from the honesty seedheads. Just add a few across the painting, otherwise it can start to look contrived.

- Use a spray bottle to wet the large plain area on the middle right, then dampen a rake brush and use it to agitate and blend the transition between the pink and green.

- Use white glue and tweezers to add honesty seeds.

- Add some final details. I've used a size 0 rigger to add some additional fine twigs with vandyke brown. Use these to extend the glued-on found materials, and break up the large plain area.

- Add indigo ink and granulation fluid on the lower part of the painting, along with some burnt umber ink touches, too.

- Prepare jaune brilliant watercolour, and use it along with white gouache to add the final highlights to the honesty seedheads. You might like to add a little spattering at this stage, too.

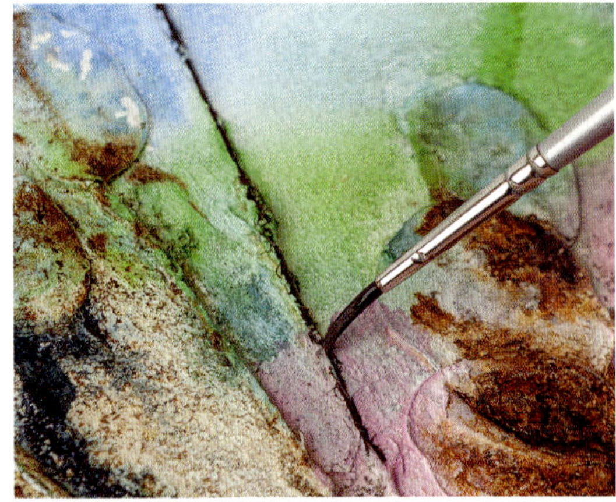

A hit-and-miss approach ensures the stems look natural: you don't want solid stems, or they'll look too severe.

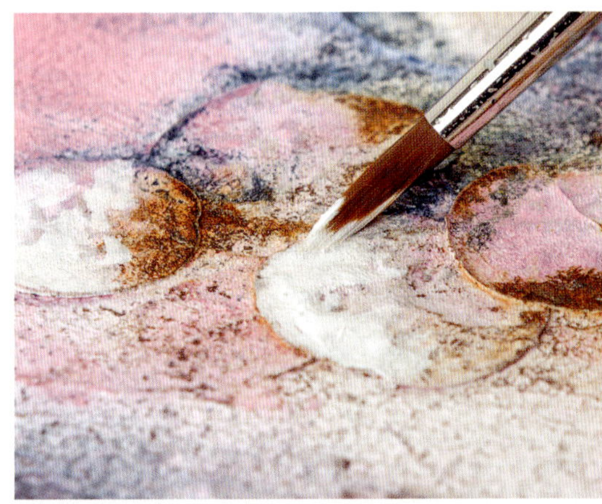

Drawing the paint from one side to another creates the impression that light is coming into the painting from the left and suggests the form of the seedheads.

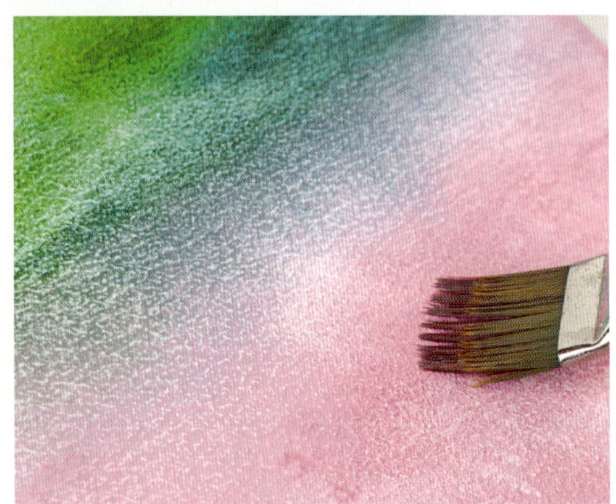

'Raking' the paint after spraying the area with clean water creates a smooth gradation between colours.

The finished painting.

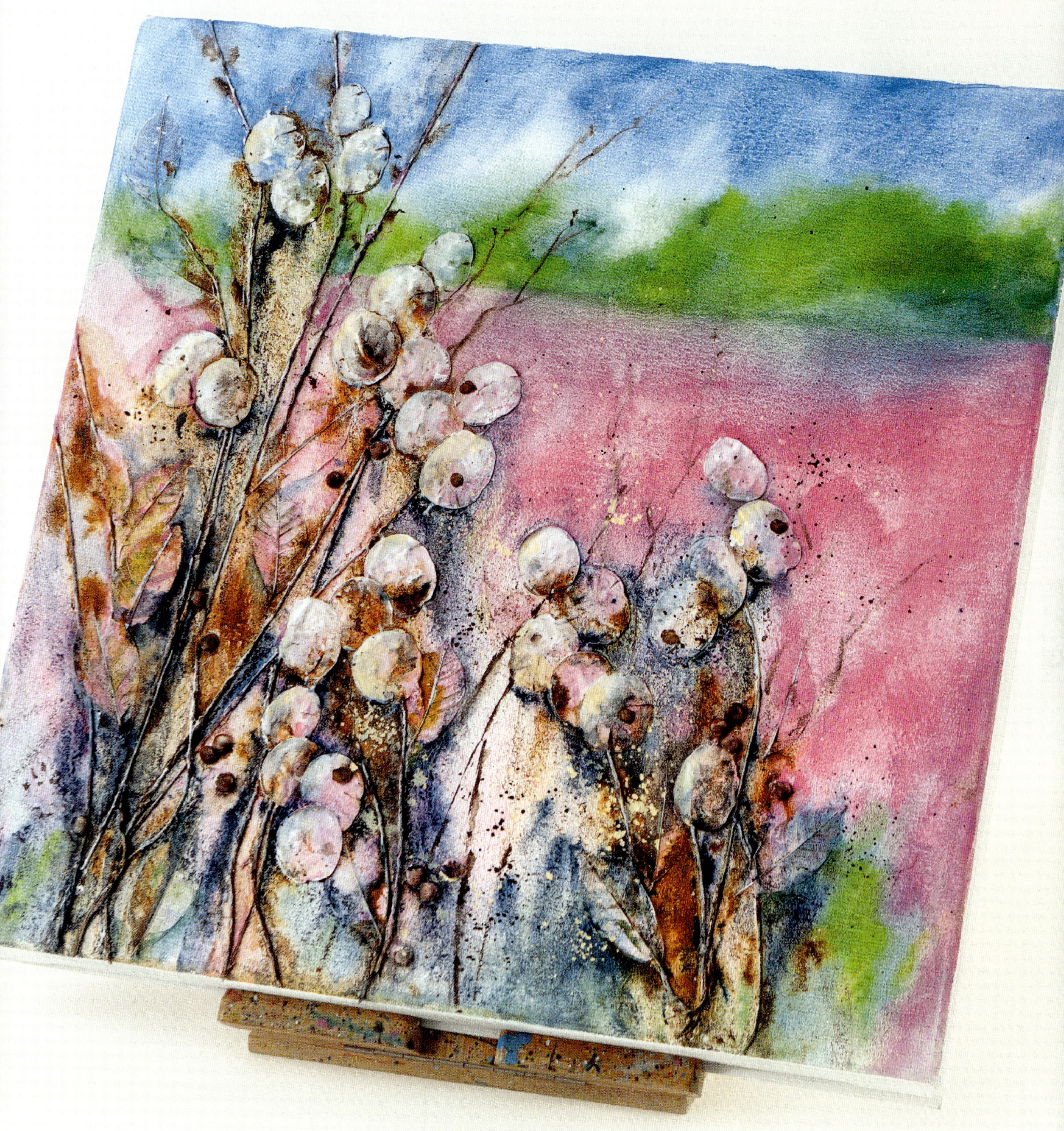

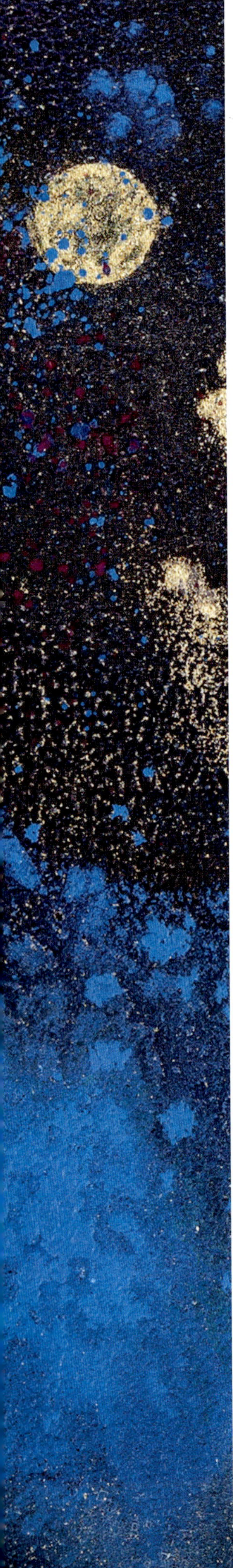

Striking a balance

When working on your art, it is always important to balance up the composition, in other words, to make sure the weight is distributed evenly across the picture. This helps the viewer's eye to move across the surface and into the rhythm of the painting. This is relatively easy in a realistic or naturalistic painting, as it's easy to assess the objects. In more abstract work, it is both harder and easier. Harder, because you have no concrete reference points, and easier because you and you alone can decide where marks are placed, and how important they are in the composition. You can plan this in advance, or allow the paint to guide you partway, before you steer the painting home.

This type of random use of pigments and other materials is a really good way of veering towards abstraction, as the more unusual use of materials and techniques is a good way to catch the viewer's eye. The viewer can then apply their own interpretation to make up their mind on exactly what the subject is. Give something like this a go with your own work; it's a very easy way to continue the journey towards abstraction.

When I developed the painting opposite, I had no subject matter in mind and took a technique-led approach. In this particular case I was inspired by some new shades of paint I'd discovered: Daniel Smith's napthamide maroon and lunar black. I dived straight in and let the paint flow and mingle on the canvas. The result was all very dark so I added some gold bronzing powder into the paint. I used a pipette to avoid disturbing the paint as it was settling and drying.

Balance can take some time to come, so don't rush. I knew the painting needed something else so allowed it to dry. After thinking about it for a couple of days, I decided to introduce some process cyan ink – a really beautiful, uplifting bright blue – to help balance the rich, deep darks. I directed the ink onto the lower third of the canvas to represent a steep rock face or hillside; then let it run down. To tie it all in I used a palette knife to spatter some of the blue into the sky area to balance everything up. It completely changed the whole painting; the invigorating swathe of bright blue adding direction, movement and interest across the foreground area and leading the eye upwards. To finish it off I painted in a full moon using the gold, providing a familiar reference point for the viewer which acts as a resting place for the eye. In this way, the painting combines darkness and light, stillness and motion, for a dynamic but balanced finish.

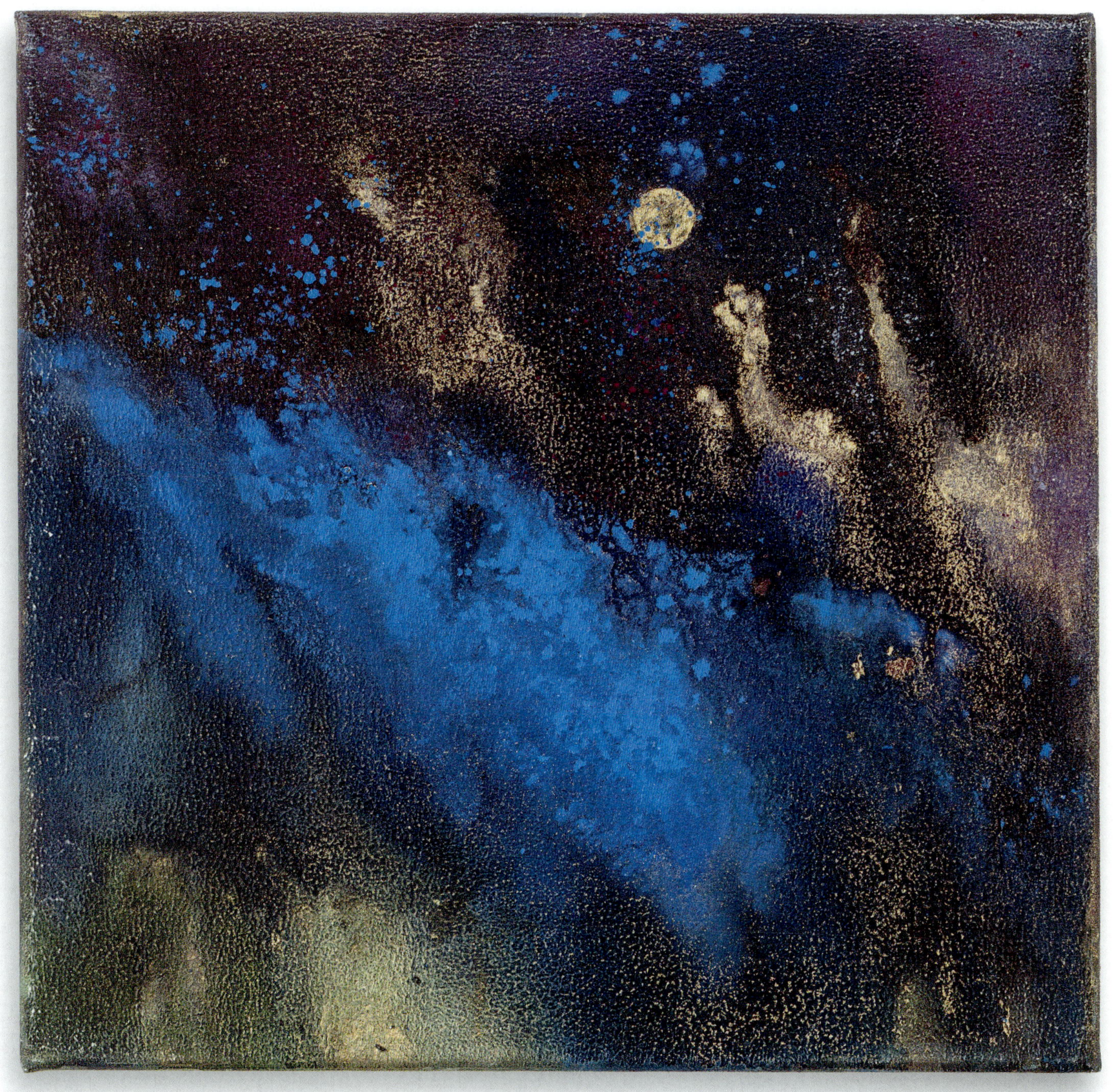

Blue Moon

30 x 30cm (11¾ x 11¾in)

*I made the sky the main focal point here, but
drew the viewer's attention further down the
page with the addition of bright blue pigment,
and the movement I created with it.*

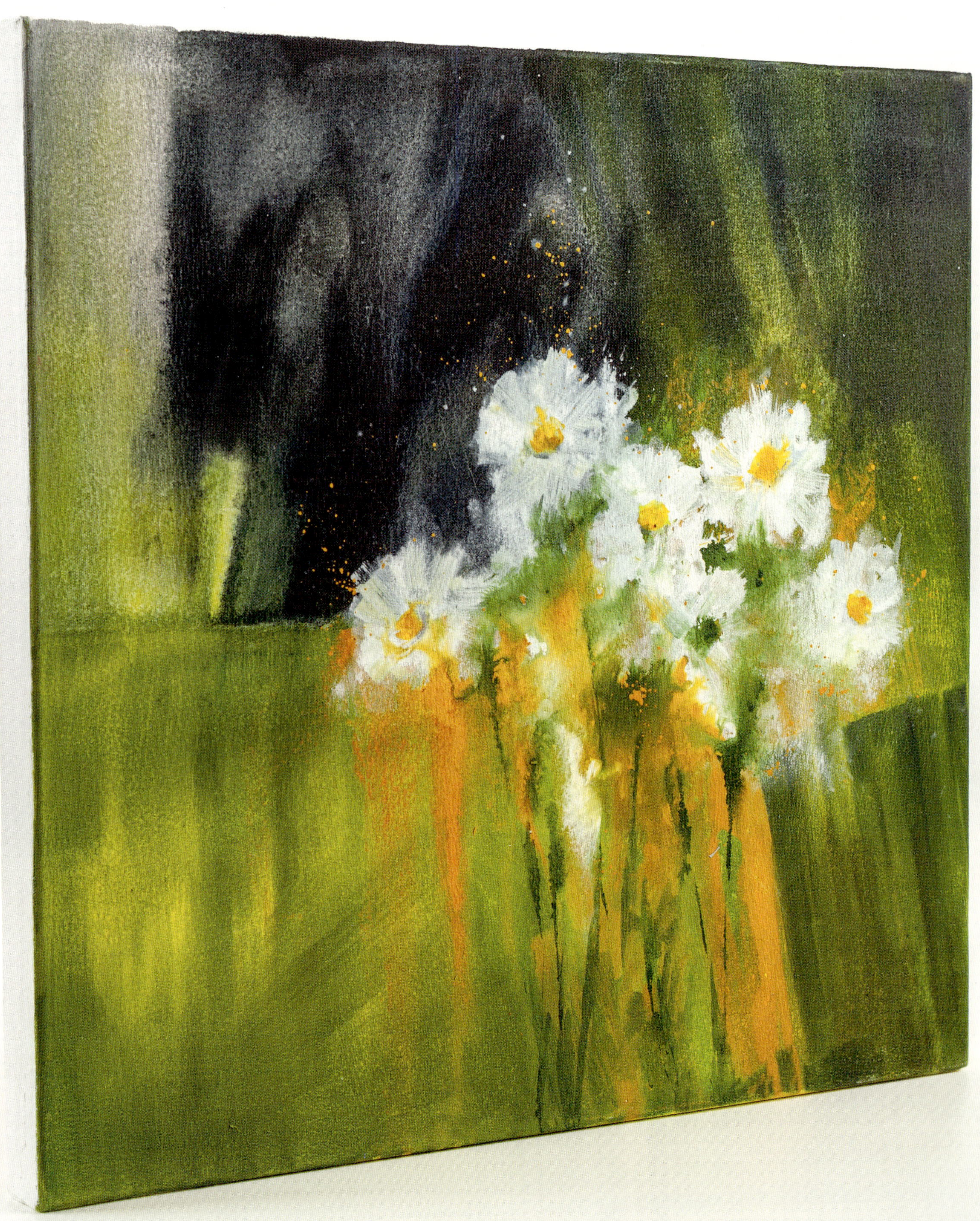

shape and line

Using contrasting shapes, colours, and a variety of hard and soft edges all add up to creating an interesting painting. We've talked about opposites on the colour wheel showing each other off to their best advantage, the same can be said for contrasting lines and shapes.

Random lines in abstract work are fine. There's no right or wrong way to draw them. However, I like to bear in mind that some lines can lead your eye out of the picture – something to watch out for. They can also help with perspective and balance, giving direction and guidance to the viewer. A straight line across the centre, for example, can suggest a horizon line to divide the sky and earth – but can equally be interpreted as the edge of a table, for example.

Consider the nature of the shapes and marks you make. Square or oblong shapes and straight, clean lines can feel hard, whereas circular and curved shapes and broken lines, or those of varying weight, can feel softer. The way you make your shapes should be considered in your painting, just as you would with colour or texture. Depending on what you want to say in your painting, you can strike a balance between the shapes and lines that you make.

Generally, I think a combination of both hard and soft lines and a variety of shapes makes for a more interesting composition.

Opposite:
Daisy Meadow
50 x 50cm (19½ x 19½in)

The round shapes of the daisies complement the structured background, where I've used various colours and sectional lines to add interest and give the painting a semi-abstract style. You will see how I added some orange for the daisy centres and a little underneath the flowers, too.

Orange is opposite blue on the colour wheel, so these touches of bright orange sing out against the deep dark blue of the background, drawing the eye effectively. Shapes are also used to direct the eye. The majority of the painting is made up of hard, straight lines – all except the flowerheads themselves, which are soft, round and diffuse. Being different draws the eye, and makes them the focus.

Uncontrolled mark-making and texture

'Why would I want to be uncontrolled?' you might ask. To paint in an uncontrolled way means your work will be a lot looser – and uninhibited. The results will be instantly fresher and more appealing and, crucially, will allow the watercolour to work best. Nothing 'kills' the freshness of watercolour – nor the enjoyment of painting with it – like trying to control where it flows and how it acts.

Of course, working in a less controlled way doesn't mean splashing randomly. You still want to use shape and line to direct the viewer's eye, but there's a balance to be struck. Randomness can help to soften your lines and will throw up unexpected shapes that you can develop, highlight or cover to better serve your composition.

Working in a less controlled way requires practice and confidence. If you're struggling to loosen up, I find one of the best ways to start is to is to use plastic food wrap to create an underpainting. The technique is shown on page 82, and this can be varied and developed to create still more ununusual effects.

Texture and freshness

When placed on top of wet paint, the wrap will form some amazing patterns. As noted on page 82, you can also add more paint, ink or granulation medium with a pipette to create more depth and definition. The plastic wrap can be manipulated to a certain extent – to create long linear marks in a particular area, for example. You never know exactly what results you will get until you peel the plastic off the surface.

Try using quite thick paint. This way, you will find it possible not only to create marks, but also to add a certain amount of texture too. This technique can be used for any subject – it adds interest, and the best thing about it is that it cannot be replicated exactly, you can do something similar but not an exact copy. I find it's a great way of getting you moving again if you are, perhaps, stuck in a rut and need a bit of inspiration.

Speed and freshness

There's a traditional oil painting technique called *alla prima*, which means 'at the first', and involves painting everything in a single session. As watercolourists, this will be familiar to us, but it is worth considering setting yourself a time limit to see if speed will help you overcome hesitancy. Canvas is the pefect surface for this – if it doesn't go to plan, then you can simply paint over the result with white watercolour medium and start over!

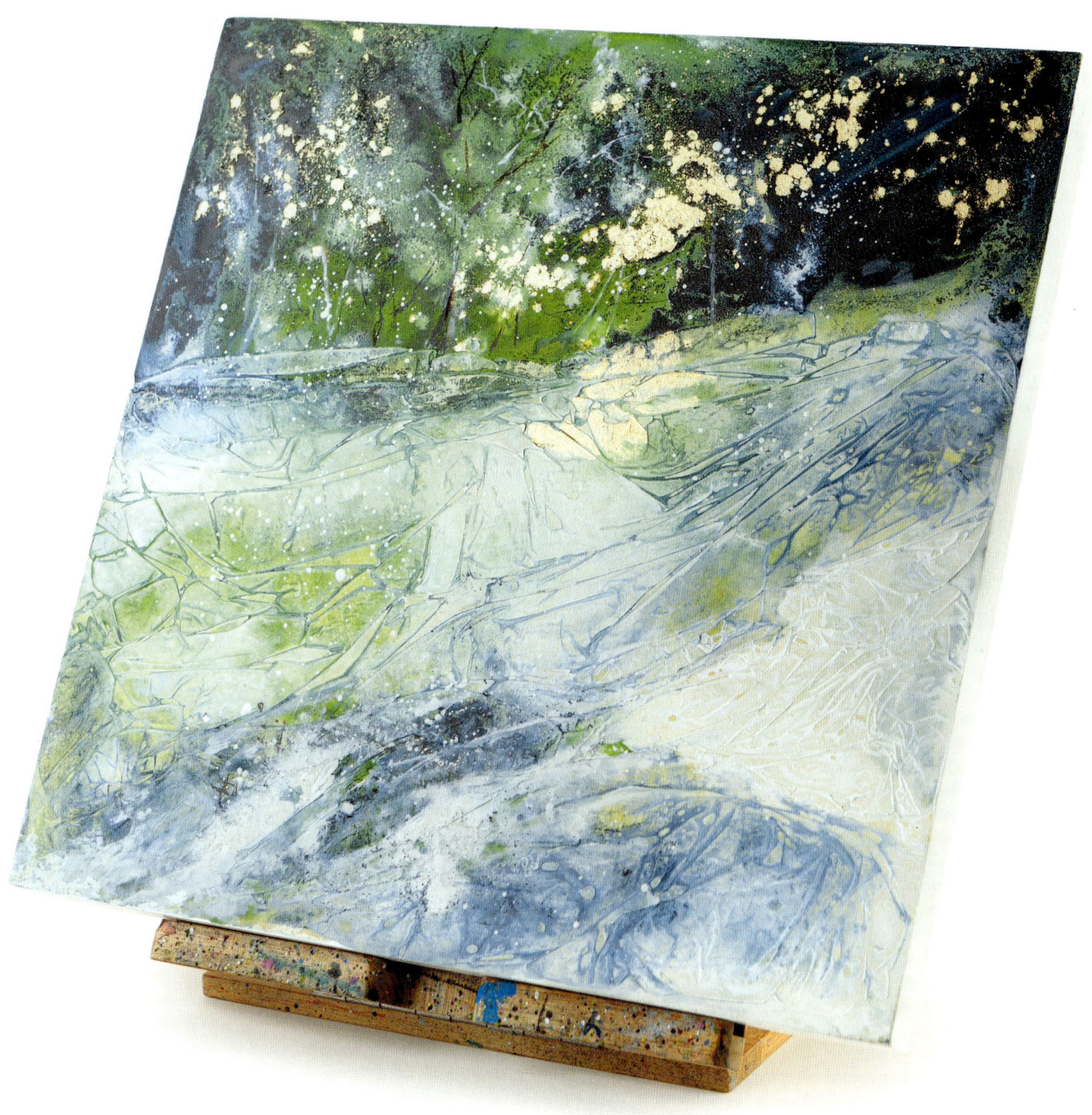

Icy Gold

30 x 30cm (11¾ x 11¾in)

This painting was completed in one go, apart from the addition of a minor bit of detail to suggest some tree trunks and branches above the horizon line, and a little gold bronzing powder spattered on the dry surface.

EXERCISE: Working over a textured surface

Loosening up on a canvas with a textured background is really fun as you don't really need to do much work! The textures created, when preparing the canvas, do nearly all of the work for you as the paint and ink will run and merge together, sinking into the crevices you created with the crackle paste – or whatever other medium you've used to texture the surface. It can be alarming to see the paint flowing seemingly uncontrollably, but after some practice you'll see that you do retain some control.

To tackle this exercise, see the chapter on texture on pages 44–49, to prepare your surface. From here, you can use purely dilute washes of paint to work over the top, but I find that the intensity of ink helps to set off the texture well.

In the painting opposite, white ink was added while the paint was still wet so that the edges were soft and then just a tiny bit of definition in the seedhead and stalk tied it all together.

After everything has dried, use a thin brush to suggest some form to the cow parsley and pick out some of the crackled shapes in gold to give that extra intensity and interest.

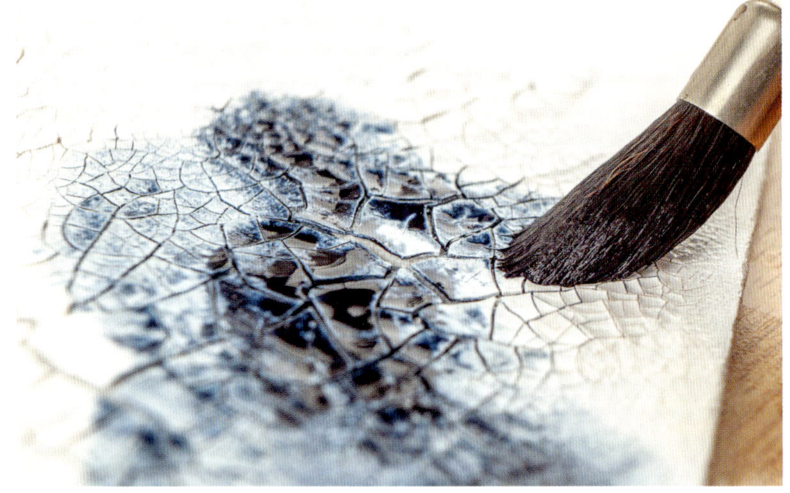

Paint flowing into the cracks strengthens the impression of texture.

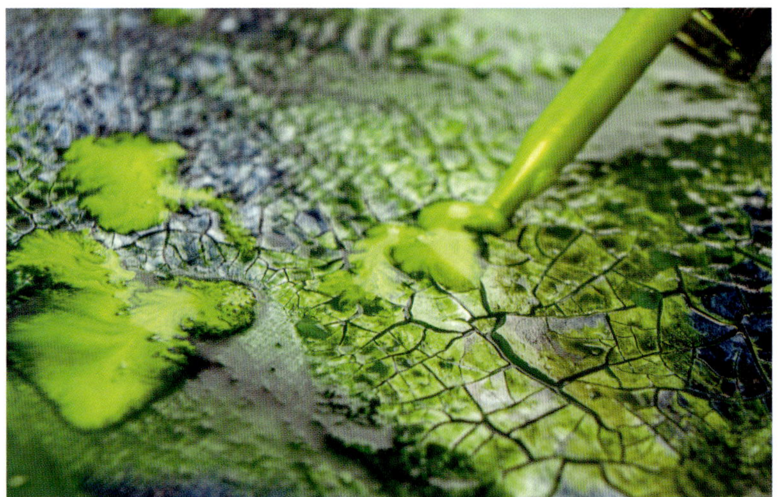

Ink added wet-on-wet displaces some of the paint, creating interesting effects.

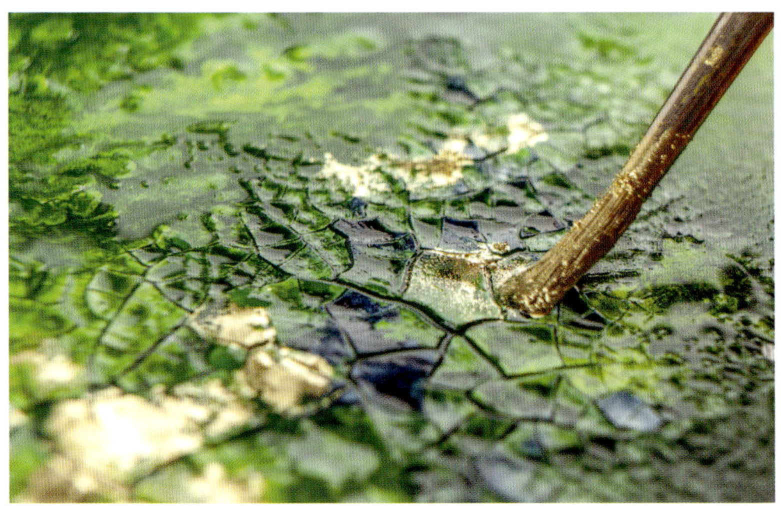

Gold ink can be added with a brush while the previous layers are still wet.

Golden Patterns
20 x 20cm (8 x 8in)

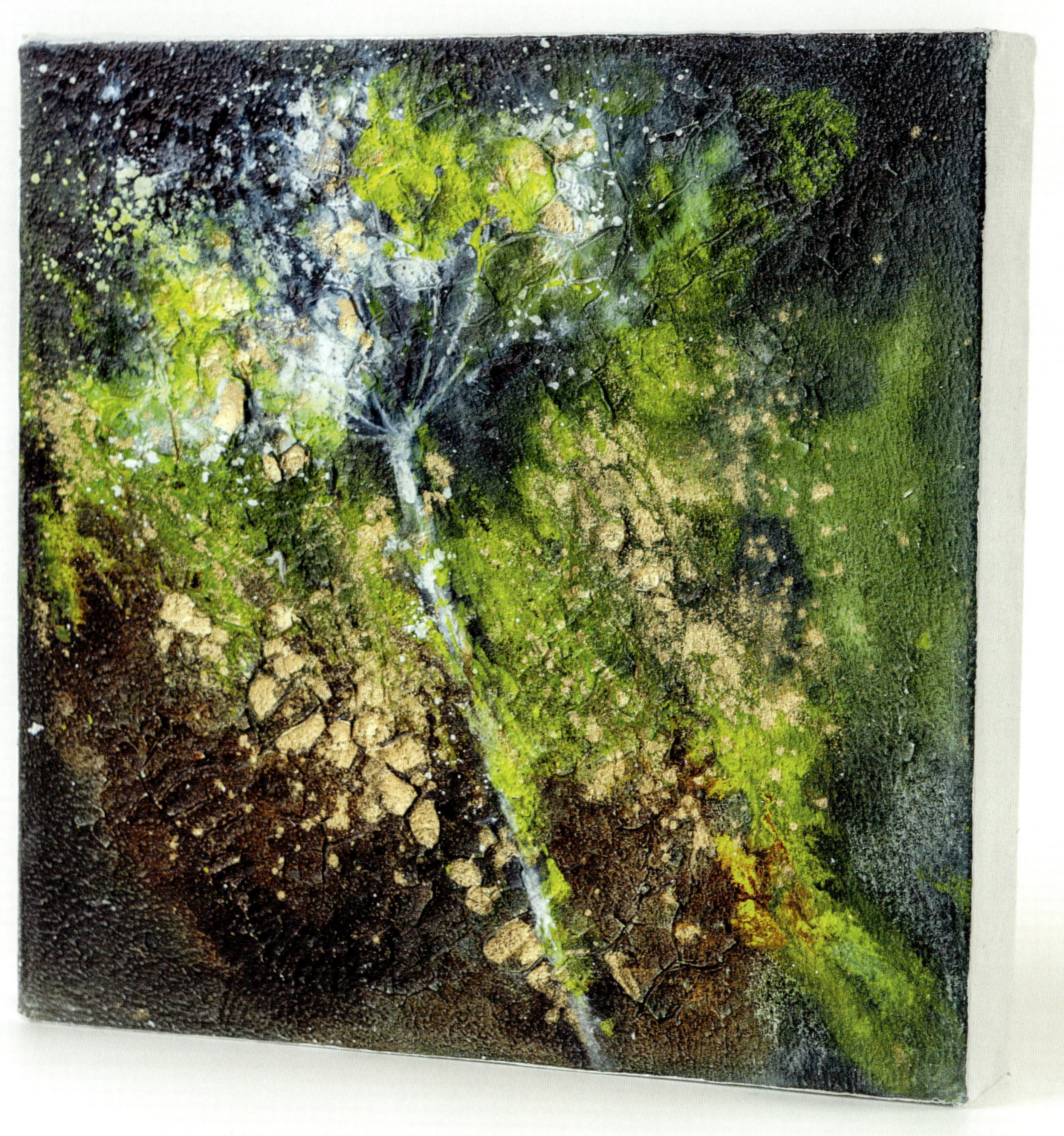

Structure and edges

Providing the viewer with a rhythm to lead their eye around your work is most important. Balance and structure inform the visual weight of objects, form, colour and space. The human eye is always seeking stability, so using a well balanced composition helps the viewer to take in the painting as a whole. Executed well, the harmony between different shapes, lines and edges creates a rhythm that helps the viewer to be transported into the painting.

Hard edges These are the very distinct, obvious breaks in colour, line or tone. Hard edges are eye-catching, and so they appear to come forward, or 'advance' in a painting. An example in the painting opposite is the left-hand side of the ship, which forms a hard edge against the sky.

Soft edges Where edges are blurred or blended, or colours and tones gradually merge into one another, we say that the edges are soft. These draw the viewer's eye and attention less, so they fade into the background a little more – we call this 'recession'. The distinction between the sea and the sky on the right-hand side is a good example of a soft edge.

For a well balanced painting, there should be nothing disjointed, such as hard edges or bright colours towards the outer perimeter of the painting as this will lead the eye off the canvas. The quality of the edges you use is crucial, as are the colours.

Having said that, if you want to suggest movement, then having a flash of hot, bright colour or sharp edges off-centre – as in the bright, colourful buoys at the top here – can draw the eye effectively. Note, however, that this is balanced by the hard contrasts in tone on the sea foam in the centre. The line of the ship draws the eye down from the buoys to this area, and then around the rest of the sea.

While the water is full of movement and energy, the central balance makes you feel reassured that the ship is not in danger, and results in a restful semi-abstract work.

Opposite:
Safe at Sea
40 x 40cm (15¾ x 15¾in)

By working on a very textured canvas, I was able to both capture movement with the sea and also create a weathered look for the hull of the boat. I liked all of the effects I created, but felt that it lacked a focal point. I decided that I would add some colour to jazz it up a bit. The addition of the warm, bright buoys instantly lifted the painting, and made the eye travel upwards to take in everything.

However, the buoys initially stood out too much as the colours were very vibrant. To rectify this, I added some plastic wrap on top of the wet paint and when it had dried, I was really pleased with the result: it had made marks reminiscent of the other textural marks in the painting and helped the buoys to blend in really well.

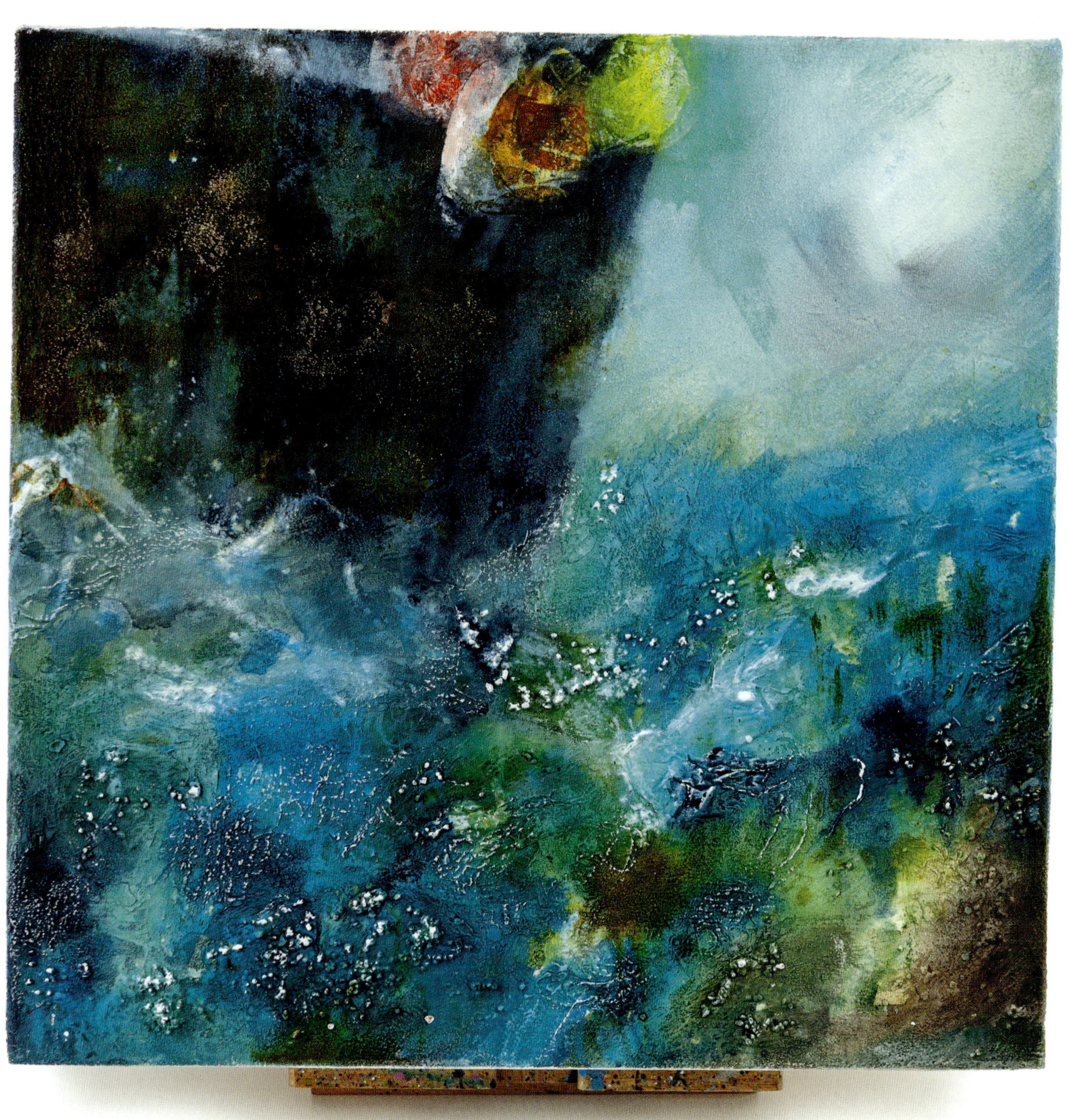

Introducing randomness

We all love surprises – and what better way to introduce a surprise element to your work than by adding something randomly that you didn't initially plan to do when you started a painting?

Randomness is an exciting dimension to add to an otherwise 'un-curious' piece of work. When working with familiar colours and textures, keep an open mind as to how you can use randomness to develop the ordinary into something exceptional. Happy chances, as wet colours mix on the textured surface of canvas, can easily spark a fresh or unexpected idea: go with it and keep things interesting; both for the painting, and for yourself.

Keep your mind open, and don't stick to your initial plans if random chance takes your inspiration elsewhere.

Painting *Sloes in the Landscape*

For this location-led painting (see page 26), I initially planned a landscape and chose some colours to use accordingly. As you can see, I combined some representational colours with more unconventional colours to get across the impression of place I had.

I carried the abstract theme further, by working over an underpainting created with plastic food wrap. The resulting semi-random marks and shapes were really pleasing. When I peeled off the wrap, the top right-hand area suggested a clump of trees on a hillside to me, while the foreground shapes formed in gold and red, reminded me of autumn leaves.

I pondered over whether to leave it alone or emphasize the leaf shapes more: should I add a few trunks and the odd branch in the distant trees or leave them alone? I left it until the next day – a pause for reflection is sometimes very useful. On further consideration, it occurred to me that it reminded me of one of my favourite photographs I had taken of a hedgerow, where some of the leaves had started to turn into their autumnal colours, with sloe berries nestled amongst them; this got my creative juices flowing, and so, I decided to add some of the berries.

I used a deep maroon colour to first paint in the shapes of the fruit and then, when that had dried, I used ShinHan lavender shade to paint over them to give that dull opaque hue that sloe berries have. I lifted out a stem here and there to join them up and, to add balance, I dampened some of the background area and dropped in some of the lovely opaque lavender colour to tie it all together. I was really pleased with the outcome. It's something different and it certainly pays to be a bit random sometimes and throw caution to the wind.

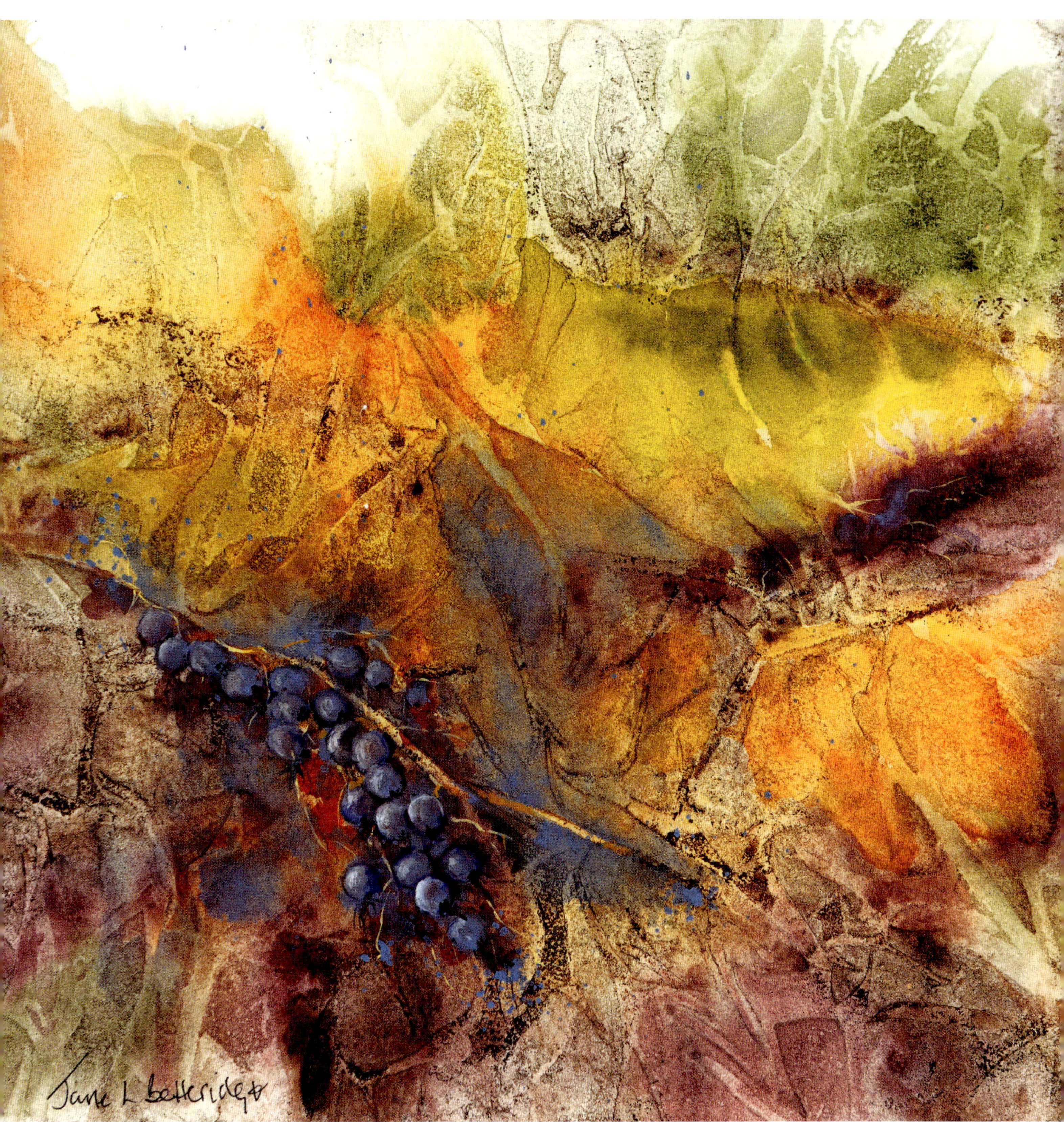

Sloes in the Landscape

25 x 25cm (10 x 10in)

EXERCISE – Loose marks for spontaneity

On page 76, I suggested you start to doodle when trying to loosen up and paint in a more abstract style. This exercise lets you try this with your new-found knowledge of shapes, lines, colour and texture. Compare your earlier doodles with those made after this exercise to see whether you can spot differences in the qualities of your lines and shapes.

This can be done first of all in a sketchbook and then, when you've created some interesting shapes and connections between them, transfer your ideas to canvas. I love to just let the paint flow and merge on the canvas or paper and then draw into it, or lift out or add other mediums. Using various tools, some really unusual effects can be achieved. It really doesn't matter if it represents a subject or not, doing this can be a warming up exercise before commencing your main painting; it really will loosen you up for future work.

After you've doodled loosely, you'll probably find some marks that you particularly like. You can either transfer them to a new piece of canvas, or develop them where they are. Be careful when working over or around them that you don't obscure what it is you found so appealing in the first place.

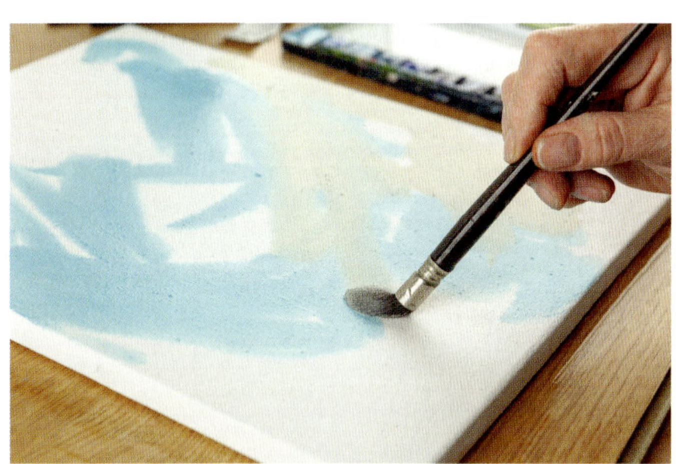

Working with loose brushstrokes – that is, by holding the brush less firmly and moving more broadly – you'll find the marks you make are fresher, and may lead to attractive surprises.

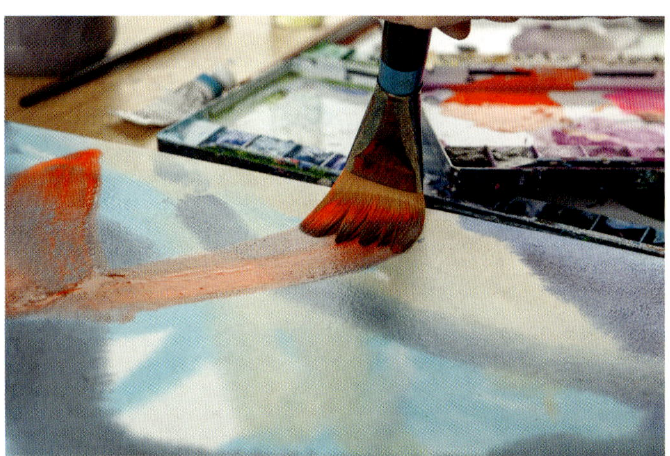

Anything that you can do to reduce the control you have over the piece can help to inject some spontaneity. Holding a larger brush at the end of the handle will mean that you can't control it as effectively – and it's this that will introduce a sense of randomness and freedom to your work.

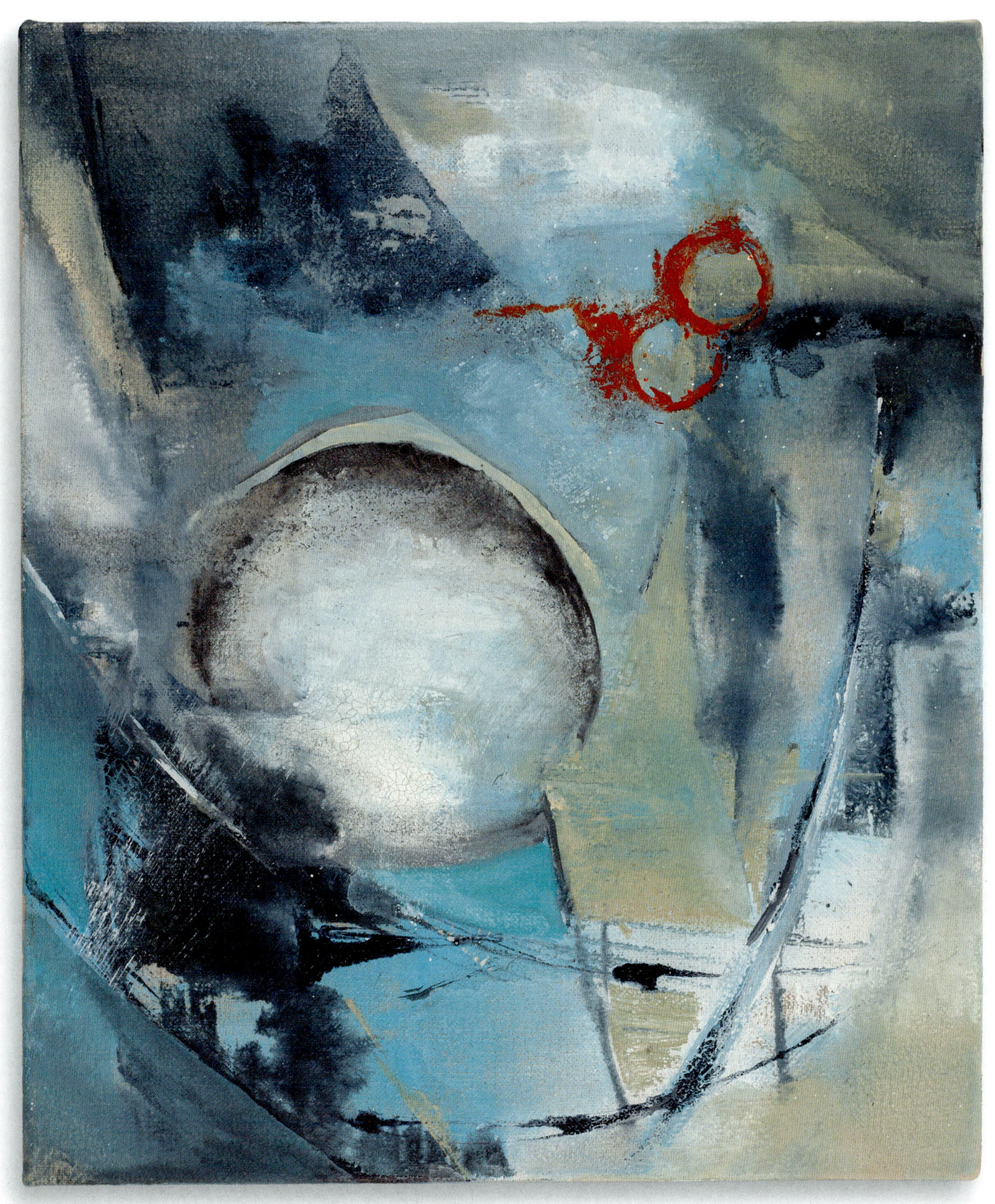

Nautical Shapes

25 x 35cm (10 x 13¾in)

flowers and fruit

Still-life subjects can be calming and restful, but this can also edge into them appearing static or – worse – dead-looking. The abstraction in this project allows us to introduce movement and dynamism into a subject that is, by its nature, motionless. Clean, choppy (but subtle) marks contrast with the overall softness, reflecting the movements that the artist's eye makes over the subject as the painting develops. The result is a still life that is vibrant and arresting.

Ranunculus are one of my favourite flowers; I love how many layers of fine, papery petals each flower head holds. Using these flowers as a starting point, here we combine a few plums and pears with an imaginary plate and beaker to creare this composition.

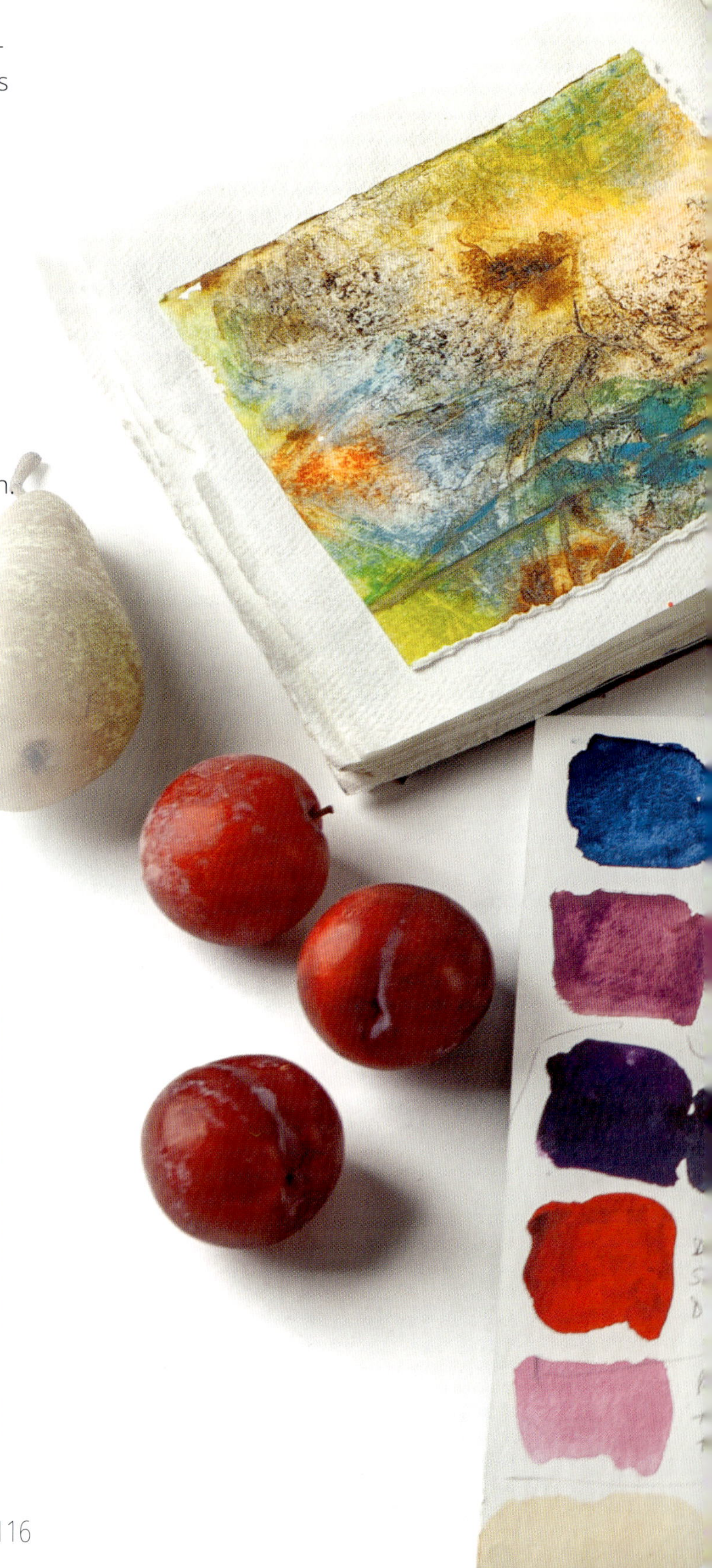

You will need

- **Block canvas** 40 x 40cm (15¾ x 15¾in)

- **Watercolour paints** Rose of ultramarine (Daniel Smith), Prussian blue (Daniel Smith), pale green (ShinHan), horizon blue (ShinHan), jaune brilliant (ShinHan), indigo (ShinHan), deep scarlet (Daniel Smith), green apatite genuine (Daniel Smith), turquoise (SAA), pink peony (White Nights), leaf green (ShinHan), royal blue (White Nights)

- **Inks** FW acrylic: white

- **Brushes** Four large (size 16) rounds, two large 75mm (3in) sponge brushes, one small 25mm (1in) sponge brush, one medium (size 10) round, one small (size 8) round

- **Other materials** Flower pattern stencil, ranunculus, plums and pear

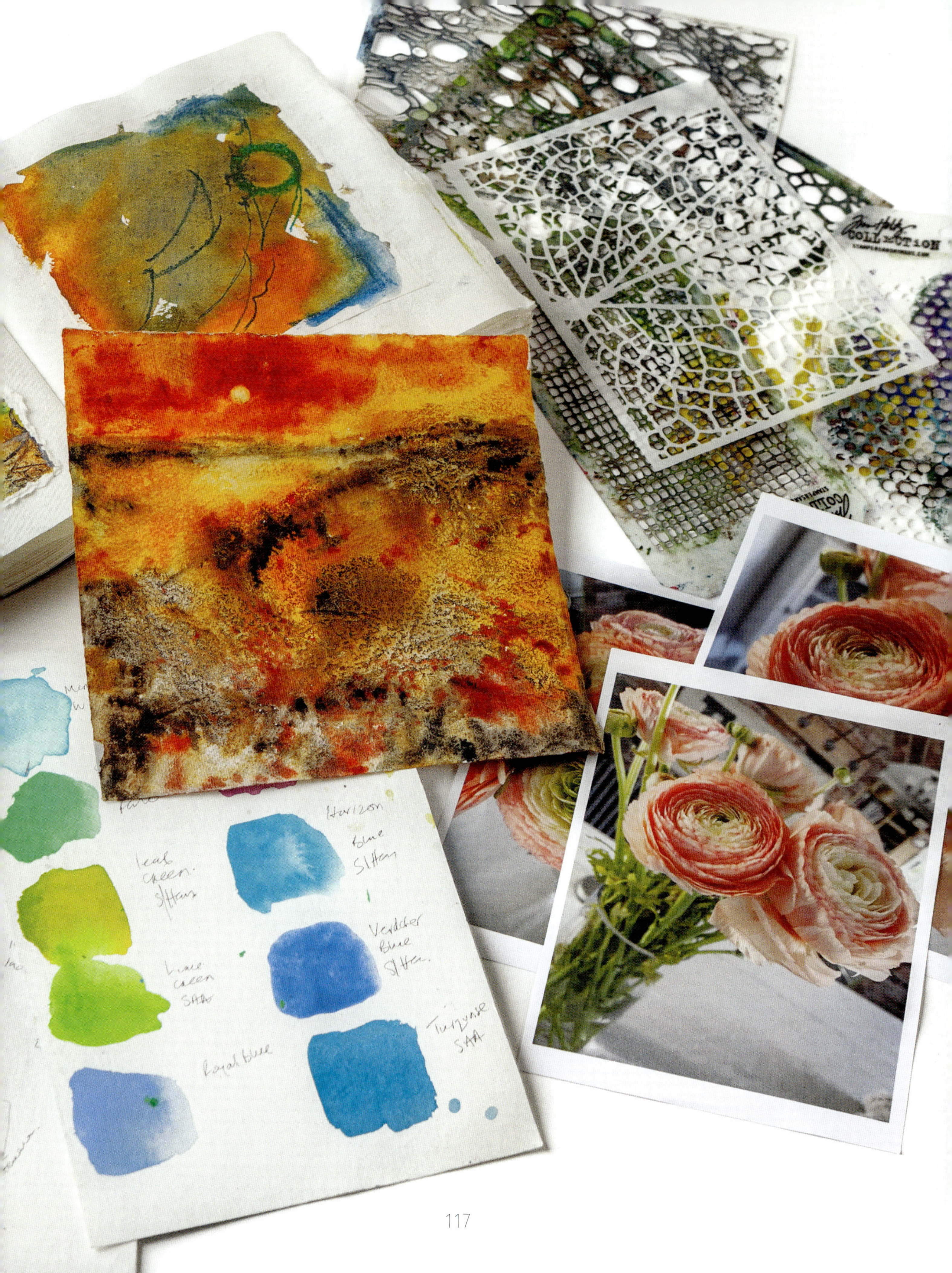

1 – the abstract background

- Start by preparing your paints: rose of ultramarine, Prussian blue, pale green, horizon blue. Glazing is important in this project, so don't forget the Aqua Fix!

- Next, paint a large, warm, dark rectangle at the bottom right with the rose of ultramarine; frame it with Prussian blue, then cover the rest of the surface with horizon blue, before introducing loose marks of pale green within the horizon blue wet in wet.

- Swap to the sponge brushes to feather the edges of the areas together with light, sweeping strokes.

It doesn't matter if the edges of the areas bleed a little, but try to keep them distinct as you paint.

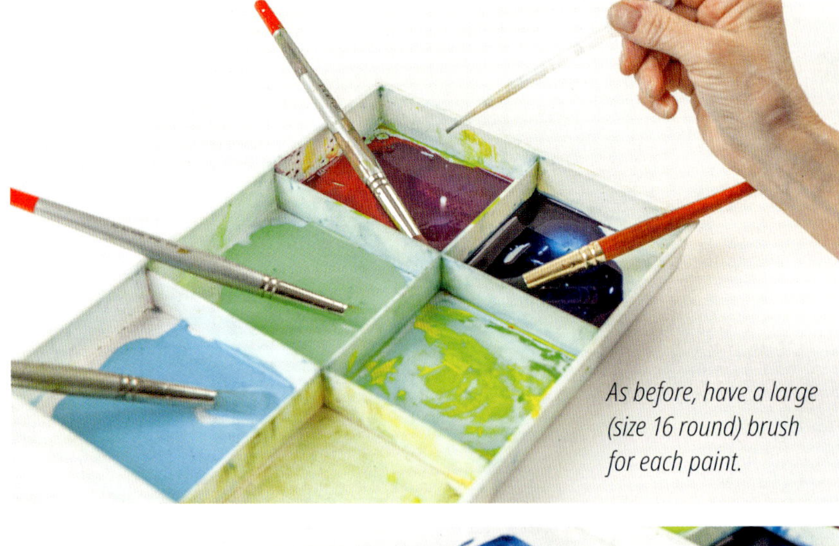

As before, have a large (size 16 round) brush for each paint.

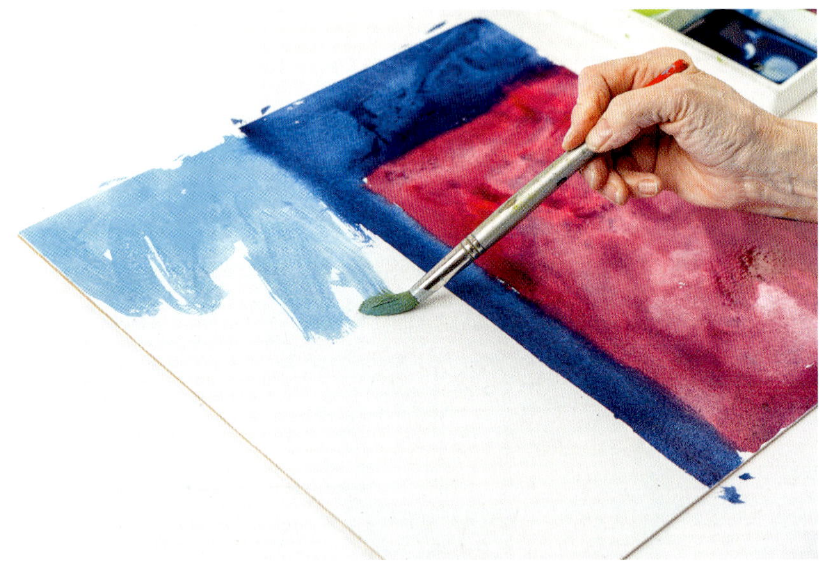

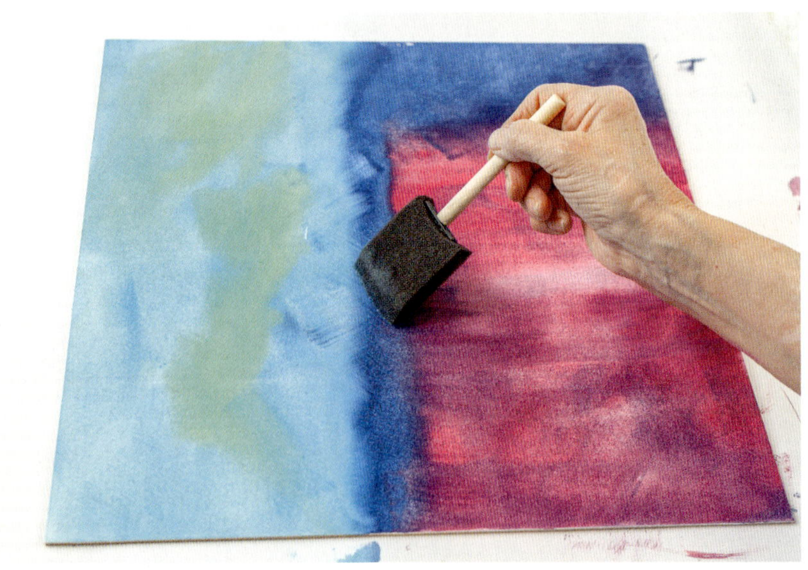

When using the sponge brushes, the aim is to merge the geometric blocks into a single area, but retain the overall impression of form.

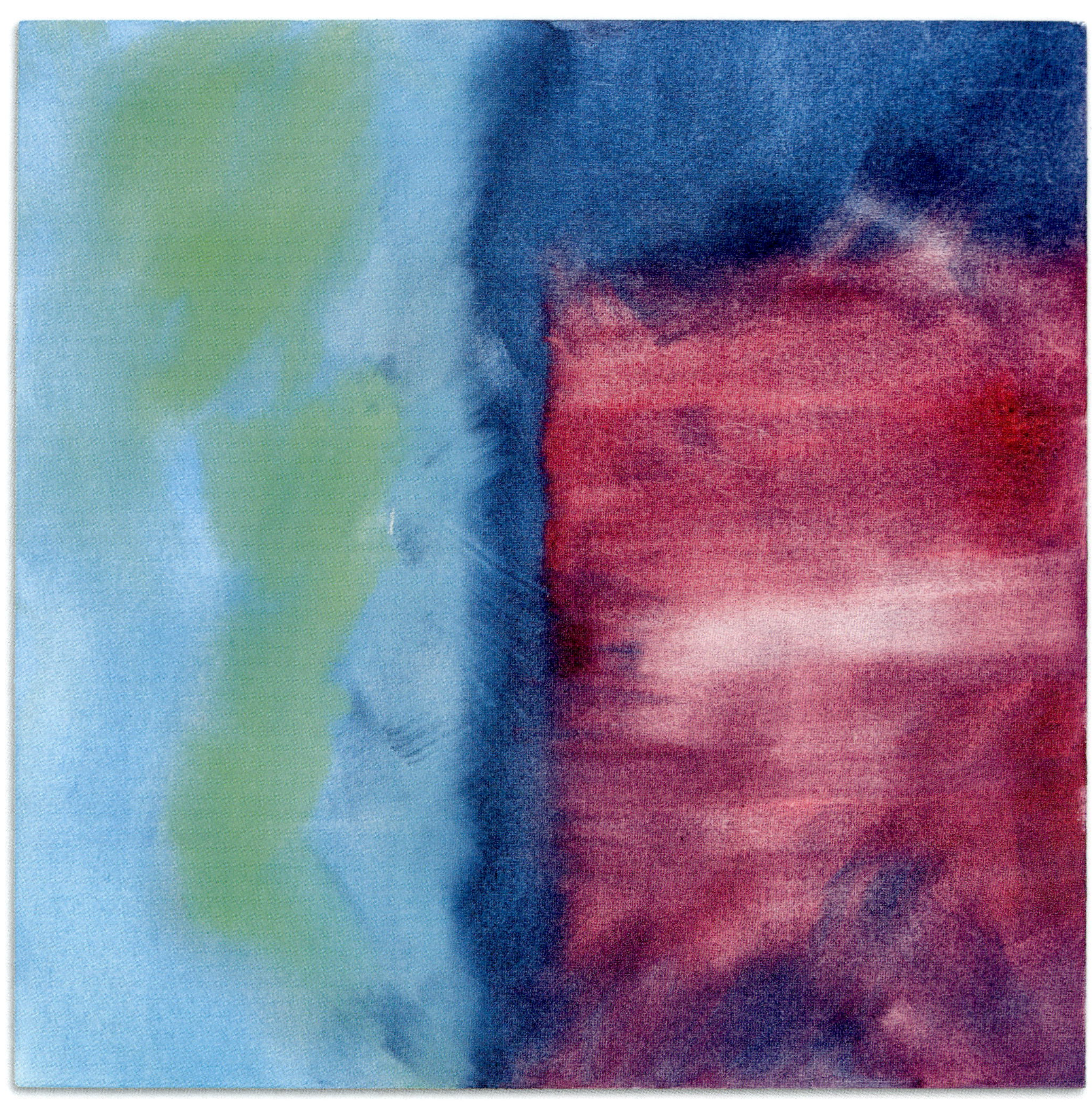

The painting at the end of this stage. The graphic, linear marks made in the background create balance and structure before we embark on painting the softer shapes of the fruit and flowers.

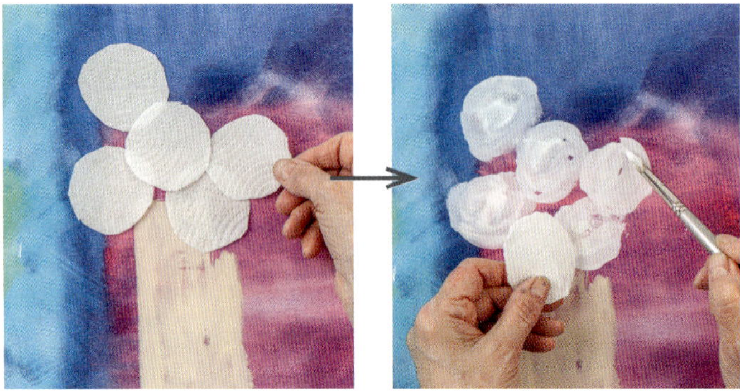

It doesn't matter if the edges of the areas bleed a little, but try to keep them distinct as you paint.

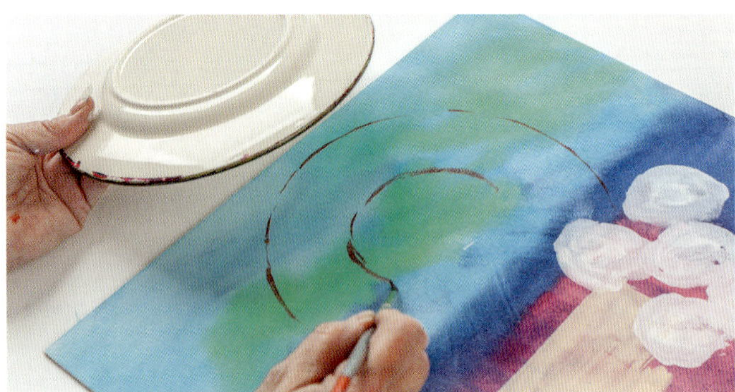

Overlapping the circles of paper (left), helps the painted result look natural. You might prefer a more stylized look, in which case keep them equally spaced.

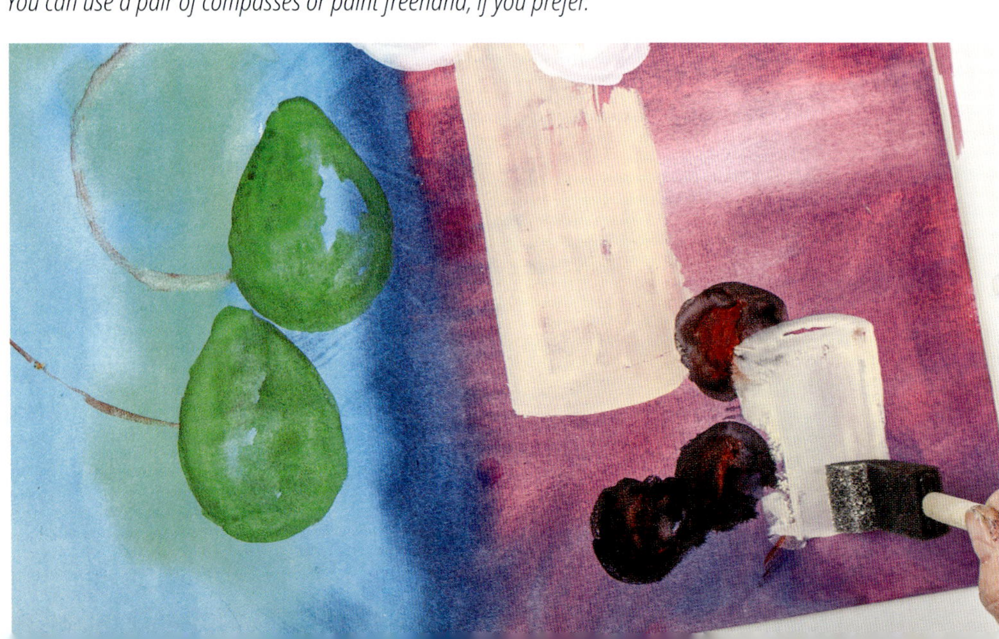

You can use a pair of compasses or paint freehand, if you prefer.

2 – establishing the shapes

• Prepare some jaune brilliant. Block out the main shape of the vase using a 75mm (3in) sponge brush, then tidy it up with the size 16 brush.

• Cut scrap paper into circles, and use them to test out placement of the flowerheads. Once you're happy with the placement, remove each circle in turn, and paint in the space with white ink and a medium brush. This will work as an underpainting to make the paint on top sing out.

• Use deep scarlet to draw round the shape of your plate, then lift it away and add a few details within.

• Use a mix of indigo with rose of ultramarine to establish the basic shapes of the plums. Add deep scarlet wet-into-wet to the plums. Next, establish the pears with apatite green genuine. Consider the scale of the fruits against the other objects.

• Add the beaker on the lower right-hand side in the same way as the vase.

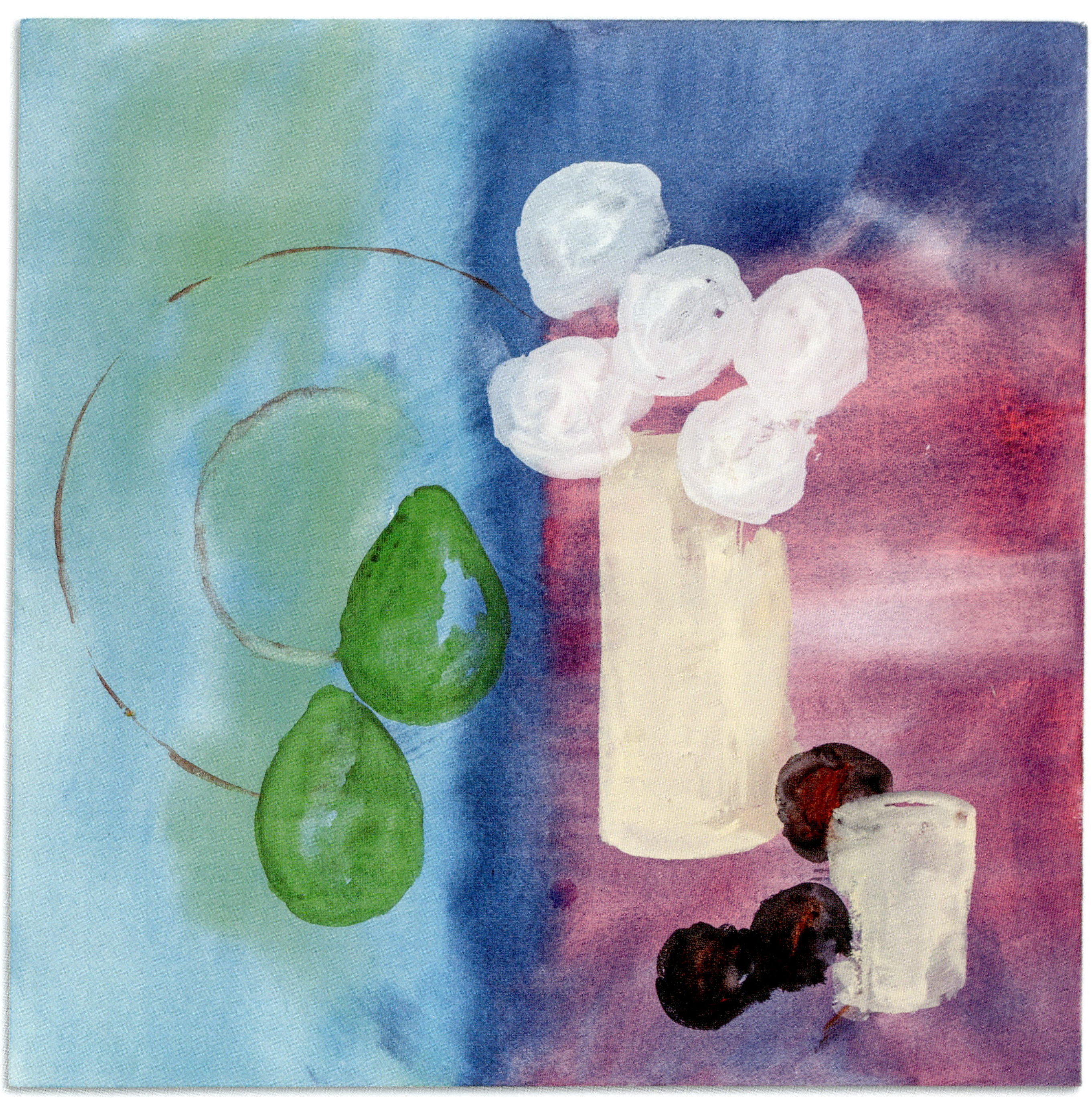

The painting at the end of this stage. Note how the circular plate helps to tie everything together, providing a visual link between the linear, blocky background and the softer shapes of the foreground objects.

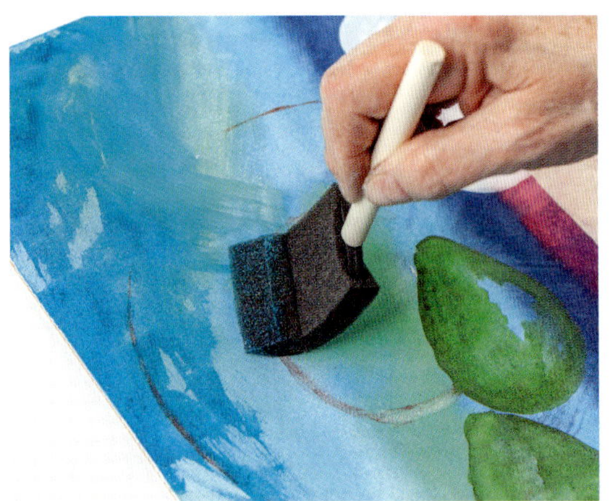

Making your sponge brush marks in a criss-cross fashion to build up the suggestion of texture. Don't be afraid to work over the plate itself.

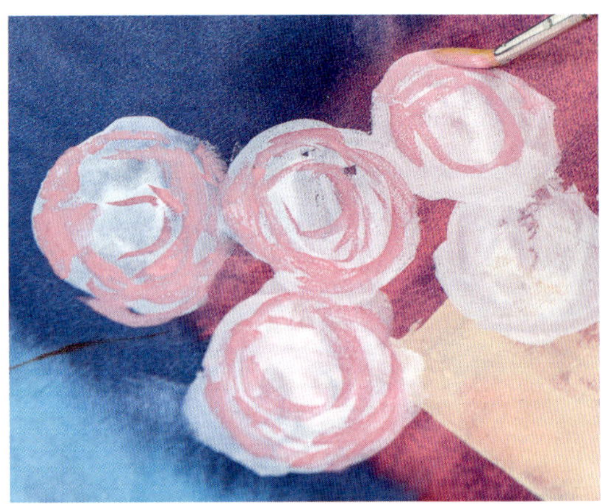

3 – glazing

- Glaze the area around the suggestion of the plate with turquoise, applying the paint with a large brush, then feathering it with a sponge brush.

- Use a medium (size 8 round) brush to apply pink peony to the flowers, using curling, curving brushmarks.

- Change to a small sponge brush and use the pale green to paint across the outline of the plate, softening it into the background until just a suggestion remains. As before, blend away with criss-cross motions. Apply leaf green to the pears, mostly on the left-hand and upper sides, using a large brush, then soften and blend across the outlines using a small sponge brush.

- Continue to build up and develop the layers across the painting using the colours on your palette. Apply the paint with a brush, then soften and feather away with the sponge brushes. You're aiming for a soft, hazy outlines – a little like those achieved through the traditional oil painting technique of *sfumato*.

- At the lower right-hand corner, feather the paint away more from the bottom and right-hand sides of the objects, and leave the upper right-hand sides more defined.

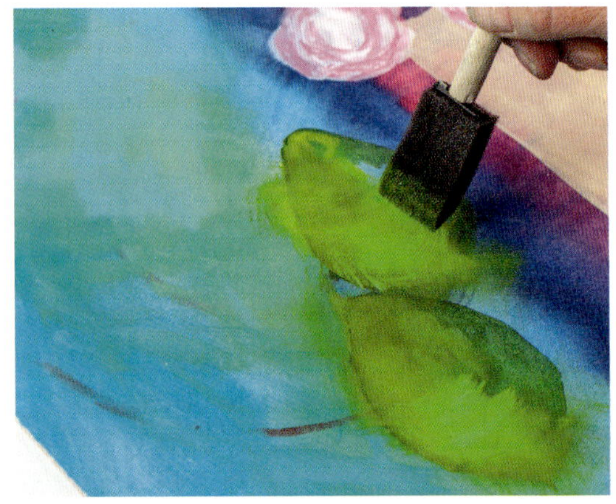

As you blend, pick up a hint of pale green on the sponge brush and add some light marks on the left-hand side, near the base of each pear.

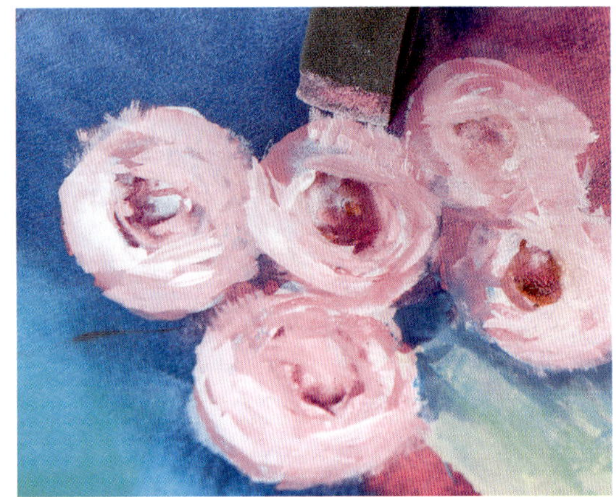

As you work the flowers, introduce rose of ultramarine in the centres, and build up the outer petals with more pink peony and white ink. Apply all the paints and ink here before feathering; and don't work over the flowerheads themselves – just feather the very edges, helping to soften them into the background.

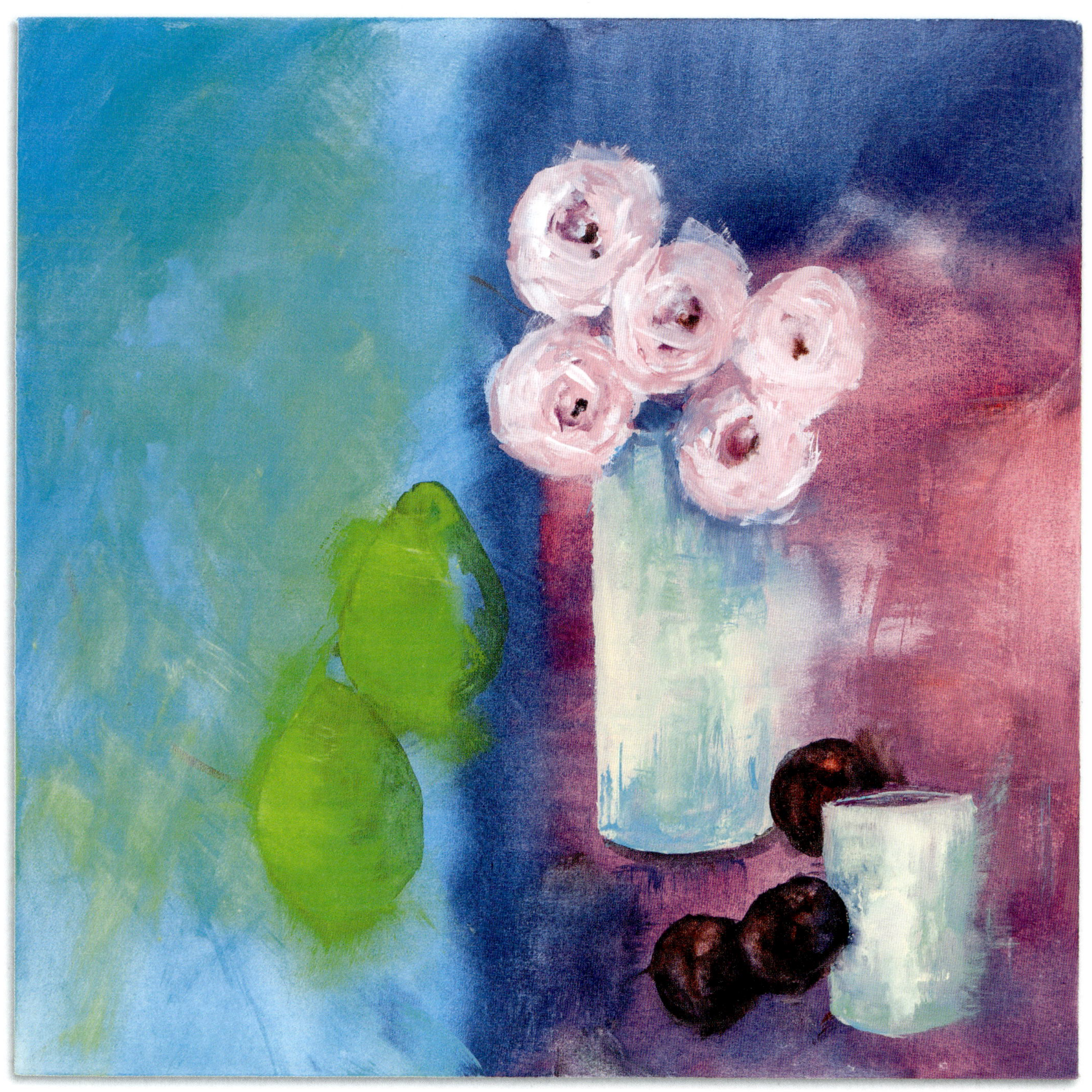

The painting at the end of this stage. Before moving on, assess the painting. If you find one of the objects is getting too eye-catching, try feathering the background colour into the object, rather than the object colour into the background.

4 – refining and adding life

- Suggest the pattern on the plate with rose of ultramarine. You can paint this freehand, but a stencil will help to ensure consistency of design. Avoid making the shapes too clear and sharp; or they'll stand out too much from the surrounding painting. Use quite a dry brush to break up the application of paint, and if things are too stark when you remove the stencil, use a little kitchen paper to lightly dab and knock back the marks.

- Use a mix of leaf green and green apatite genuine to suggest some foliage around the flowerheads with short, choppy marks. Add Prussian blue to the green mix wet-in-wet on the canvas for shading.

- Develop the plums by lifting out a little paint from the upper left-hand sides of the plums using a damp brush, then add light, choppy marks around the plums using a small sponge brush and pink peony. Keep these small and subtle.

- Build up the pears with the greens on your palette and choppy marks. Use the same approach on the flowers, but soften these less.

- Mix horizon blue and turquoise together, and use this to add subtle choppy marks over the left-hand side.

- Mix vandyke brown with jaune brilliant, and paint in the stems on the fruits, and a few light touches in the foliage around the flowers.

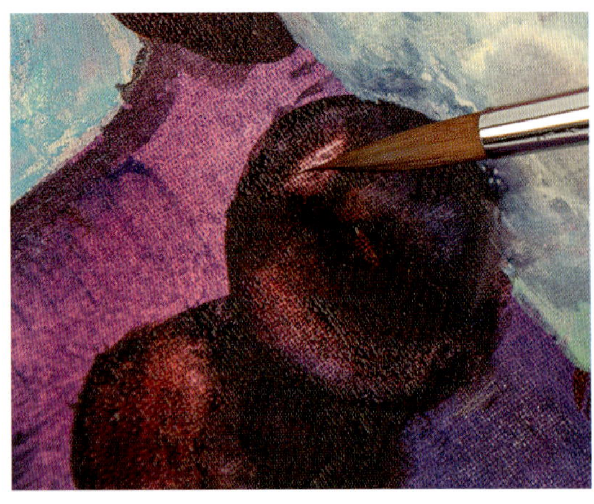

Removing colour by lifting out helps to suggest the shape and detail of the fruit.

The finished painting

40 x 40cm (15¾ x 15¾in)

The flowers are the focal point of the composition, so note that the contrast and impact of the marks elsewhere (such as around the pears and plate) are intentionally less noticeable to avoid drawing the eye from the ranunculus blooms.

To finish, make any adjustments you feel necessary – in my painting, I felt that the pears looked a little flat initially, so I refined them with highlights on the top and right, and shading on the bottom and left. I was, however, careful not to over-develop them to the detriment of the flowers. I also added some further choppy marks with pink on the left-hand side to lead the eye up towards the flowers – and more importantly to ensure that both sides were joined with colour.

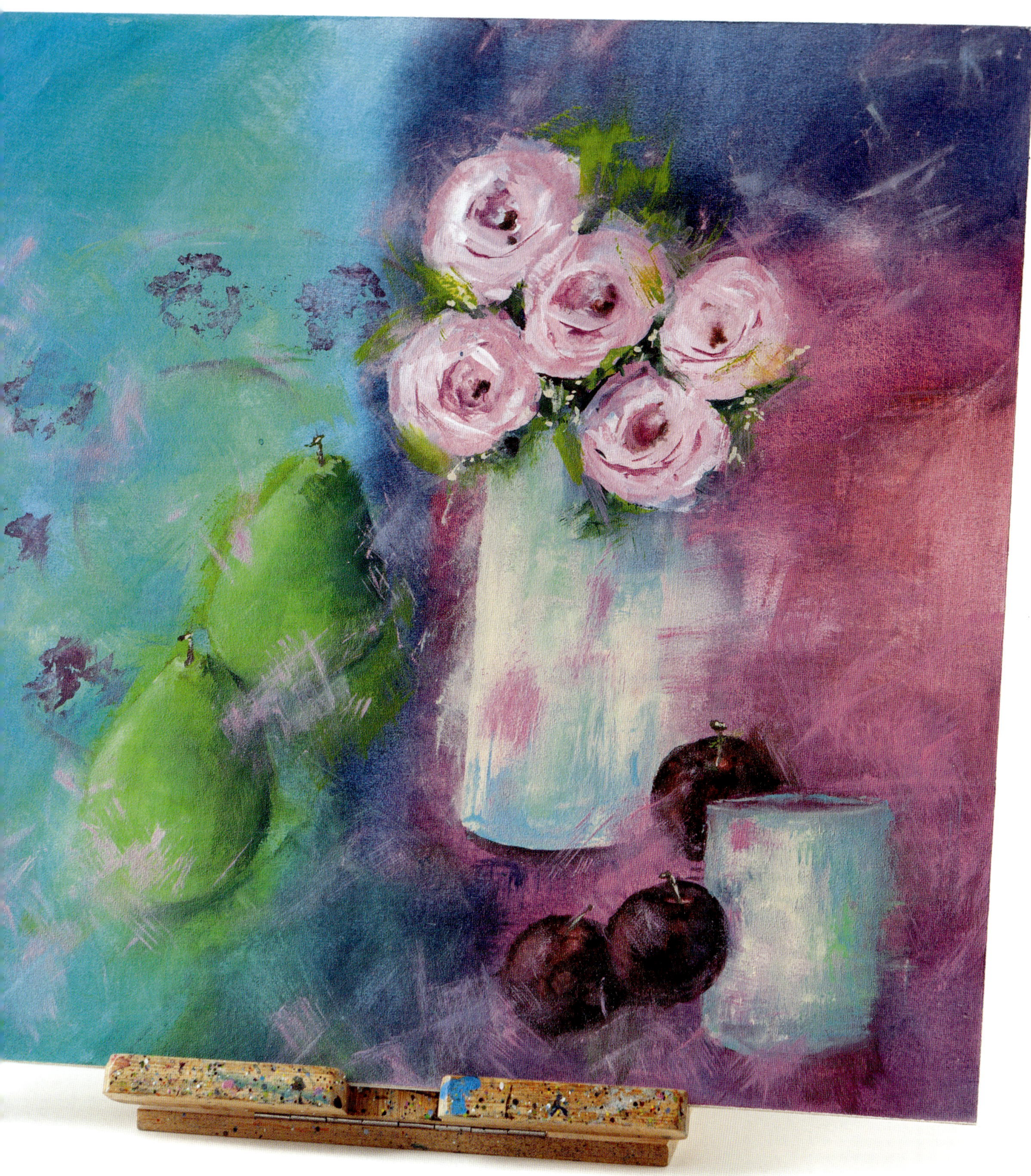

afterword

I want this book to encourage you, and to help you experiment with a looser style of painting. From my experience of teaching painting for the last twenty-five years, I know it's what a lot of students and even established artists strive to do. It isn't as easy as it looks – nothing ever is – but I really hope that the ideas, exercises and projects here have set you on the path to give it a go and get the results you want.

As my closing advice: continue to experiment, simplify where possible, don't overwork your painting, and think 'dynamic'. Remember colour, line, shape and texture – start with a few basic ideas to see what suits you and then expand. Try to leave your comfort zone, your normal style of painting and veer into the unknown. I think you will be very surprised at what you can do.

I sincerely hope that you will open up your mind and be more daring with your art. Instead of thinking, 'Oh, I can't do that,' just do it and see what happens – what have you got to lose?

As for myself, I will continue to try even harder to loosen up my loosened-up work further! My own goal is to steer myself gradually towards total abstraction. As with any goal, it will take time. While it seems daunting at first, by taking risks, being spontaneous, using my intuition and being adventurous I will reach my goal, I'm sure. I hope you will reach your own goals, too.

Wildflower Meadow
40 x 40cm (15¾ x 15¾in)

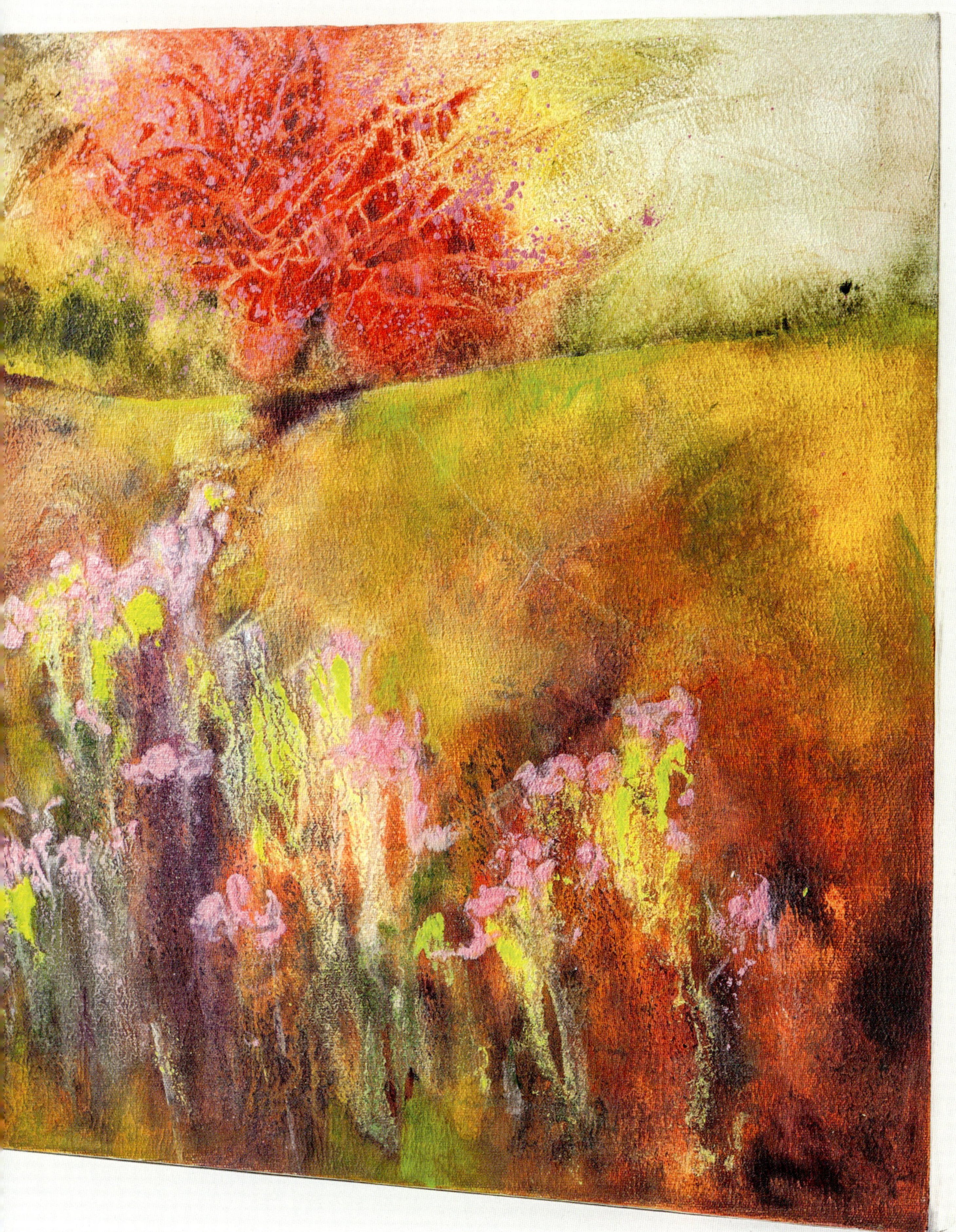

index

Aqua-Fix 12, 13

background 14, 17, 52, 72, 82, 84, 90, 100, 105, 108, 110, 112, 118, 119, 121, 122, 123
balance 57, 62, 70, 88, 102, 105, 106, 110, 112, 119
blend 15, 64, 66, 96, 100, 122
bronzing powder 16, 28, 44, 102, 107

canvas 8
  bare canvas 64
  block canvas 58, 92, 116
  box canvas 8, 9, 10
  canvas board 8, 9, 64
  loose canvas 8
  preparing canvas for watercolour 10
collage 16, 24, 84
colour 12, 13, 16, 17, 20, 23, 26, 28, 30, 34, 35, 40, 51, 52, 54, 56, 62, 72, 74, 75, 78, 88, 96, 100, 105, 110, 112, 114, 123, 124, 126
  complementary colours 52, 56
  unusual palette 78
composition 17, 20, 24, 57, 64, 72, 78, 94, 102, 105, 106, 110, 116, 124
crackle paste 23, 28, 29, 44, 46, 47, 58, 60, 108

doodle(-ing) 17, 38, 76, 114
drama 17
drawing 28, 36, 38, 105, 124

edges 11, 14, 26, 35, 60, 71, 105, 108, 110, 118, 120, 122
  hard edges 110
  soft edges 26, 110
embedding material 48
energy 19, 40, 64, 110
exercises
  evoking peacefulness and calm 42
  experimenting with techniques 82
  foxglove collage 84
  getting your impressions down while fresh in your mind 38
  loose marks for spontaneity 114
  minimal detail 90
  movement and energy 40
  poppy seedheads 90
  simple poppy 88
  take just the critical parts 80
  taking photographs 31
  working over a textured surface 108
experimenting 17, 20, 28, 33, 34, 36

feathering 60, 118, 122, 123
flowers 14, 22, 28, 31, 36, 74, 92, 105, 116, 119, 122, 124

focal point 26, 103, 110, 124
foliage 16, 54, 78, 80, 82, 124
found materials 48
foxglove 81, 83, 84, 85
freehand 120, 124

gauze 16, 17, 48, 49, 92
gesso 8, 47
glass bead gel 46, 58, 60
glazing 12, 13, 28, 98, 122
gouache 48, 58, 92, 100
granulation 28, 46, 58, 64, 70, 82, 88, 98, 100, 106
granulation medium 46

harmony 17, 110
honesty 5, 54, 92, 100

imagination 76, 78, 80
impasto 28
initial impressions 35
ink(s) 17, 26, 28, 33, 39, 44, 46, 51, 58, 64, 66, 70, 72, 74, 82, 88, 90, 92, 95, 98, 100, 102, 106, 108, 120, 122
inspiration 22, 24, 30, 32, 36, 40, 54, 76, 106, 112
interpretation 20, 74, 84, 102

leaves 16, 17, 23, 24, 26, 31, 38, 48, 78, 80, 92, 100, 112
lifting out 14, 64, 66, 97, 114
line(s)/linear marks 14, 16, 20, 26, 28, 36, 52, 60, 76, 80, 88, 90, 94, 96, 98, 100, 105, 106, 107, 110, 114, 119, 126
location 12, 26, 30, 35, 36, 40, 54, 112

making notes 36
mark making 16, 20, 24, 40, 76, 106
  mark making materials 16
masking fluid 46
mediums 8, 16, 46, 47, 60, 68, 70, 114
modelling paste 46, 47, 58, 60, 66
mood 26, 54
movement 40, 64, 66, 71, 76, 102, 103, 110, 116
muted mixes 56

object 23, 24, 36, 40, 123

paintbrushes 14
pattern 23, 116, 124
personal 20, 22, 51, 72, 76, 86
photographs 24, 26, 31, 34, 80, 112
  using photographs 80
plastic food wrap 48, 82, 112
portable kit 33

randomness 82, 112, 114
reference 24, 30, 31, 32, 33, 35, 36, 37, 40, 42, 76, 80, 102
representational 7, 17, 20, 23, 28, 51, 66, 72, 76, 78, 92, 112
routes into abstraction 22

salt 16, 17, 28
sample book 32, 37, 40, 42
  making a 32
shape 17, 20, 34, 47, 74, 80, 89, 90, 105, 106, 120, 124, 126
simplicity 33, 34, 36, 56, 74, 75, 84
skeleton leaves 48
sketchbook(s) 17, 24, 26, 30, 32, 33, 35, 36, 37, 39, 76, 78, 80, 82, 114
sketches 32, 33, 35, 36, 38
softening 96, 106, 122, 124
sponge brush 116, 118, 120, 122, 124
starting points 23, 24, 26, 28, 30, 40, 58, 116
  location 23
  object 23, 24
  technique 23
stencil 48, 116, 124
still-life 116
structure 28, 90, 110, 119
subject 7, 17, 20, 28, 30, 34, 38, 51, 54, 58, 72, 74, 75, 76, 78, 80, 82, 86, 88, 102, 106, 114, 116

technique 28, 40, 64, 66, 78, 82, 84, 100, 102, 106, 122
textural 8, 17, 44, 46, 61, 68, 110
texture(s) 10, 12, 16, 17, 20, 23, 24, 30, 31, 3, 37, 40, 44, 47, 58, 60, 62, 66, 68, 70, 82, 88, 90, 92, 94, 96, 105, 106, 108, 112, 114, 122, 126
thread 48
tip and tilt 64, 98
tree(s) 14, 17, 26, 28, 29, 37, 38, 42, 74, 78, 107, 112

vibrancy 13, 51, 56, 58, 64

wash(es) 12, 14, 16, 23, 28, 47, 48, 108
watercolour ground 8, 10, 11, 16, 39, 47, 48, 49, 58, 94
watercolour paints 12
  consistency 13
  keeping clean 13
  mixing 13
  preparing watercolour for canvas 13